# breakthrough

## DISCOVERING THE KINGDOM

*Derek J Morphew*

VINEYARD INTERNATIONAL PUBLISHING
PO Box 53286, Kenilworth, 7745
Cape Town, South Africa
Email: vip@vineyardbi.org

Reg. No.CK94/26543/23

First published 1991, Struik Christian Books, Cape Town
Re-published 1998, Vineyard International Publishing, Cape Town
Third publication 2001, Vineyard International Publishing, Cape Town
Fourth revised publication 2006, Vineyard International Publishing, Cape Town

Cover by Mercy Arts Studio, USA
Printed and bound by R R Donnelley, USA

ISBN 0-620-23469-5

*Derek J Morphew*

*(BA Rhodes, Ph.D UCT)*

# Breakthrough
## DISCOVERING THE KINGDOM

# Table of Contents

# Introduction

My own discovery of the kingdom of God occurred during the late 1970s. It was one of the reasons I felt an immediate affinity with John Wimber in the early 1980s, since the writings of George Ladd on the kingdom had been a formative influence for both of us. John was bringing the message of the kingdom to Anglican leaders and churches at the same time. The first decade in the genesis of a number of movements (The Association of Vineyard Churches, New Wine, and Holy Trinity Brompton) saw the kingdom of God being established as the primary theological model. Since then a new generation of Christians and Christian leaders has emerged. We have tended to assume that this generation has been raised on the same foundation.

Assumptions and reality do not always coincide. During the last ten years I have found myself teaching on the kingdom in conferences linked to the same movements in 16 countries and multiple languages. The perception of the leaders has been the same everywhere. We need to lay this foundation once again. The subject is so fundamental to scripture and to our spiritual genesis that we cannot allow a single generation, church or group of churches to miss it.

I generally try to explain how crucial the kingdom is to this emerging tradition, or these networks of churches. Although Jesus has been known and worshipped as Lord and Saviour by countless generations, in another sense he has been rediscovered, for the first time since the first century, following the modern discovery and translation of the literature of his era. He has been rediscovered as the Jewish prophet/messiah, who came announcing and demonstrating the kingdom of God, a reality that belongs to the end of the age. It was this rediscovered, eschatological Jesus that Ladd introduced to the evangelical church. It is now common in theological circles to speak of the ministry and message of Jesus as 'inaugurated eschatology'. However, it is not at all common to have churches and leaders believe that we should do the same today, or enact the message and ministry of Jesus, or make this theology the basis of their whole agenda. This was the particular step taken by John Wimber and it is this legacy that leavened the two church networks.

Karl Barth, the great Swiss theologian, warned us not to make any biblical theme or principle other than the name 'Jesus Christ' the focus of Scripture.[1] Christ alone unifies all Scripture. When we look at the Word of God from the perspective of the centrality of Christ, we realise that the message, ministry and self-understanding of Jesus are inseparably linked to the kingdom. Jesus came announcing the kingdom. His parables explained the kingdom, and his miracles bore witness to its presence. In fact, the theme of the kingdom as preached by Jesus Christ unites the whole flow of biblical truth, from Moses, through the Prophets, the Writings, the Gospels, the Epistles and the Revelation of John.

# Confrontation

God's rule is eternal and universal in the sense that he is, he was and he always will be the supreme ruler of all things. He rules the heavens, the angels, the planets, nature, history and all reality, yet we do not necessarily experience his rule in our lives. The coming of the kingdom involves God's intervention in the course of human history. His power breaks into the affairs of men, confronting the forces that withstand him and imprison people, and interrupting the normal course of society.

This is what happened to the Israelites when they were in bondage in Egypt, ruled by the occult powers operating through the cruel system of Pharaoh's government. The gods of Egypt, Pharaoh's rule and his army kept Israel in slavery. Then the kingdom came. Moses spoke, and the 'I am' of Israel judged the gods of Egypt through plagues, signs and wonders and his 'outstretched arm'. Two powers were locked in conflict: the power of Egypt crumbled, and Israel was set free.

The same thing happened when Israel invaded Canaan. The armies of Israel clashed with the forces of the land, but God went before them to secure the victory. When the Spirit of God anointed David as king, he defeated every power that held Israel in subjection. The peace of David's rule was synonymous with the peace of the kingdom. It reached its peak in the glorious rule of Solomon, his son. The Lord of Israel ruled in and through his anointed kings.

These interventions of God led Israel to confess: 'Our God reigns!' As Israel experienced the rule of God, they grew to understand that it extends over nature, foreign nations, the course of history, the heavenly beings, the sea, indeed, over all. But God's rule is not a guarantee of his blessing. He intervenes according to his sovereign will. When Israel misused and misconstrued God's reign, he intervened in a new and painful way: he raised up foreign nations to judge Israel and bring her into bondage again.

In this context, the prophets received the promise of the kingdom, not as an immediate event as in the time of Moses, but as the assurance of the dawning of a new age. This promise eclipsed everything that had gone before. God would break through into human history once more, in a comprehensive revelation of his kingly rule.

The prophets spoke of wonderful, dramatic things. A stone would fall from heaven, pulverise all the kingdoms of this world, and grow to cover the earth. The glory of God would outshine the sun. The Spirit of God would make the wilderness into the Garden of Eden. God's anointing would rest on a descendant of David and he would rule in universal power. All nations would bow at his feet. The prisoners would be set free, the blind would see, the lame would walk and a new, special peace would come to God's people. This would be God's final day, the event of his coming. The result would be a new people of God living in a new world. Life in this age would be transformed into that of a new age where God alone would reign and all his enemies would finally be defeated.

Prophet after prophet spoke of this new covenant, of a new priesthood, a New Jerusalem, a new nation, and a new day. They waited, ruled relentlessly by one foreign power after another. Was God's anger so great that he had turned his back on them forever? Centuries passed until even the voices of the prophets grew still. God's blessings in the times of Ezra and Nehemiah and the war of independence led by the Maccabees was a glimpse of what had been promised. When would the kingdom come?

Suddenly and unexpectedly, strange and mysterious things began to take place. A wild-looking prophet appeared in the desert, predicting the arrival of the anointed one. He introduced a carpenter from Nazareth as the fulfilment of all Israel's dreams. Yet in and through this carpenter something new began to take place. The pharaohs of his age were spared for the moment, but the powers of darkness came under heavy attack. The lame walked, the deaf heard, cripples walked, sinners were forgiven, demons were cast out, the dead were raised, demonic storms were calmed with a word, and the nearness of the kingdom was announced with an authority that had never been heard before.

Multitudes came to hear this man. Everything he did and said testified of the revelation of God. He spoke continually of the kingdom, in parables and beatitudes, in sayings and stories. There was no doubt that an event of great importance was taking place. He spoke of the kingdom in mysterious ways, as though it were already present and yet still to come. In some ways he seemed to burst the confines of what the prophets had expected, yet he seemed unwilling to reveal the total expectation of the kingdom, pointing instead to a final, cataclysmic intervention.

The mysterious way in which he manifested the kingdom was one thing. The blindness of the nation and its leaders was another. Was he the Messiah? Was he a pretender? The blind affirmed the latter; God authenticated the former. Events that were only expected in the future, final breakthrough of the kingdom kept occurring in and through Jesus Christ. The mystery of his person and the blindness of the nation created a confrontation expected by the prophets but understood by few – his message and his following began to collide with the religious authorities.

Jesus took on the role of the servant, described by Isaiah as the one who would suffer for the nation. He was crucified, but he rose again, manifesting a form of life that was only expected in the age to come. After the resurrection he spoke continually of the kingdom, promising a further intervention of God's reign in power. He commissioned his disciples to proclaim the kingdom to the ends of the earth. Then he ascended, and the power of the Holy Spirit came upon the early disciples.

The events that followed Pentecost resembled those that had occurred during Jesus' life and ministry. Once again, the breakthrough of the kingdom was manifested in confrontation. The good news confronted the darkness of the ancient world. Demons were cast out. The sick were healed. The dead were raised. Sinners experienced forgiveness. Towns and villages were cast into turmoil as Jesus was proclaimed king. The testimony of the disciples who witnessed these events, recorded in the Gospels, Acts, the letters and the Revelation of John, speaks of the kingdom.

Jesus commissioned his disciples to proclaim the kingdom to all nations to the end of time, and we live in a time when the message is spreading as never before. Church history has given evidence of continued interventions of the kingdom, in nation after nation and from generation to generation. On the one hand we await the ultimate breakthrough of God into human history when this age will finally give way to a new age and God will rule supreme in a new heaven and a new earth. On the other hand, the end has already come in Jesus and through the outpouring of the Spirit. The church lives by the powers of the future age while the powers of this age continue around us. The kingdom calls to us from the future and breaks in on us with a final summons. It is worth selling all we have to purchase this one pearl of great value. Let us respond therefore to the word of Jesus to 'seek first the kingdom of God' (Matt.6:33).

# PART I

## The Old Testament Revelation of the Kingdom

The teaching of both Testaments on the kingdom of God can be summarised in short sentences that enable us to encapsulate the overall theme.

The Old Testament teaching can be summarised in two statements:

*The Lord is king. The Lord will become king.*

These will be replaced by four statements that encapsulate the New Testament teaching:

*The kingdom of God will come.*
*The kingdom of God has come.*
*The kingdom of God is coming immediately.*
*The kingdom of God will be delayed.*

You will notice that these statements relate to time, both present and future. For the Old Testament people of God the kingdom was first present (the Lord is king) and then future (will become king). For the New Testament people of God the nature of the kingdom was more mysterious.

The two statements that summarise the Old Testament teaching relate to the major sections of the Old Testament. *The Lord is king* reflects the pre-prophetic writings (Pentateuch, Historical books and Wisdom Literature) that bear witness to the Exodus event, the conquest and the Davidic monarchy. *The Lord will become king* reflects the promise of the prophetic writings, which looked forward to the Messianic coming of the kingdom after the loss of the kingdom during the exile.

# Pictures of the Kingdom

The thinking of the biblical writers was shaped by the great tradition of the Hebrew prophets who saw reality in a unique way. Their visions were symbolic pictures of the visible world. Scripture is therefore filled with the pictures of the kingdom.

The Exodus provides us with the first picture of the kingdom: the collision of two powers.

The covenantal relationship between Yahweh, the victorious king, and Israel, the vassal nation, presents us with the next picture of the kingdom.

In the conquest of Canaan we again see two powers in conflict, one invading the other. The rise of the kingdom under David and Solomon is the final result of conquest. It gives us a third picture. This time the collision of powers develops into a golden age.

Let us explore these historical events and begin to see what the prophets saw: events pointing ahead to the kingdom of God.

## The Exodus

The first explicit mention of the kingdom of God is found in Exodus. There are implicit references as far back as Genesis chapter one, where the use of the plural (Gen.1:26) may imply 'throne language' for God the creator.[2] One could follow such implicit themes prior to the Exodus event. However, the intention here is to expound the more obvious biblical teaching on the kingdom.

The way the kingdom is presented in Exodus has much to do with the structure of the narrative. The actual text that confesses, 'The Lord will reign for ever and ever' (15:18), forms the climax of a deliberate build-up. Examining the text backwards from this climax reveals much.

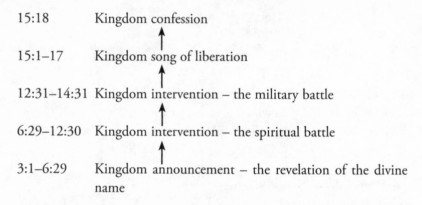

15:18         Kingdom confession

15:1–17       Kingdom song of liberation

12:31–14:31 Kingdom intervention – the military battle

6:29–12:30   Kingdom intervention – the spiritual battle

3:1–6:29     Kingdom announcement – the revelation of the divine name

The base of the whole development is the revelation of the divine name. From this point the narrative flows until it reaches the climax of the confession of the kingdom. The connection between the divine name and the revelation of the kingdom runs as a theme through scripture. The revelation of the divine name constitutes the announcement of the coming reign of God. Inherent in the name of God is his nature to come down and intervene in the affairs of men. His intervention takes place at two levels: first the spiritual-invisible and then the military-visible. The result of the two-dimensional battle is liberation for God's people. The climax of their song of liberation is the confession of the kingdom. The whole narrative, from chapter three, is therefore the prior commentary on the key text, namely Ex.15:18.

## Kingdom Announcement
## The Revelation of the Divine Name

The Exodus reveals the name or character of God the king. The naming of a person in Hebrew thinking involved more than the mere act of selecting a name. A name encapsulated the character of a person. For Moses to ask, 'What is your name?' was therefore to ask, 'What is your nature, or character?'

When Moses asked this question, God said to him, 'I am who I am' (Ex.3:13–14). The Hebrew name for God in this text is YHWH. It was considered so holy in subsequent centuries that few ever pronounced it, leading to the loss of the vowel signs. No one really knows how it was pronounced. Older translators used Jehovah. More recent ones use Yahweh. Whatever its pronunciation, its meaning is much more significant. It derives from the Hebrew verb 'to be' (I am), which carries the unique ability to refer to 'being' in the past, present or future tense. Hence when Moses asked about the divine name the reply, 'I am', can be translated:

- I Was Who I Was
- I Am Who I Am or
- I Will Be Who I Will Be.

Notice the emphasis on the name in Ex.6:6. Literally it reads, "Therefore, say to the Israelites: 'I am the I Am Who I Am, and I will bring you out from under the yoke of the Egyptians.'"

Further, if one examines how this verb is used in the Old Testament, one discovers that it often described the word of the Lord coming to a certain prophet (Jer.1:4; Ezek.1:3). In each case it carried the idea of 'becoming present'. When the word of God came to prophets it meant that what they said unleashed events. Their words were deeds, or event-words. One could say that the word carries the idea of being dynamically present or 'coming' to be present. It signifies that God has entered the situation. He has invaded history. He is manifestly present.

He is now present – He 'is' in a special sense. It introduces us to the profound theme of the God who 'comes' to his people.[3]

Words have meaning in contexts. The context here is vital. The cry of the Israelites in their slavery has reached God. He is announcing his purpose to come down and intervene with signs and wonders. In so doing, he will confront and interrupt the historical situation (3:7–15; 6:2–8). The whole passage is the commentary and explanation of the divine name.[4]

If one could put the whole meaning-field of this name into a sentence it would be,

> *I was, I am, and I will be, from generation to generation, the becoming present one, coming down into the situation of man, to deliver and transform, from bondage to liberty.*

## Kingdom Intervention – The Spiritual Battle

The message of the Exodus is of two kingdoms in collision: the power of God against the power of darkness, the power of Yahweh against the power of Egypt. To say 'kingdom of God' is therefore to say something about power, battle, conquest and victory.

The way of scripture is to show the invisible before the visible. Once the invisible battle has been won it translates into the visible battle, a point understood by intercessors. Behind the political and military might of Egypt were the spiritual powers of darkness. The story of the snakes (Ex.7:10–12) is a striking example of the spiritual battle. The snakes of the magicians symbolised their occult powers. Aaron's rod swallowed their rods. The symbolic meaning of this could not be missed.

The Lord declared that he would execute judgement against all the gods of Egypt (12:12). Each Egyptian god had a physical representation or symbol. The plagues (7–11) were a carefully devised way of saying 'your gods are defeated'. Let us look at some of the more evident examples.

The Nile was believed to be the sacred abode of the Nile god Ha'pi. In the first plague the Nile god died: Ha'pi turned to blood. In the second plague frogs, the symbol of Heqit, goddess of fertility, multiplied beyond control. Instead of making the crops and the livestock fertile, Heqit herself began to multiply. In the fifth plague, the livestock began to die. The bull was sacred to Apis, cows to Isis and the ram to Ammon. The representations of three Egyptian gods were exterminated. In the seventh plague heaven, the home of the gods, was cast into disarray. One of the highest deities in Egypt was Ra, the sun god. In the ninth plague Ra was blotted out. Probably most important in Egyptian belief was the fact that Pharaoh and his firstborn were held to be of divine conception. This was the basis of his authority. The death of Pharaoh's firstborn in the tenth plague represented the death of a deity.

Each plague was preceded by Moses' prediction that it would take place. This made it impossible for the Egyptians to believe that the events were coincidental. Pharaoh could not contest the fact that a superior power lay behind the events. The God of Israel was revealing himself as the sovereign Lord of nature. The prediction, timing and intensity of events took place at his behest. He showed himself to be king over nature and over the gods of Egypt.

## Kingdom Intervention – The Military Battle

Having defeated the powers of Egypt in the heavenly realm, the Lord defeated them on the military front. When the horses and horsemen of Pharaoh went into the sea with their chariots, the Lord brought back the waters and drowned them. This victory of God was the final act of deliverance for Israel.

## The Kingdom Song of Liberation

The first thing that strikes one about this song is the repeated use of the divine name. If one reads the introduction to the New International Version (NIV) one will see that whenever Yahweh appears, the NIV uses LORD, rather than Lord, which is used when the Hebrew name

*Adonai* (Lord) appears. Notice how often LORD/Yahweh is uttered in this song (15:1, 2, 3a, 3b, 6a, 6b, 11, 16, 17b, 17c, 18). The song is an exposition of the name, or character of God, as promised and revealed to Moses at the burning bush, now known and experienced by the people of Israel. It celebrates the Warrior God who wages war against Pharaoh and defeats him. It is a song of liberation. Now, for the first time, a population of slaves was a free people. Pharaoh, king of Egypt, had held the children of Israel in bondage. The Lord confronted Pharaoh with the demand that he let Israel go. Pharaoh refused, and the result was all-out war, decisively won by the LORD.

## The Kingdom Confession

The climax of the song is Miriam's confession: 'The LORD will reign for ever and ever' (15:18).

The Hebrew word *Melek*, 'king', comes from *Malak*, 'to be king, to reign'. As with the divine name, the concept is a dynamic one referring to dominion, rule and power. The 'kingdom of God' refers only in a secondary sense to the realm or area over which the king reigns.[5] The reign of God is not a place but an event: God's intervention or break-through in the affairs of men. [6]

### *What does this mean?*

The king is *for* his people: he hears their cry and intervenes on their behalf. The king is *against* the oppressor of his people: he declares holy war on the gods and powers of Egypt. The king is a *mighty man of war* bringing deliverance through battle. Moses pictures the Lord invading Egypt from the direction of Sinai, his holy mountain, with 'myriads of holy ones' (Deut.33:2–5). He comes because he loves his people. The king's rule means *freedom* for his people. Between them and bondage lies the sea. As they realise that they are finally free, they begin to celebrate. The God of Israel is king and redeemer. His kingdom brings liberation.

People who have been oppressed identify with the Exodus. When the early settlers felt trapped and oppressed by British imperialism at the Cape, they trekked into the hinterland. They saw themselves as the children of Israel being led out of Egypt. The Latin American oppressed see their quest for liberation from oppressive structures as another Exodus. African Americans and the leaders of the liberation struggle in North America and of South Africa have found the Exodus picture helpful in the same way. These identifications are possible because the Exodus is a powerful symbol of God's intervention in history and the affairs of men. He is not a distant, faraway God. He is the active, invading, dynamic God who is very much involved with man. We must add, though, that there were many oppressed peoples during the time of Moses. God chose to liberate Israel because she was his covenant nation.

The picture of the kingdom in the Exodus points forward to the fulfilment of the kingdom in Jesus Christ. Matthew's Gospel shows how Jesus is the second, greater Moses. Just as God came down and intervened for his people Israel so, in Jesus Christ, God intervened for the sake of lost humanity. The same sense of powers in collision emerges in the ministry of Jesus. As he cast out demons, healed the sick, stilled the storm and raised the dead, he was invading the prison house of the strong man and setting the captives free.

Christians are people who can look back on the Exodus as the first picture of the liberation they have experienced in Christ. As you read this you may remember what your life was like before Christ intervened. You may, on the other hand, find yourself oppressed by the pain and misery of a life lived without the reality of God. You too can experience the breakthrough of the kingdom, in and through Jesus Christ. Just as the Exodus intervention was an expression of God's grace, so too, in Jesus Christ God has revealed 'grace upon grace'.

*Jesus came to save us from a life of sin + death*

## Kingdom and Covenant

The second picture of the kingdom is found in the Sinai covenant, introduced by Yahweh calling to Moses, 'You will be for me a kingdom of priests and a holy nation' (Ex.19:3, 6). The Lord delivered Israel in the Exodus so that they could become his people and enter a covenant with him. Israel was under treaty to Pharaoh as contract or slave labour. Yahweh defeated Pharaoh in battle and, as the conquering king or suzerain, entered a treaty with the conquered nation – yet not with Egypt, but with Israel. The Sinai covenant is a kingdom covenant. It is a treaty laying down the terms upon which the conquering Lord is prepared to relate to the conquered nation.

At the beginning of the last century archaeologists unearthed the archives of the ancient Hittite empire at a village called Bogazkoy. This followed numerous similar discoveries in Ancient Mesopotamia and Egypt. An interesting aspect of the Hittite archives was their international treaties. Sometimes nations entered into friendship treaties with undertakings of mutual respect. These were parity treaties. At other times a suzerain or ruling king of a conquering nation entered into an unequal treaty with the conquered nation. Ancient oriental scholars called these 'suzerainty treaties'.

These international treaties followed clearly defined conventions in whatever nation they occurred. A modern example would be the forms used in hire-purchase contracts. The fine print always follows certain legal and social conventions with only names, addresses, terms and interest rates differing.

The Sinai treaty followed the conventions of the day. Egypt was conquered to liberate Israel from her contract labour treaty so that she could enter a new covenant with Yahweh. Israel moved from the status of a slave nation to that of a kingdom nation. No other suzerain lived among the people he had conquered. He lived in his own land and ruled the conquered nation from a distance. This suzerain, the Lord, came to live in the conquered nation as king. His relationship with Israel was an unheard of new kind of suzerainty treaty (Deut. 4:32–34).

God entered the social and legal conventions of the day to enable Israel to understand the nature of their relationship. His intervention created a new, clearly defined relationship with oaths, testimonies, blessings and curses, stipulations, statutes and commandments. Once he became their king, their relationship with him was secure (7:7–9; 10:14–17).[7]

We should pause here to consider the relationship between kingdom and covenant. Traditionally the covenant theme has been regarded as the most fundamental biblical theology. Reformed theologians have drawn attention to the Old and New Covenants, or Testaments, as testimony to it. Within the Old Testament the covenants of creation, Noah, Abraham, Moses and David are taken as a key to unlock the comprehensive teaching of scripture. While such views are still largely valid, one needs to affirm that the covenant relationship between Yahweh and Israel is an outworking or expression of the coming of the kingdom. Because the 'I am' became present and enabled them to make the confession, 'The LORD will reign,' and because he delivered them from Egypt as a conquering suzerain king, therefore they became his covenant people. The terms of the covenant are simply the terms of the Lord-vassal relationship. The kingdom creates the covenant.

## Kingdom and Conquest

The third clear picture of the kingdom is found in the conquest and the Davidic monarchy. The Lord, the king in the midst of Israel, gives them victory as they invade Canaan. Psalm 47 describes the Lord as the 'great king over all the earth' who 'will subdue the peoples under us, and the nations under our feet' (verses 2–3). Under Joshua each tribe obtained its portion, the inheritance provided for Israel (verse 4). If, in the Exodus, Israel came to know God as king over Egypt and nature, they encountered his rule over 'the nations' in the conquest. Through his power, each nation Joshua invaded was subdued.

## The Davidic Monarchy

Although the period of the Judges is a hiatus between the conquest under Joshua and the victories under David, the Davidic monarchy is the real fulfilment of the promises made to Moses of the good life in the Promised Land. There are three primary texts for the Davidic monarchy: Psalm 2, 2 Samuel 7–8 and 1 Kings 4.

### *Psalm 2*

This time the confrontation is not between two kingdoms. Instead, all the kingdoms of this world rise up against the Lord, the supreme king (Ps.2:1–2). But the Lord's power is overwhelming. He laughs as he rebukes and terrifies the nations because they are easily destroyed (verses 4–5, 12).

In the Davidic monarchy God would no longer speak through a prophet like Moses. He would rule from heaven through the representative king he had established on earth. This was a break with the past, which Samuel could not understand. For him only Yahweh could be king. To have an earthly king like the other nations was to depart from the unique relationship Israel had with the Lord (1 Sam.8:4–9; 19–22). But Samuel had to change his ideas and lay down the terms of a new manifestation of the kingdom (10:25). There would, in fact, be two kings: one in heaven and one on earth, the Lord reigning through the king he had ordained.

The term Messiah, 'anointed one', was the Israelite name for their king. David was the first 'anointed one'.[8] Psalm 2, the Messianic Psalm, lays down the calling and authority of the king of Israel. It is his letter of appointment. 'I have set my King on my holy hill of Zion' (verse 6). God says to him: 'You are my Son, today I have begotten you' (verse 7). From this privileged position, the representative king can ask for power from the king under whose authority he stands. With this anointing he will rule the nations and even crush them into submission (verses 7–9).

## 2 Samuel 7–8

There are obvious parallels between the Exodus event and the establishing of the Davidic monarchy. The sequence of the Exodus was:

- The kingdom announcement inherent in the divine name,
- The kingdom intervention through spiritual and military battle,
- The kingdom song of liberation.

With the Davidic monarchy we have

- The prophetic promise of the kingdom,
- The kingdom wars of David, followed by
- The golden age of the kingdom under Solomon.

2 Samuel 7 and 8 are the texts for the first two stages. 1 Kings 4 is the major text for the third stage.

## 2 Samuel 7

The chapter deals with the promise of the kingdom through the prophet Nathan. It is sandwiched between two stages of victorious battle. David had just completed the battles required to establish him as king over all of Israel (7:1). The following chapter describes his victories over the surrounding nations. The chapter itself falls into two obvious sections: the prophetic promise (verses 5–17) and the response of David (verses 18–29).

The prophetic promise has various key elements.

- There is a play on the word 'house'. David wants to build a physical 'house' or temple for the Lord but the Lord is going to build a 'house' or dynasty for David (verses 5–7, 11b–16).

- Giving David a 'house' or dynasty means giving him a great name, 'like the names of the greatest men of the earth' (verse 9). This anticipates the focus of David's response, which is to exalt the great name of the LORD. So there is 'house' and 'House' and 'name' and 'Name'.

- The essence of the 'house' and the 'name' is the establishing of the kingdom. The dynasty, or sonship, or line of kings to follow David has the divine promise spoken over it, 'I will establish the throne of his kingdom for ever … your house and your kingdom shall endure for ever before me, your throne shall be established for ever' (verses 13, 16). House, name and kingdom are interchangeable concepts.

- The basis of the kingship, as with Psalm 2, is adoptive sonship. The same formula is spoken, 'I will be his father and he shall be my son' (verse 2; Ps.2:7).

The response of David matches the nature of the promise.

- The exaltation of the name of David by the Lord (verse 9) now leads David to exalt the name of the Lord. We have noted that where LORD is found in the NIV the Hebrew YHWH is in the original. Where YHWH and Adonai are found together the NIV translates 'Sovereign LORD'. Where YHWH is used with Sabaoth ('hosts') it translates 'LORD Almighty'. 'These renderings convey the sense of the Hebrew, namely, "he who is sovereign over all the hosts (powers) in heaven and on earth, especially over the hosts (armies) of Israel".'[9] Once again the idea of kingship is inherent in the name of God. The most pervasive thread running through David's response is this name. 'Sovereign LORD' is found in verses 18, 19 (twice), 20, 22, 28, 29. 'LORD Almighty' is found in verses 26 and 27. 'LORD' is found in verses 24 and 25. God has done something to 'make a name for himself' (verse 23). Clearly David is using all his verbal skills to speak the divine name, in every way he knows how!

- David is supremely aware of the unusual privilege of being a recipient of the coming kingdom. The kingdom interventions of God are not his 'usual way of dealing with man' (verse 19), but his extraordinary way. They are the times when Yahweh becomes manifestly present, revealing the essence of his mysterious name. This is a 'great thing' (verse 21). It not only sets Yahweh apart, so that no other God can be compared to him (verse 22), but it sets Israel apart, as a truly unique people, delivered through the first great coming of the kingdom in the Exodus (verse 23). The language echoes the Song of the Sea (Ex.15:11).

• The basis of the coming kingdom is the promise of God. Almost all of David's response is worship and praise. The only sense of intercession is when David says, 'Do as you promised' (verse 25). This is hardly a difficult request, because for Yahweh to fulfil his promise he simply has to be himself, to be true to his great name.

• Although the word 'covenant' is not specifically mentioned, it lies submerged behind the whole passage. It is most clearly implied in what many have called the covenant formula: 'Israel has become your people and you have become their God' (verse 24), which finds its final expression in the eternal city of God (Rev.21:3).

## 2 Samuel 8

The spiritual, invisible basis of the kingdom has been revealed in the prophetic promise, where the name and names of God are clustered together as the foundation of the Davidic house, or monarchy. Chapter 8 takes us through the visible, military expression of the kingdom. It has a recurring refrain: 'The LORD gave David victory wherever he went' (verses 6, 14), enabling him to subdue his enemies, make them subject, and cause them to bring tribute (verses 1, 2, 6, 11, 14). The chapter gives a chronicle of David's victories over all the surrounding nations. The climax is found in verse 15: 'David reigned over all Israel, doing what was just and right for all his people.' It functions in the same way as Exodus 15:18. The whole of the previous narrative is its commentary.

## Solomon's Reign

*1 Kings 4*

1 Kings 4 describes the kingdom of Solomon at its zenith and provides us with a picture of what God's kingdom is supposed to be like. Each section describes a different aspect of Solomon's rule. Because Solomon was the representative king, his rule describes the various facets of the kingdom of God manifest in his time.

• Kingdom celebration and multiplication

God promised Abraham that Israel would be like the sand on the sea-shore; under Solomon it began to happen. This was a growing nation who ate, drank, and were happy (verses 20–21). It was party time – God's party. They were tasting the Messianic banquet, living to the full and prospering because Solomon's reign reflected God's rule – because Israel had the kingdom of God, they had it all!

• Kingdom prosperity

An oriental monarch was judged by the magnificence of his court. The greater the table at his court and the more state officials, foreign dignitaries and ambassadors he had, the greater the king. Solomon ruled from Tiphsah to Gaza, and his influence extended way beyond his direct rule. His court must have exceeded the full United Nations in session! One day's provision in Solomon's court included 30 kors of fine flour, 60 kors of meal, 10 fatted oxen, 20 pasture-fed cattle, 100 sheep, deer, gazelles, roebucks and fatted fowl. What a buffet! The queen of Sheba was overwhelmed at Solomon's wisdom and prosperity (1 Kgs.10:4–7).

• Kingdom peace

The Hebrew term for peace, *shalom*, means much more than the absence of war. It means total well-being in every aspect of your life – your health, marriage, children (lots of them!), your relationship with your neighbour, your crops, herds, vines, fruit trees, the weather, feasts, worship, and celebration. Not only was the royal court something to behold, but also every Israelite family lived under their own vine and their own fig tree. They experienced *shalom* because of the sheer power of Solomon's rule expressed in his military machine and efficient economy (1 Kgs.4:25–28).

• Kingdom lifestyle

Israel never distinguished between the material and the spiritual. The glory of the kingdom included far more than material prosperity. God gave Solomon wisdom and great insight (verses 29–31). Because he was God's king, he saw things from the perspective of the kingdom. When a man's mind is shaped by the kingdom, he becomes a great visionary, an expansive thinker. The text draws our attention to this through a deliberate comparison: the nation is compared with the sand on the seashore (verse 20). So is the mind of their king (verse 29). The enlarged size of the nation is a measure of the enlarged mind of their king. It is not possible to see the world, creation, mankind and life through the eyes of the kingdom and remain petty or small-minded.

Solomon spoke 3 000 proverbs (verse 32). As one reads the book of Proverbs, most of which is attributed to Solomon, one is struck by the practicality of his guidance for everyday life. Kingdom living is both glorious and profoundly simple and practical.

His songs numbered 1 005 (verse 32), a further expression of the Messianic anointing. We should remember that the Song of Songs, attributed to Solomon, is one of the most uninhibited pieces of romantic and sexually explicit literature. Like his father, most of his songs would have been for worship. However, the fact that the songs of Solomon, both romantic and spiritual, are an expression of the kingdom, is testimony to the Hebrew world view that incorporates the whole of life under the rule of God. When the kingdom comes to you, all your relationships are transformed – not just the 'spiritual' ones.

He was also a biologist, zoologist, ornithologist, herpetologist, and ichthyologist (verse 33). There was no aspect of creation that he could not comprehend. This is the epitome of the Hebrew understanding of the wholeness of life that flows from the rule of God. The kingdom involves the whole experience of man as the servant of God. The rule of God applies to every possible area of our endeavour.

The Davidic monarchy ushered in a period of great worship. David established the tradition of musicians and singers and Solomon built a magnificent temple. This is the context of many of the Psalms – the faith of Israel that sprang from this golden age of kingdom power. As subsequent generations suffered foreign occupation and defeat, they declared their faith in God the king, beginning with the Exodus, conquest and re-conquest under David. God is king of all the earth (Ps.47:7), seated on a glorious throne in his heavenly temple (verse 8). The Lord is king because he intervenes in the course of history. The better we understand the extent of God's reign, the more glorious we perceive his throne to be. Myriads of angels surround him and his presence is awesome. He is 'clothed with majesty' (Ps.93:1), reigning in power. His rule is eternal and universal, extending over all nations and all of nature (145:13).

## How Do We Experience God's Reign?

God's intervention always brings liberty: from slavery in the Exodus, from wandering in the desert, and from foreign oppression before David. The kingdom brings the rule of justice. Knowing God as your king means living under his wise, righteous administration rather than under oppressive rule (Ps.96:10). He upholds the cause of the oppressed and gives food to the hungry. He sets the prisoner free, watches over the alien and sustains the fatherless and the widow (146:7, 9, 10; 99:4). God's rule encompasses our entire lives – our family life, community life, international relations, prosperity, poetry, philosophy of life and the wonders of nature. This Davidic *shalom* points beyond itself to its full expression in Jesus, Son of David.

The Davidic picture teaches us to avoid all attempts to reduce the rule of Jesus to a purely 'spiritual' and personal experience. If the kingdom had such massive scope for ancient Israel, how much more should the reign of Jesus fill his church? Christ should be Lord over the whole of our lives.  We know that the golden age will elude us prior to the final coming of the kingdom. It will only really emerge when the kingdoms of this world have become the kingdom of our Christ. But once we have grasped this picture of the kingdom, we can never settle for less. Our vision of reality will always be pushing towards the ultimate goal, shaping our whole approach to life.

# Promises of the Kingdom

The reign of David and Solomon was a peak experience for Israel, but the peace did not last. Israel and Judah entered a period of apostasy that resulted in the Babylonian exile.

A refrain echoes through the history of the kings of Israel: A certain king did evil in the sight of the Lord and worshipped Baal. He died and his son ruled in his stead. He also did evil in the sight of the Lord, worshipping Baal and Asherah. Periodically a good king emerged who reversed the process, but the slide towards apostasy continued. Prophet after prophet warned Israel of certain doom, but none was really heeded. Eventually the judgement of God had to fall. Israel was invaded and subdued by the Assyrians and then the Babylonians, and the nation returned to bondage. Babylon became the new Egypt. The kingdom was lost.

This dark night of the soul for Israel is expressed in Psalm 137, 'By the rivers of Babylon we sat and wept when we remembered Zion' (verse 1). They were asked by their captors to sing the songs of Zion, but how could they sing songs of joy in a foreign land? The Psalm was popularised by Bony M in their hit, *Rivers of Babylon*.

*In these dark circumstances the prophets of Israel received the promise of the kingdom: 'the Lord will become king'. As they looked back at the deliverance from Egypt and the Davidic monarchy, the conviction grew that God would again redeem his people. Had he not promised David: 'Your house and your kingdom shall endure forever before me. Your throne shall be established forever ...' (2 Sam.7:16)?*

The prophets saw that the future breakthrough would be far greater than the previous interventions of the kingdom. There would be new elements in the final intervention of God in human history, eclipsing the entire previous history of redemption. This time the kingdom would involve more than the Middle East. It would cover the whole earth and reach cosmic proportions, eventually including a new heaven and a new earth.

## The Language of Promise

The study of the final intervention of God's kingdom at the end of the world is known as 'eschatology', from the Greek *eschatos*, 'last' and *logos*, 'discourse'. Eschatology examines the destiny of the individual and mankind in general. Another term closely associated with eschatology is 'apocalyptic'. As life became more and more negative and depressing for Israel, visions about the eschaton became more graphic and a specific type of prophetic symbolic language emerged. The word 'apocalypse' *(apokalypsis)* means a 'revelation' or 'unveiling'. Apocalyptic writings reveal things that are hidden and unveil the future. Although the apocalyptic writings came after the prophetic writings (BC 200–AD 100) and represent a later development in thought, many apocalyptic passages can be found in the prophets.

Isaiah and Daniel are the two major Old Testament books about the kingdom. They are important because Jesus drew frequently from them and understood his role in terms of their kingdom promises. Both couched their prophetic word in the context of deliverance from the Babylonian exile. To some extent their predictions were fulfilled in the return from exile and the restoration of the land in the time of Ezra and Nehemiah, but their promises ranged far beyond this historical period, reaching to the ultimate horizon of world history. If the Lord had made previous promises and kept them he could make new ones and keep these as well. The prophets realised that the future would eclipse the past. The God who made a way through the Red Sea, who destroyed the chariots and horses of Pharaoh, told them to forget the former things and not to dwell on the past; for he would do a new thing (Is.43:16–19). Habakkuk looked back at the Exodus and prayed for a glorious new coming of God (Hab.3:1–15).

While the prophets looked to the future, they were firmly rooted in the past. Exile was a traumatic experience for Israel as it called into question everything she believed about God, but she remembered the first experience of kingdom intervention in the Exodus. God did not bring Israel out of Egypt because she was a great nation, 'but it was because the Lord loved you, and kept the oath he swore to your fathers' (Deut.7:8). If God had fulfilled his promises in the past, he could make further promises and fulfil them too. Also, this God had revealed himself as 'the First and … the Last' (Is.44:6), Lord of all time. This language was to be echoed in the New Testament: '"I am the Alpha and the Omega," says the Lord God, "who is and who was and who is to come, the Almighty"' (Rev.1:8). Only such a God could reveal the meaning of history and declare what is yet to come.

The future orientation, based on the past, is so widespread in the prophets that instead of explaining over and over what they were talking about, they developed stock phrases that summed up the promise of the kingdom. The 'day of the Lord', 'the latter days' and 'in that day' all referred to the final revelation of God's power and glory at the end of human history. Because the prophets were seers they were not strictly logical or systematic in their thinking. Dreams and revelations do not operate on that level. They did not lay down neat timescales or define whether the events God was showing them were near or distant – exactly how and when God would fulfil the promise was up to him. As a result, they were able to hold together the immediate and the distant future and to describe events that were fulfilled in the deliverance and restoration from exile in the same context as events that occurred at the first coming of Jesus Christ or are yet to take place at the Second Coming of Jesus.

'That day' would not only be a day of blessing. Many passages speak of the end as a moment of devastating judgement. It was naïve to believe that it would be a purely positive experience. For some it would be as if a man fled from a lion only to meet a bear, or as though he rested his hand on the wall only to have a snake bite him (Amos 5:18–19). It would be a cruel day for many, a time of wrath and anger, a time of doom for the nations. Further, as part of their sense of anticipation, the prophets often felt 'the day' to be very near.

## The Promise in Isaiah[11]

Isaiah was one of the Old Testament books most quoted by Jesus and much of his language has been carried into the New Testament. He weaves together various themes like a classical composer. The major theme, the coming of the kingdom or of the Messianic era, runs throughout but emerges in a multiplicity of movements and finer details. His starting point is one he holds in common with the general prophetic view of the future: God, the king, will come and the Spirit will be poured out, bringing salvation. In Isaiah's terms, salvation includes the whole spectrum of God's mercy and peace in creating a new people of God who will enter the new order.

### God Will Come

Isaiah announces the good news that God will come to save and comfort his people. This is where the idea of 'gospel' or good news can rightly be said to have originated. The good news to Zion is that God will deliver his people (Is.40:9–10). 'How beautiful on the mountains are the feet of those who bring good news, who proclaim peace, who bring good tidings, who proclaim salvation ...' (52:7). God has been waiting for this moment. He will come like a pent-up flood. The glory of this coming will eclipse every previous coming. It will be like people who have been walking in darkness seeing a great light. The moon and sun will be abashed because they will be unable to compete with the glory of the Lord Almighty. The impact will be so great that all mankind will see it together. The people of God will 'arise' and 'shine' because the glory of God has come to them (60:1–2, 19–20).

## The Coming King

The Davidic monarchy had become firmly established as the permanent expression of the kingdom. The new Davidic king would come – the anointed one, the 'Branch of the Lord', the 'stem of Jesse' (4:2). The government would be placed on his shoulders and he would bear all the Messianic titles: Wonderful, Counsellor, Mighty God, Everlasting Father and Prince of Peace (9:6–7). As the justice of God flowed through David to Israel bringing freedom from oppression, the new David would come with justice and righteousness for all nations in the new, eternal covenant inaugurated through his death (11:4–5).

## The Coming Spirit

Some of the most beautiful passages in Isaiah are about the coming of the Spirit. He uses the symbols of water, rain and rivers to signify the life-giving quality of the Spirit's work (32:15; 35:1–7; 41:16–17; 43:19–20; 44:1–5).

In South Africa we have the annual phenomenon of the Namaqualand flowers. After the spring rains, the dry, semi-desert area just south of Namibia is transformed into a carpet of flowers stretching as far as the eye can see. The source is water, the miracle-working power of rain. Isaiah pictures people blossoming and growing in abundant life because of the outpouring of the Spirit. The descendants of Israel would spring up like grass, the desert would burst into life, and water would gush forth in the wilderness for the poor and needy.

The knowledge of the Trinity – the fact that God is Father, Son and Holy Spirit – was revealed through the life, death, resurrection and ascension of Jesus Christ and the outpouring of the Spirit at Pentecost. One cannot see this in the Old Testament without New Testament hindsight, but in describing the coming of God, the coming of the king and the outpouring of the Spirit, Isaiah makes it clear that it is the Triune God who will finally break through into human history. God will come in the fullest sense, bringing salvation.

## The Coming Salvation

Isaiah promised that God's salvation would reach the ends of the earth. It would be universal and last forever (49:6; 51:4–6). We said that the word *shalom* conveys a sense of total well-being. The term 'salvation' is equally all-embracing. It implies complete wholeness. The reign of God would affect man's entire being and his total environment. There would be the forgiveness of sin, the liberation of the captives, *shalom* for God's people, the resurrection of the dead and the joy and praise of the end times.

- There would be the forgiveness of sin and healing. No one living in the city of God would be ill and the sins of all who dwell there would be forgiven. God would blot out their transgressions (33:24; 43:25).

- Salvation would bring freedom: the deaf would hear, the blind see, the lame leap like deer, the dumb shout for joy and those imprisoned would be set free (29:17–19; 35:5–6; 42:6–7; 49:8–9). The anointing of the Spirit gave the Messiah the authority to proclaim this freedom (61:1; Luke 4:18).

- Salvation would mean peace for God's people. For the writer of Kings and Chronicles, peace was the term that best described the quality of David's rule. For Isaiah peace is part of a salvation that includes healing, forgiveness, liberation and resurrection. He describes this peace graphically:

*The wolf will live with the lamb, the leopard will lie down with the goat, the calf and the lion and the yearling together; and a little child will lead them. They will neither harm nor destroy on all my holy mountain, for the earth will be full of the knowledge of the Lord as the waters cover the sea.* (11:6, 9)

Every symbol of danger and depravity would lose its power to harm. The serpent would eat dust and the lion straw, and the wolf and the lamb would feed together. Man's work would no longer be in vain. In effect, the results of the fall would be reversed. God would provide peaceful, secure homes and an end to violence and destruction (65:20–25).

• Salvation would include the resurrection of the dead. 'He will swallow up death forever. The Sovereign Lord will wipe away the tears from all faces; He will remove the disgrace of his people from all the earth' (25:8). Death will be abolished in the end time: 'Your dead shall live; their bodies will rise' (26:19).

• Isaiah spoke of this time of salvation, forgiveness, healing and resurrection as a time of great joy, the joy of the future age. When salvation comes to the people of God they will want to shout aloud and sing for joy. Because salvation will be universal, the sound of joy will be heard from the ends of the earth. The heavens, the earth and the mountains will burst into song together (12:3–6; 24:14–16; 49:13).

In Jewish thinking a time of great joy and celebration meant a feast. As the prophets continued to speak about the future Messianic age, the idea developed of the final feast to eclipse all feasts with God himself as the host. Solomon's table formed the basis for this anticipation of the future.

Isaiah also had the joyous return from exile in mind. 'The ransomed of the Lord will return. They will enter Zion with singing; everlasting joy will crown their heads. Gladness and joy will overtake them, and sorrow and sighing will flee away' (51:11). The ruins of Jerusalem would join with the mountains, the hills and all the trees of the field in the great celebration.

As a result of this powerful salvation, God's people would be completely reconstituted. There would be a new people forming a new nation, living in a new city with a new temple.

## The New People

The new people would be formed out of every nation and all the tribes of Israel scattered abroad. At God's final, decisive summons – a great trumpet blast whose sound would reach to Assyria and Egypt and to the ends of the earth – God's scattered people would return to Jerusalem from the four corners of the earth (27:12–13). All the nations would be gathered to Jerusalem, the city of God, which would become the capital of the world. Jerusalem is depicted as a great mother, suckling God's people at her comforting breasts (66:10–14). The wealth of nations will flow into the city. The whole world will see the glory of God. David's just rule will extend to all nations as the salvation of God reaches to the ends of the earth. The peace and joy of the kingdom will be found in all nations.

## The New Order

A redeemed people, forgiven, healed, liberated, and raised from the dead, gathered into a new Jerusalem, consisting of people from every nation, requires a totally new context. Isaiah does not shrink from taking the message to its ultimate conclusion: there will be a new earth and new heaven – a totally new order (65:17; 66:22–23).

We said that the prophets spoke of both the positive and the negative dimensions of the 'day of the Lord'. It would be a great day and, simultaneously, a day of devastation. Alongside this glorious new order we learn of devastating judgement. God will lay waste the earth and devastate it. He will scatter its inhabitants. Terror awaits those who face God's punishment (24:1–13, 17–22; 66:15–16). His anger is directed at the pride and arrogance of man: the worm will not die and the fire will not be quenched for those who have rebelled against God (2:12–18).

Isaiah's vision of the coming kingdom is massive in its scope. He saw the coming of the kingdom as one great event: God in his glory, the king in his justice, the Spirit in abundance, salvation, forgiveness, healing, liberation, joy, resurrection, the new international people of God, the new Jerusalem, the new order and the final judgement were all part of the 'day of the Lord'. All this together is what Isaiah meant by the Messianic hope or the kingdom of God.

The first breakthrough of God in the Exodus led to the calling of a covenant people. This covenant people only really achieved a covenant lifestyle during the Davidic monarchy under Solomon, a golden age that led to a more complete picture of *shalom*. This in turn became the basis for Isaiah's further understanding of the Messianic era of salvation culminating in the new world order, a development pregnant with expectation.

## The Promise in Daniel

Jesus referred to himself as the 'Son of Man'. This is the key to his understanding of the kingdom. We find one of the major sources of this name in Daniel, and the context in which it appears is crucial to our understanding of Jesus' teaching. We will discuss the visions in Daniel 2 and 7.

### Daniel 2

Nebuchadnezzar, king of Babylon, had a dream that no one but Daniel could understand. He saw a large human image that was struck by a stone that fell from heaven. The stone grew until it covered the whole earth. Daniel's interpretation concerned the fate of the kingdoms of this

world and the breakthrough of the kingdom of God (Dan.2:31–45).
The image is that of a man representing various human kingdoms
– the successive manifestations of governments and powers in history.
Traditionally, the image is interpreted as follows:

| | |
|---|---|
| Head of gold | Babylonian Empire |
| Breast and arms of silver | Medo-Persian Empire |
| Belly and thighs of bronze | Greek Empire |
| Legs and feet | Roman Empire[12] |

We could add the names of great human empires: Charlemagne, Ottoman,
Napoleonic, German, Russian, and American. The image is a symbolic
way of describing all the kingdoms of this world as they succeed one
another to the end. By way of contrast, the stone is not cut by human
hands. It falls from above, initiated by the God of heaven, and fills the
whole earth as God's everlasting kingdom.

• There are two kinds of kingdom, totally different in nature.

One is earthly and human, the other heavenly and divine. The contrast between the kingdom of man and the kingdom of God is the
basis of one of the most fundamental concepts of biblical eschatology,
the difference between this age and the age to come. The four world
empires in the vision represent the history of this world, this present
age. The coming of the kingdom of God refers to a new world, the age
to come.

This is the basic conceptual framework of all the New Testament writers. Jesus, in the parable of the two kinds of seed (Matthew 13:24–30,
36–43), speaks of the 'end of the age' and the 'kingdom of their Father'
which is to come. In Mark 10:30 he speaks of 'this present age' and the
'age to come', as does Paul in Ephesians 1:21.

A word about the 'new age' may be appropriate here. The devil, and
occult movements in general, counterfeit the works of God. Many
interpreters have noted in Revelation the false trinity of the dragon, the
beast and the false prophet that sets itself up against the Triune God.

The genuine revelation of God is paralleled by a demonic counterfeit. The idea of a new age is one such instance. The idea has its origin in the Old Testament prophets and comes into particularly clear focus in Daniel. This age will be superseded by the new age or age to come, the age of the Messiah. False pretenders to Messiahship have attempted to initiate such a period. Hitler proclaimed a thousand-year reign (the Third Reich) focused on himself. Today an occult movement proclaims its own 'new age'. The phenomenon is therefore not new.

The issue is not the language one uses, but what one means by that language. I will use the 'age to come' or the 'new age' to mean the promise of the kingdom of God. Others may use the term to refer to an occult utopia, but the two usages could not be more different. The one is the very antithesis of the other. Christians are in danger of throwing away their birthright, the 'new age' in the Scriptures, out of fear that they may absorb some of the ideas of the New Age movement. Why should we allow the devil to steal our language and then be afraid to use it ourselves? I will continue to speak of the 'new age' or 'Messianic era' or 'age to come'! Those who accuse me of being 'new age' because of this would be guilty of a deliberate misrepresentation. Can Christians speak of the kingdom of God in an unbiblical manner and be deceived into occult new age thinking? We will tackle this in the next section. At this point I simply wish to clear the way on the question of terminology.

- The transition from this age to the age to come is cataclysmic.

The stone pulverises the image (2:34–35). The kingdom of God 'crushes all those kingdoms' (2:44). This is no gentle, evolutionary change. The transition is radical and drastic – very different from its occult counterfeit.

  - The human and divine kingdoms of Daniel 2 are viewed both individually and corporately.

Nebuchadnezzar, the head, is an individual king, but the fourth kingdom is described as two groups that intermarry but never merge into one. The same applies to the heavenly kingdom. Commentators use Daniel 2:34 to refer to the divine origin of Christ, but the kingdom brought by the individual stone grows into an empire that covers the globe. This point becomes more explicit in Daniel 7:1–28.

## *Daniel 7*

Daniel 7 parallels Daniel 2. Once again we have four world empires culminating in an empire with ten subdivisions, the ten toes (2:41) and the ten horns (7:7). These empires end abruptly with the coming of a heavenly kingdom of everlasting duration. The beast is slain, ushering in the future, everlasting kingdom. As with the former vision, the beasts, following the traditional interpretation, represent the four great world empires.

| | |
|---|---|
| Lion | Babylonian Empire |
| Bear | Medo-Persian Empire |
| Leopard | Greek Empire |
| Fourth beast | Roman Empire |

- There is a total contrast between the earthly and heavenly kingdoms.

The beasts rise out of the sea, an apocalyptic symbol for the people of the earth, the sea of humanity. This is why they are also said to rise out of the earth. The kingdom of the age to come is heavenly in origin. It is initiated by the court sitting in heaven. One comes on the clouds of heaven and the people of this kingdom are the 'saints of the Most High'.

- The bringer of this kingdom is the Son of Man.

The Son of Man is a heavenly, pre-existent, divine figure (Ezekiel 1:26). He appears out of heaven as though he has always been there and has no origin in time, a heavenly man who is both human and divine. He comes with the clouds of heaven and takes his place before the throne. To him is given dominion and glory and kingdom (7:14).

The idea of this heavenly man developed in the apocalyptic writings where the Son of Man rises out of the sea and comes riding on the clouds of heaven for the great day of revelation. He will deliver creation and judge the world. He is sometimes identified with the Messiah.[13] To the Jewish mind therefore, to say 'Son of Man' was to refer to the pre-existent, heavenly man who would come from heaven to destroy the kingdoms of this world and set up the eternal kingdom of God.

• The Son of Man is a corporate personality.

This was a concept to which the Hebrews were quite accustomed. The Son of Man is both individual and corporate. In Daniel 7:13 an individual man appears. To him is given dominion and glory and kingdom. However in Daniel 7:18 we are told that the 'saints of the Most High' will inherit the kingdom and in verse 27 that the 'kingdom and sovereignty ... will be handed over to the saints, the people of the Most High'. The text speaks about an individual Son of Man and in the same passage about a corporate body.

The heavenly man is a representative figure. Though individual, he contains within himself an entire people. His name is really 'mankind'. This is exactly the way Paul speaks of Adam in Romans 5. Adam (meaning 'man') is both the individual husband of Eve, who sinned, and the representative of the human race. When he fell we fell in him. All men are either 'in Adam' or 'in Christ'. In fact, Christ is called the 'last Adam' or 'second Adam' (1 Cor.15:45–48). Just as Adam contains the fallen human race within himself, so the Son of Man contains a new, heavenly, redeemed human race within himself. When he comes, a new humanity begins. A heavenly 'mankind' or human race comes to reign. We have then, two kinds of human race: the sea of humanity in this age out of which beastly or subhuman empires arise and the heavenly race out of which an everlasting kingdom emerges. The first human race is depraved or beastly; the second is redeemed or heavenly.

## To Sum Up

God deals with man in terms of two ages, this one and the age to come. The dawning of the new age is the same as the coming of the kingdom promised in Isaiah. The kingdoms that exist now are of human origin, corrupt and consigned to divine judgement. The kingdom that is coming is the work of God. It is eternal. The change from this age to the age to come will be violent and cataclysmic. The one who ushers in the kingdom, the Son of Man, is a heavenly, divine, human figure who contains within himself the future redeemed humanity that will occupy the kingdom of God.

What is the promise of the kingdom? It is a vision that grew out of Israel's understanding of the breakthrough of the kingdom in the Exodus, the Sinai covenant, and the Davidic monarchy. The vision burst the bounds of past experience to include a future coming of God that will be final, the 'day of the Lord'. It sees God breaking through again, this time more gloriously, once and for all. God will come in all his glory. The king will come with justice. The Spirit will be poured out in abundance. And the result will be salvation, forgiveness, healing, liberation, resurrection and eternal joy that reaches the whole world. This will create a new people of God in a New Jerusalem, a new heaven and a new earth. Human rebellion and sin will be judged. And all this will come about decisively and suddenly, violently, like a stone falling from heaven and pulverizing the world we live in. The one who ushers it in is the Son of Man.

*The Lord is king, and he will become king!*

We are now ready to turn to the New Testament.

# PART II

## The New Testament Revelation of the Kingdom

*The kingdom of God will come.*
*The kingdom of God has come.*
*The kingdom of God is coming immediately.*
*The kingdom of God will be delayed.*

*Herein lies the mystery of the kingdom.*

# Fulfilment of the Promises

The Old Testament drew to a close with a sense of great expectation. Isaiah and Daniel pictured the kingdom as vast and majestic. The day of the Lord would be the complete, final revelation of God to mankind. Every previous coming of the kingdom involved confrontation between the power of God and the oppressor of his people. The living God would again demonstrate his supreme power and authority. This kingdom breakthrough was expected at any moment, but instead hundreds of years of silence, oppression and waiting followed.

Can you imagine a people waiting for centuries for the fulfilment of such a promise? As time passed their expectations became desperate and bizarre. The promises of God were exaggerated, politicised, or trivialised. The literature of the intertestamental period illustrates this. Some writings said that when Messiah came, each vine would bear a hundred clusters of grapes, each cluster with a thousand grapes, and every woman would have a hundred children. A frightening thought for the ladies! Pretenders arose, claiming to be the Messiah. Each claim was proved false, but their attempts made a mockery of a dying hope. Others accepted the Roman status quo as the Roman system continued its relentless control. Only a few kept the hope of the kingdom alive. Those who were moved by the births of John and Jesus were the last glowing embers of a fire that was almost extinguished. Zacharias and

Elizabeth, Simeon and Anna were old people, holding on to an ancient promise.

A prophet arose in the desert, and for the first time in hundreds of years the people heard the ring of authority. Someone had actually heard from God! His words of judgement and promise echoed those of the Old Testament prophets. People must repent. The time was short. The kingdom of God was near. He would be followed by the One who was to come. He announced this event in terms that spoke unmistakably of the end, the day of the Lord. The axe was laid to the root of the trees. Wrath was coming. The bad fruit would be thrown into the fire.

As John preached a repentance that required moral change, Jesus arrived and received the anointing promised for the Messiah. The voice of God spoke from heaven, authenticating him as the Son of promise. The message of John and the baptism of Jesus fulfilled the promise of Isaiah (Mk.1:2–3, 11).

The confrontation was immediate. This time the enemy was not Pharaoh, nor the nations that had held Israel captive in her own land, nor the Babylonian kingdom, but the ultimate enemy of God's people, the devil himself. The Spirit drove Jesus into the wilderness to do battle with him for 40 days, a Hebrew way of describing a fairly short period (1:12–13). Jesus returned from the desert triumphant, 'filled with the Holy Spirit' (Lk.4:1). He proclaimed the same message as John, the language of Isaiah placing his words unmistakably in an 'end of the world' context. The time of waiting had ended. The good news had arrived. People must repent and prepare to meet their God because the kingdom was near. The breakthrough had come!

## Mark's Gospel

This sense of rapid, dramatic fulfilment is made particularly plain in Mark's Gospel. His story reads like an exciting eyewitness account. Three words characterise the coming kingdom:

- Immediately,
- Authority, and
- Mystery.

## The Immediacy of the Kingdom

Everything seems to happen immediately, the next day or, at the most, a few days later. Jesus was driven into the wilderness 'immediately'. He called Simon and Andrew and they followed him 'immediately'. James and John followed him without hesitation. People were amazed at Jesus' teaching in the synagogue. A demon began to manifest, but Jesus rebuked it and it left 'immediately'. This was all-out spiritual warfare. 'As soon as' he left the synagogue, Jesus went to Peter's house and healed his mother-in-law. That evening the whole community gathered and more healings occurred. Jesus was driven by a sense of urgency. Very early the next morning he was on the go again. He had to preach in all the villages. When a leper asked for mercy, he was healed 'immediately'. Jesus sent him away 'at once'. A few days later the story continues in another area.

All this happens in the first chapter of Mark's Gospel, and the point is obvious. The kingdom came suddenly, dramatically and unexpectedly.

## The Authority of the King

The Old Testament prophets had been calling out for centuries to a rebellious people who would not obey. Now Jesus called men with the authority of God, and they dropped everything to follow him. Through him they heard the final summons of God.

- When Jesus spoke in the synagogue, the people recognised an authority they had never heard before. According to Matthew, Jesus spoke with an authority that *superseded the Law of Moses*. In Jewish culture only God could do that. That is why the people were amazed.

51

- He had authority *over demons*. They immediately recognised it. With a word he rebuked them so that the people could understand the authority of God.

- His authority extended *over sickness*. He told a fever to go, and it did. He healed a leper and a paralytic.

- His healing of the paralytic demonstrated that he had the authority *to forgive sins*. The scribes believed that God alone could forgive sins. Jesus made his claim abundantly clear: 'But that you may know that the Son of Man has authority on earth to forgive sins … I tell you, get up, take your mat and go home' (Mk.2:10–11).

Daniel spoke of the 'Son of Man', the heavenly One who would come to earth with the full authority of God. God's rule had drawn near. His authority was breaking through and destroying every power that stood in its way.

- The account of the stilling of the sea (4:35–41) reveals that Jesus' authority *over nature* was that of God himself. What Jesus did amazed the disciples and made them ask: 'Who is this? Even the wind and the waves obey him!' (4:41). In Hebrew thought the roaring of the sea symbolised the chaos and disorder that challenge the rule of God. Only the living God could intervene against such a power. Jesus spoke to the storm in the same way that he spoke to demons, indicating that the same evil power had caused the storm. A cosmic battle was raging between the rule of God and the power of Satan. Jesus dealt with it with complete authority.

Just as the sea raged, so the demoniac raved amongst the tombs, totally out of control (5:1–20). As with the storm, no human power could still him. He was powerfully controlled by a legion of demons. The demons pleaded for mercy because they feared the rule of God that had drawn near in Jesus. Delivered, the man was calmed as the sea had been.

- The account of the demoniac is followed by the healing of the woman with the twelve-year bleeding problem (5:21–43). When she touched him, power went out of Jesus, showing that the new authority was resident in him. The woman approached him while he was responding to Jairus's plea to heal his daughter. His daughter died and Jesus promptly demonstrated that he had authority *over death* as well. The people were completely astonished (5:42).

Each account of Jesus' authority has one common element: men are set free from whatever binds them. The other Gospel writers show how these events fulfil Isaiah's promise. Luke tells us that Jesus read the passage about the liberation of the captives at his opening address in Nazareth (Lk.4:16–19). According to Matthew, Jesus consciously fulfilled Isaiah's expectations (Matt.11:1–5).

## The Mystery of the Kingdom

Running through the entire ministry of Jesus is the same sense of confrontation that we saw in the Old Testament picture of the kingdom. But the enemy now assumes a different shape. He is no longer identified with particular nations and the gods that rule them, but with all the evil of the world and all opposition to God. The final cosmic battle has begun. The strong man himself comes into view: his fortress or headquarters is being attacked (Mk.3:26–27). The presence of Jesus confronts him at every point. The demons recognise what is happening to a far greater extent than the people, and they are caught off guard.

Has the end arrived? (Matt.8:29). Everything about Jesus indicates that the final judgement has drawn near. Yet strangely, other aspects of the ministry of Jesus seem to run counter to this dramatic realisation. Perhaps the end has not arrived.

## It Is Here!

Jesus' acts of authority and his confrontations with Satan force people to ask ultimate questions: Who is this? What is happening? As we look at Jesus, we find that his every action speaks of the fulfilment of the promise of the kingdom. This becomes clear with the feeding of the multitude.

Moses had led Israel to safety in the wilderness. There God taught and miraculously fed them. When they wandered, God was their shepherd. Moses prayed that another shepherd would be raised up to give the nation ultimate security (Num.27:17). Ezekiel promised that the Davidic Messiah would shepherd the people of God in the wilderness (Ezek.34:5, 23, 25). The wilderness symbolised the place of Messianic rest for the people of God. Jesus therefore chose to take his disciples to rest in the wilderness (Mk.6:31–32). The people came to him and he had compassion on them like the true shepherd of God (6:34). He taught them many things and fed them miraculously from a few loaves and fishes. The Messiah was revealed to the common people.

The previous passage (6:11–29) depicts the wealth and luxury of Herod's court. Herod was a king who exercised his power by executing the prophet of the kingdom. His sumptuous feast compared very badly with the glory of God, revealed to the common people at another, heavenly feast, prepared in the wilderness.

Jesus commanded the crowd to sit down in groups of hundreds and fifties, just as Moses had done (Ex.18:21). Although they were in the wilderness, there were patches of grass for them to sit on. Already the wilderness was turning into green pastures where the Shepherd would feed his flock (Ps.23) and they could partake of the Messianic banquet. The 12 filled baskets spoke of overflowing abundance, and the 12 disciples of the new nation of God.

This event was followed by another stilling of a storm. This time Jesus showed his authority over nature in an even more dramatic manner by actually walking on the water. The disciples were amazed because 'they had not understood about the loaves' (Mk.6:52). If they had realised that the feeding of the multitude revealed that Jesus was the Messiah, they would not have been so surprised at his command of nature.

The feeding of the five thousand took place in a Jewish environment. The miraculous feeding of the four thousand took place in the region of the Decapolis, a Gentile environment (7:31, 8:1–12). As Isaiah had anticipated, the Messianic salvation was reaching beyond Israel to include the nations.

## It Is Not Here

In these and so many other ways, the Gospels testify to the fact that the kingdom of God broke through in Jesus. What had been expected for so long was now really taking place. But there was much about Jesus that the disciples and his followers found mysterious and difficult to understand. They were looking for the kingdom and were deeply excited by the signs of its presence in Jesus, but they were confused about the veiled way in which Jesus revealed it. The demons seemed to know more than the people did. They failed to grasp who Jesus really was.

Jesus bemoaned their dullness. 'Do you still not see or understand? Do you have eyes but fail to see, and ears but fail to hear? And don't you remember? When I broke the five loaves for the five thousand, how many baskets of pieces did you pick up?' (8:17–19).

There was more to the mystery of Jesus' identity than the disciples' blindness. He forbade some from saying too much about who he really was (1:43–44) and did not share the secrets of the kingdom openly with everyone (4:11). When it was revealed to Peter that Jesus was the Christ, he was warned to 'tell no one about Him' (8:30). The revelation of Jesus' glory was limited to the inner circle of Peter, James and John (9:2–13). He forbade them from sharing the secret until he had risen from the dead.

Why did the Messiah choose to hide himself in this way? Why did some of the things promised by the Old Testament prophets take place and others not? When would the nations be judged? When would David's Son overthrow Caesar and rule as universal king? Why did Jesus not allow the crowd to take him by popular acclaim and declare him to be king (Jn.6:15)? Had the kingdom really come? John the Baptist himself struggled with this mystery (Matt.11:3). And yet there was dramatic, exciting evidence that the kingdom had finally dawned.

How should we understand what happened in Jesus Christ? How does his coming relate to the coming of the kingdom? We will need to examine the mystery of the kingdom in more detail.

# The Mystery of the Kingdom

Jesus often prefaced his teaching about the kingdom with the statement: 'He who has ears to hear, let him hear!' He said that the parables of the kingdom were closed to the minds of some but open to others. The kingdom was wrapped in a cloak of mystery. Jesus explained some of the secrets of the kingdom to his disciples (Matt.13:11–13), but its nature was not obvious. Understanding it required special insight.

The summary statements now begin to make more sense. As noted, the Old Testament view of the kingdom can be summarised in two statements:

- The Lord is King
- The Lord will become King.

The New Testament view can be summarised in four statements:

- The kingdom will come
- The kingdom has come
- The kingdom is coming immediately
- The kingdom will be delayed.

These statements seem contradictory. How can an event be simultaneously future and present? Yet this is precisely where part of the mystery lies.

Wherever there are truths in Scripture that are in creative tension with each other, the danger exists that people will try to explain away one side of the tension in favour of the other. This is especially true of the kingdom. Many have wanted to choose certain texts about the kingdom and use them to explain away others. It is important to understand that the four strands of teaching we have identified cannot be dealt with in this way. Let us consider how they can all be true at the same time.

## The Kingdom Will Come

Jesus thought in terms of two ages or two worlds: the present and the future (Mk.10:30). Like Daniel, he saw this future kingdom in terms of the coming of the Son of Man. This means that the kingdom is eschatological – of the end times.

Towards the end of his life, Jesus and his disciples sat on the Mount of Olives. They asked him about the sign of the end of the age. His answer is one of the lengthiest of his teachings recorded in the Gospels (Matthew 21–25 and the synoptic parallels). This teaching falls into three sections:

- The build-up to the tribulation and the beginning of sufferings (24:1–14),
- The time of great tribulation (24:15–28), and
- The coming of the Son of Man after the tribulation (24:29–25:46).

The Jews believed that a time of crisis would precede the coming of the Messiah. These were to be the birth pangs of the future age. His teaching fits into this context. The Son of Man comes in the last period.

The glorious coming of the Son of Man will be like lightning that 'comes from the east' and 'is visible even to the west' (24:27). He will come on the clouds of heaven to gather his people (24:30–44). The faithful are warned to be ready at all times (24:45–25:13). Jesus explained that unbelievers would be taken by surprise at the sudden judgement, but believers should read the sign of the times, the budding of the fig tree (24:32–35), and be ready to share the glorious destiny of the Son of Man. He will sit on the throne and judge all the nations (25:31–32). He will appoint a kingdom for his disciples and they will judge the 12 tribes of Israel (Lk.22:29–30). The passages in Matthew, Mark and Luke about the gathering of God's chosen and the judgement of the wicked at the coming of the Son of Man are repeated in similar statements in Paul's letters, especially 1 Thessalonians 4:13–5:11 and 2 Thessalonians 1:3–12. The Lord will come with a loud command, the voice of the archangel and the sound of the trumpet of God (1 Thess.4:16). He will be 'revealed from heaven in blazing fire with his powerful angels' (2 Thess.1:7–8). These passages are clearly about the future, final coming of Christ at the end of the world.

Revelation follows a similar pattern. The time of great world tribulation will precede the coming of the Messianic kingdom. The power figures of this world will want to hide away from the 'wrath of the Lamb' (Rev.6:15–17). The rider on the white horse will come with eyes like 'a flame of fire' and destroy the enemies of God (19:11–16). This will be the climax of the coming of the kingdom. Heaven will begin to sing: 'The kingdom of the world has become the kingdom of our Lord and of his Christ, and he will reign forever and ever!' (11:15).

The idea that the kingdom is a joyous feast (Lk.22:29–30) is developed more fully in the context of the marriage supper of the Lamb (Rev.19). This will be followed by the future order, a new heaven and a new earth, with the bride of Christ as the New Jerusalem (20–21). The prophecies of Isaiah find their fulfilment in this future kingdom.

A whole school of thought developed that attempted to 'explain' or even remove these passages, creating the impression that Jesus spoke only of the present kingdom and not of a future kingdom. But the evidence is overwhelming. Jesus and all the apostles believed in a future, final, dramatic intervention of God, which will end this world and inaugurate the next.

## The Kingdom Has Come

The emphasis in the New Testament on the futurity of the kingdom is balanced, in almost equal proportion, by the emphasis on the presence of the kingdom as the fulfilment of the Old Testament promises. We have seen that the Old Testament prophets spoke of the 'day of the Lord', the future breakthrough of the kingdom. The whole Jewish nation waited for hundreds of years for this promise to be fulfilled. Many Messianic pretenders had claimed to fulfil the promise (Ac.5:35–36), but not until Jesus said, 'The kingdom of God is among you' (Lk.17:20–21), had the Messianic age finally arrived.

The fact that a future kingdom can suddenly be present is unexpected and strange. It breaks through like the stone in Daniel 2. The most probable translation of Matthew 11:12 is 'the kingdom of heaven has been forcefully advancing' or 'the kingdom of heaven has been coming violently'. This unsettling nature of the kingdom is felt especially by the demonic powers. Isaiah promised the release of the captives. In fulfilment of this, Jesus violently invaded the dominion of the strong man and plundered his goods (Mk.3:21–27). The casting out of demons is a sign of the presence of the kingdom (Matt.12:28). They cry out in confusion because this event has begun 'before the time' (8:29).

### *Matthew 11:11–15 & Luke 16:16–17*

The New Testament is saturated with 'fulfilment' statements. Matthew 11:11–15 and Luke 16:16–17 describe the dramatic moment when John the Baptist handed on the burden of his ministry to Jesus. The voice of God had been silent for centuries. Suddenly John appeared, with a power and anointing equal to that of any Old Testament prophet. Jesus captured the sense of drama in this event:

> *What did you go out into the desert to see? A reed swayed by the wind? If not, what did you go out to see? A man dressed in fine clothes? … A prophet? Yes, I tell you, and more than a prophet …*

*Among those born of women there is no one greater than John.*
(Lk.7:24–28)

Equally dramatically, John announced the coming of the Messiah and pointed to Jesus: 'Look! The lamb of God, who takes away the sin of the world!' (Jn.1:29) Then, quite suddenly, John was beheaded and the power and authority the people had seen in John resided in Jesus. Some even thought John had come to life again in the person of Jesus.

This transition enacted the classic Jewish expectation of the messenger followed by the Messiah and is the reason why Jesus' explanation of this turning point is so crucial. Jesus said of John the Baptist: 'He is Elijah who was to come' (Matt.11:14), explaining that the messenger predicted by Malachi had come. It was widely accepted in Jewish belief that this messenger would be Elijah. He was taken up from the earth in a fiery chariot and therefore never really died. The Jews believed that he would return to complete his ministry just before the coming of the Messiah.

The words 'is' and 'was to come' indicate that the presence of the kingdom does not in any way deny the futurity of the kingdom. The turning point from the old to the new came with the ministry of John the Baptist. John is Elijah, yet Elijah is still to come. In other words, a future kingdom reality is now present in fulfilment. How the kingdom can be both future and present is a mystery, hence the statements '... if you are willing to accept it' and 'He who has ears, let him hear' (11:11–15).

According to Luke 16:16, 'The law and the prophets were proclaimed until John. Since that time the good news of the kingdom of God is being preached.' The words 'until' and 'since that time' indicated that the great transition had taken place from promise to fulfilment. No longer was the kingdom a future hope. It had become a present reality. The whole Old Testament dispensation is summarised as the time of 'the law and the prophets'. That time was over. A new time had arrived: the presence of the kingdom. As John announced the coming of the kingdom, redemptive history changed dramatically from the era of promise to the era of fulfilment. This transition is the basis of the concept of 'before Christ' (BC) and 'after Christ' (AD).

The traditional point of transition is the death and resurrection of Jesus, but there are a number of turning points between the old age and the new: the birth of Christ, the ministry of John the Baptist that was passed on to Jesus, the death and resurrection of Christ, and the ascension of Christ leading to the outpouring of the Spirit. We have looked at the ministry of John. A few comments about the other three points will explain what is meant.

As one reads the accounts of the birth of Jesus, one cannot escape the repeated emphasis on fulfilment: 'Today in the town of David a Saviour has been born to you; he is Christ the Lord' (Lk.2:11). This brings 'good news of great joy'. God has remembered his holy covenant (1:72). Simeon can die in peace because his eyes have seen the salvation of God (2:29–32). Anna gives thanks in the temple for the child Jesus who is an answer for all those who have been looking for the 'redemption of Jerusalem', recalling the promises in Isaiah (2:38). The hope of the coming of the kingdom, which these two old people had lived for, had finally arrived.

The cross is the traditional point of transition. Jesus spoke of it as the hour of world judgement (Jn.12:31). As he died he announced: 'It is finished!' (19:30).

The ascension of Christ and the outpouring of the Spirit on the day of Pentecost marks a fourth turning point. Isaiah and Joel promised the coming of the Spirit as one of the phenomena of the end. Peter could say that Pentecost was what Joel had prophesied (Acts 2:16). We will examine these turning points in greater detail in the next chapter.

## The Kingdom Is Coming Immediately

The fact that the kingdom has come and yet will come in the future, is a mystery. These two points seem to be contradictory and represent the two 'extremes' of New Testament teaching on the subject. They stand in creative tension with one another. To say that the kingdom is coming immediately goes almost as far as saying that it has arrived; to say that the kingdom is delayed does not go as far as saying that it will only arrive in the distant future. These two statements therefore lie somewhere between the statements about the kingdom being totally future or totally present.

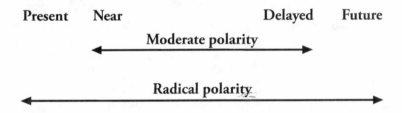

Jesus said that the kingdom was imminent. It was about to come at any minute, but so close that its immediacy touched the present. Radical decisions must be made because the kingdom was about to come. The phrase 'the kingdom of God is at hand' (Mk.1:15) has been translated the kingdom of God is 'upon you', 'at hand' or 'near' (NIV). The New International Version is probably the best translation. The kingdom of God has not yet arrived but it is so near that 'the time is fulfilled'.[14]

Jesus told his disciples that the kingdom would come in their generation, before they had finished going through the cities of Israel (Matt.10:23). Luke 21:32 says: 'Assuredly, I say to you, this generation will by no means pass away till all things are fulfilled.' The promise in Mark 9:1 falls into the same category. Given the explicit nature of these statements, it is not surprising that some writers have maintained that this was the essential belief of Jesus and that statements about the kingdom being present are a misunderstanding of what he really meant.[15]

## The Kingdom Will Be Delayed

Jesus taught, in his great discourse on the end times in Matthew 21–25, that the kingdom of God will be delayed.

The Son of Man comes after the tribulation (24:30–37), but before the tribulation a considerable period is required for nation to rise against nation (24:7) and for the gospel to be preached to all nations (24:14). In the parable of the virgins (25:1–13), the foolish were caught without oil because the bridegroom was delayed. In the parable of the talents (25:11–30), we are told that, 'After a long time the master of those servants returned' (verse 19). The parable of the nobleman in Luke 19:11–27 is similar to Matthew 25:11–30 but includes different details. It was taught specifically in answer to those who supposed that the kingdom of God was to appear immediately.

Because of the texts about the kingdom being imminent and those about the kingdom being present, there are any number of commentators and biblical scholars who are quite convinced that these texts cannot be original to Jesus. A whole 'theology of the delay' has developed in some circles, arguing that Jesus and the disciples believed in the imminence of the kingdom, but when time went by and the end did not materialise, the disciples had to find an explanation. This caused them to read back into the teaching of Jesus statements about a delay.

It is all too easy to 'remove' texts arbitrarily, because of one's own assumptions. The fact is that none of these removals have any textual basis in the ancient manuscripts. They have to be removed through complex theories about how the Gospels came to be written. It is preferable to face up to the New Testament witness as it stands. These four kinds of statement are contained in the teaching of Jesus. If we cannot understand how they all fit together, the problem lies in our limited spiritual perception, not with the text. What we need is a healthy dose of prophetic insight.

## The Mystery of the Kingdom

Jesus stated categorically that no one but the Father knew the exact timetable of the kingdom, not even he. How should we then understand the four different strands of biblical teaching?

We saw that the Old Testament prophets often held together events of the immediate and the distant future in one prediction. For instance, the promise of liberation in Isaiah 40:26 was fulfilled both in the return from exile and in the ministry of Jesus. The essence of the prophetic view of history is to grasp God's dealings with man. The exact chronological distance is not particularly important. Jesus was a prophet and could therefore see the kingdom as both immediate and distant without any sense of contradiction.

We must hold on to each strand of Jesus' teaching. The kingdom of God is future, immediate, present and delayed. Only when we hold these 'contradictory' strands together can we really understand the glory and power of the kingdom of God in Jesus Christ. Perhaps it is only the prophetic vision that can begin to see things through the eyes of God with whom a thousand years are as one day. Armed with this prophetic view of history, we can come to terms with the mysterious nature of the kingdom:

> It breaks through from the future into the present in successive interventions of God.

The event that took place in Jesus Christ burst the confines of ordinary human thinking and expectations. No Old Testament prophet could have conceived of something like this happening. It completely transcended the   expectations of Jesus' generation. Biblical scholars and theologians have written numbers of books to explain what happened, but even those explanations that do full justice to every strand of New Testament witness, only provide a human model to explain the inexplicable. That which is of the future, of the end itself, is about to come immediately. In fact, its power is already present in an unexpected intervention of God so that we can say that it is actually present, but its presence is not exhaustive. The mysterious nature of the kingdom consists of the fact that it is always here, almost here, delayed and future.

The fact that the kingdom has come, and yet is still to come, creates an unexpected period of delay in which this world continues while the next world is already present. The Old Testament prophets expected that the arrival of the age to come would coincide with the termination of this present age. But because of what happened in Jesus, we are forced to conclude that the age to come began, in some mysterious way, prior to the termination of the present age. An interim period exists between the coming and consummation of the kingdom. The kingdom is 'already' here but 'not yet' here. Two ages coexist. The age to come is present, but the present age has not ended.

It is a mistake to divide the promise of the kingdom into fragments and say this promise was fulfilled in his first coming and that promise will be fulfilled at his second coming, like someone who cuts a slice of cake and leaves the rest. This cake cannot be divided. Everything that is still to happen at the Second Coming has already happened in Jesus Christ. It has not taken place in complete finality, but in a real, anticipatory sense.

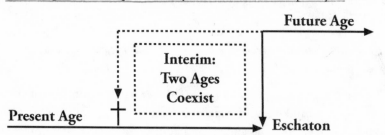

Oscar Cullmann provides one of the most helpful illustrations of this truth. The final 'push' of the Allied invasion of Europe was called D-Day. As later history has shown, this was the decisive battle of the Second World War. Once the Allies had successfully set up a military position within Europe, it was only a matter of time before Hitler's armies were defeated. However, D-Day was not the end of the war. It took months before all the Axis powers were mopped up and Hitler finally surrendered. This was V-Day, the moment of final victory. The time in between was a period of delay when the war was won but not yet won. The army that invaded on D-Day was precisely the same army that took the final surrender. The same generals, divisions and troops that invaded on D-Day pushed forward and took the war to V-Day.

The kingdom that will break through in the future is the kingdom that broke through in Jesus Christ. In his death and resurrection, the victory has been won. The end of the world has already taken place. Yet we still find opposition troops all around us. From where we are, a French town behind enemy lines, it often seems as though the enemy still has the upper hand, but we know that we are on the winning side. What took place in Jesus was the 'last days' in every sense. We cannot divide the last days into the beginning of the end, the end before the very end, and the very end. The 'last days' came with Jesus and ever since we have been living in the last days. The Second Coming will just bring the last days to final consummation.

## Fulfilment Without Consummation

The expectations of Daniel and Isaiah must be viewed as one indivisible whole. While the full revelation of the kingdom as described in Isaiah will come only at the second coming, in Jesus every element of that kingdom broke into this present world, in fulfilment yet not in consummation. In Jesus, God came to save and comfort his people and to reveal his glory. The King came to establish justice, restore the covenant and minister as God's Servant. With Jesus, the Spirit came to bring forth life in the wilderness. Men received the salvation of God, the forgiveness of sins, the liberation of the captives, the Messianic peace, the resurrection of the dead and the joy of the kingdom. As a result of his coming, there is a New Jerusalem populated by Jews and Gentiles from every nation. The Day of Judgement took place and a new order was brought into being.

In a word, Jesus is the eschatos, the end of this age and the full revelation of the age to come. This, in turn, is the full revelation of God. Therefore, since Jesus is that revelation, Jesus is God. Those who receive Jesus are taken out of this age and partake of the powers of the age to come.

'Fulfilment without consummation' is the phrase Ladd used. There are now a number of catch phrases used by theologians. A well-known one is the title of Ladd's book, The Presence of the Future. The most popular is probably 'inaugurated eschatology'. Another phrase is 'living in the interim' or 'living between the times'.

The mystery of the kingdom is the key to understanding the New Testament and the Christian life.

- It is the only perspective from which one can understand why healing occurs sometimes but not at other times.

- It is the basis of the experience of the Christian in this world. We are simultaneously 'new creatures' in Christ, with new natures, and those who have to struggle with the 'old man' and its continual reasserting of its influence in our lives. We are glorious contradictions, at the same time victorious in Christ and beset with weaknesses.

- This is also true of the church. The church is militant and frail. There is the continual struggle between the city of God and the city of man. Yet at every point the powers of the age to come are overcoming the powers of this present age. The new man in us is taking over the old man. The church militant will rise above the church divided. Jerusalem will defeat Babylon.

All these implications of the kingdom will be worked out in later chapters. Once we have understood the kingdom in this light, it becomes the plumb line for evaluating all sorts of doctrinal and practical issues and extremes. There are very few excesses in church teaching and practice that cannot be either corrected or clarified once we have understood the measuring rod of the kingdom.

# The Centrality of Christ

The phrase 'the presence of the future' sums up the point we have made in the previous chapter. This means understanding the life and ministry of Jesus eschatologically. In other words, the whole of Christ's ministry, from beginning to end, was an 'end of the world' event. We mentioned four moments that stand out as turning points between BC and AD. We now examine in greater detail:

- the *breakthrough of the kingdom in the ministry of Jesus,*
- the *Day of Judgement in the cross,*
- the *resurrection* and
- the *coming of the Spirit.*

## The Ministry of Christ

Once we have understood how the future kingdom is present in Jesus, we can view almost every aspect of his ministry in the same light. All the expectations of Isaiah were fulfilled in him.

One of the most illuminating moments in the life of Jesus was when he opened the scroll of Isaiah in the synagogue (Lk.4:16–19), deliberately explaining what he understood his ministry to be. He selected a passage that refers not only to the liberation motif in Isaiah but ends with a statement about 'the acceptable year of the Lord'. This refers to the Year of Jubilee in the Law of Moses, a special time of universal liberation. Jesus described his entire future ministry in terms of this season of liberation. In his answer to John the Baptist's question: 'Are you the Coming One?' he deliberately alluded to the promises in Isaiah and pointed to the events taking place in his ministry. 'The blind receive sight, the lame walk, those who have leprosy are cured, the deaf hear, the dead are raised, and the good news is preached to the poor' (Matt.11:2–6).

Jesus came to set people free from every kind of bondage, true to the all-embracing understanding of salvation that Isaiah had outlined. This made it good news. The Gospel writers show that Jesus was the embodiment of good news long before he announced it in the synagogue in Galilee. In the account of his birth, special mention is made of the 'good news'. The angels brought 'good news of great joy' (Lk.2:10), the good news that God had come to live among his people. In fulfilment of Isaiah, Jesus was called Immanuel, 'God with us' (Matt.1:23). Jesus' first sermon about the kingdom exhorted people to 'believe in the gospel' (Mk.1:14–15).

The good news causes people to rejoice. The joy of the end time is qualitatively different from any other joy. It is the joy of the future world. Peter speaks of 'an inexpressible and glorious joy' (1 Peter 1:8). The New Testament writers find this element from the very beginning of the breakthrough of the kingdom. John the Baptist, the prophet to announce the end time, leapt for joy while still in the womb (Lk.1:44). The good news of the birth of Jesus brought 'great joy' (2:10). Those who met the risen Christ were filled with 'joy and amazement' (24:41). Jesus promised his disciples a special kind of joy that would be complete and fulfilled (Jn.17:13). Paul defined the kingdom of God as 'righteousness, peace and joy in the Holy Spirit' (Rom.14:17).

Isaiah said that the good news of the kingdom would comfort God's people. To say that comfort or consolation had come in Jesus is to say that the Messianic era was present in him. Simeon and Anna recognised that Jesus was the promised One who had come to 'comfort' or redeem

God's people (Lk.2:25–29, 38).

Isaiah's announcement of comfort was closely associated with the concept of peace, the *shalom* of the Davidic monarchy. This theme can also be traced in the life of Jesus. At his birth the angels proclaimed peace on earth and goodwill towards men (2:14). We noted how *shalom* and salvation, in Isaiah, were both holistic concepts, touching the whole of life. Jesus brought healing to people. The Greek word for healing is *soteria*, which is also translated as 'salvation'. Jesus saved people, and told them to 'Go in peace' (7:50) and bring peace into the lives of others (10:5). The crowds understood that Jesus was ushering in the Messianic rule when they cried, 'Peace in heaven and glory in the highest!' (19:38). When Jesus showed the disciples the wounds in his hands and feet, the symbols of their forgiveness, he said, 'Peace to you' (24:36).

We saw in Isaiah that the future coming of God would be his final self-revelation, when his glory would outshine the sun. Jesus' life and ministry was filled with glory. At his conception we are told that the 'power of the Most High' overshadowed Mary (1:35). This is a way of describing the glory of God. The shepherds experienced the glory of the Lord all around them (2:9). John tells us that the Word dwelt amongst us and we saw his glory (Jn.1:14). John's Gospel describes the whole life of Jesus in these terms. Each successive sign reveals the glory of God until it is finally revealed in the cross. While John sees the cross as the culmination of the glorification of Jesus, Luke sees this in the ascension. Christ's journey to Jerusalem is the beginning of his ultimate glorification through death, burial and resurrection. This process began when his glory was revealed on the mount of transfiguration.

The restoration of the Davidic monarchy through one greater than David is a common New Testament theme. Matthew's genealogy shows that Jesus came from David's line (Matt.1:1–17). This is why he was born in Bethlehem of Judah (2:1–6). During his ministry people called Jesus the Son of David. His official crime was that he claimed to be the King of the Jews (27:37).

An integral part of the Davidic monarchy was the administration of justice to the people of God once oppressive rulers had been overthrown. The justice of God can be seen in Jesus. His ethical teaching exposed the motives of the human heart. In his denunciation of materialism and his merciless exposure of hypocrisy, Jesus reflected the great tradition of social justice revealed in the Old Testament. He provided a better righteousness in his teaching on grace, later fulfilled in his substitutionary death, which revealed the righteousness we receive, by faith. Those who accepted his offer of grace were called to a standard of ethics that exceeded that of the scribes and Pharisees.

As a result of the coming of the day of salvation, Isaiah expected a new order incorporating a new people of God, made up from Israel but augmented by people from every nation. This new order would be inaugurated on the Day of Judgement and would culminate in a new heaven and a new earth. How does this find its fulfilment in Jesus? The New Jerusalem that John saw (Rev.21) was the New Jerusalem expected by Isaiah. This future city has already arrived in Jesus. The writer to the Hebrews says that believers have 'come to Mount Zion, to the heavenly Jerusalem, the city of the living God' (Heb.12:22–24). Paul speaks of the future City of God as a present reality. 'The heavenly Jerusalem that is above is free, and she is our mother' (Gal.4:26). The trumpet will summon the scattered people of Israel to the city of God at the end time. The day of Pentecost was just such a moment. Jews had gathered for the feast from the 'Diaspora' throughout the ancient world and were represented in the Pentecostal experience. The scattering of Babylon was reversed in the gathering at Pentecost. Peter addresses the believers in Asia Minor as 'the pilgrims of the Dispersion' (I Pet.1:1).

This theme merges with that of the ingathering of the nations. The gospel must reach all nations as the witness of the church goes to the ends of the earth. Luke has a deliberate progression in mind as the gospel goes from one circle to the next and spreads around the Mediterranean basin from Jerusalem to Rome (Ac.1:8). Paul works out, in some detail, the doctrine of the new people of God comprising both Jews and Gentiles in one new man (Eph.3:1–6). The interesting thing about this fulfilment of Old Testament expectation is that instead of nations being gathered to Zion, Zion is spread among the nations. The new world also gains reality in the personal experience of every Christian. In Christ we are new creations. The old has gone, the new has come (2 Cor.5:17).

## The Cross

The day of the Lord is a day of judgement. Isaiah predicted universal judgement with the coming of the kingdom. This is also the expectation of the New Testament. When Jesus went to the cross, he said: 'Now is the judgement of this world' (Jn.12:31). He understood the cross to be the Day of Judgement. This explains why the heavens were darkened and the earth was shaken as Christ was crucified. Such cosmic events are the pangs of the end times. In Jesus the end has occurred.

This is the basis of the substitutionary death of Christ. All men will be judged at the end, but in his death Jesus has already been judged by God for our sin and borne our future judgement. Someone who chooses to identify with the cross 'has eternal life and will not be condemned; he has crossed over from death to life' (Jn.5:24). You cannot be tried, found guilty and executed for your crime twice. Once you have been executed, your punishment has been settled. In Jesus we were tried, found guilty and executed. We no longer have to look ahead to the moment when our lives will be judged. We look back to what Christ has already done for us. That is why it is absolutely essential for us to acknowledge our sin and accept that God dealt with it on the cross. The Christian who has been judged in the cross can face the future with confidence.

Existentialist thinkers were preoccupied with being 'open to the future', but the gloom of the twentieth century meant that people lived with a sense of foreboding. Aspects of modern life such as the atomic threat, ecological disasters, AIDS and the pollution of our environment combine to make people feel that there is no future. A spate of apocalyptic motion pictures has given graphic detail to this gloomy outlook. The kingdom understanding of the cross gives the Christian testimony a unique edge. Of all people, kingdom believers can be open to the future because its forbidding aspects have already been settled in the cross.

## The Resurrection

In biblical thinking, the resurrection of the dead is something that will happen universally at the end of the world. Death itself will be abolished. When Jesus was raised from the dead he entered the eternal life of the age to come. What will happen to all men at the end happened to one man in the present. His resurrection is therefore the beginning of the universal resurrection and abolition of death occurring before the time. It is the first fruits of the final harvest. Death will be swallowed up then, but in Christ death has already been vanquished.

Jesus explained this to Martha when Lazarus died. Martha believed in the resurrection at the last day (Jn.11:24). Jesus said: 'I am the resurrection and the life. He who believes in me will live, even though he dies; and whoever lives and believes in me will never die' (11:25–26). For those in Christ, the transition from death to life has already occurred. A future event is present for us. We have eternal life because we have already crossed over from death to life. The phrase 'eternal life' in the Greek is literally 'life of the ages', i.e. life of the future ages.

This is the basis of Paul's teaching on our identification with Christ. We were dead in trespasses and sins, but we have been 'made alive with Christ' (Eph.2:5). Through our union with Christ, we have passed through the barrier between this life and the next. We have entered the eternal life of the age to come. It is possible because the next life has broken through into this life in Jesus.

74

## Pentecost

Joel and Isaiah expected the outpouring of the Spirit in the last days as an integral part of end-of-world events. Many Christians know Joel's prophecy by heart but fail to notice that the statements about the sons and daughters prophesying and old men dreaming dreams are followed by statements about blood, fire and smoke, the sun turning to darkness and the moon to blood (Joel 2:28–32). The context of Joel's statement is thoroughly eschatological: the cosmic signs are events of the end. Matthew 25–29 and Revelation 6:12–17 make this clear, as does the parallel to Joel 3:13–15 in Revelation 14:14–20. Yet Peter, on the day of Pentecost, could say, 'this is what was spoken by the prophet Joel' (Ac.2:16). This means that the end of the world broke through in the coming of the Spirit at Pentecost.

An old Pentecostal preacher is said to have put it like this: 'Peter said that *this* is *that*. If *this* is not *that*, then what is *this*? But if this *is* that, then that's that.'

He probably did not understand his comment in terms of the kingdom, but it states the position very well. Those who receive the Spirit experience the powers of the age to come. The baptism of the Spirit is a taste now of what we will experience then. Paul explains that the seal of the Spirit is the down-payment or first instalment, the guarantee of our future inheritance (Eph.1:13–14). This inheritance includes the future redemption of our bodies – the total transformation of the human body by the Holy Spirit. That is why the Pentecostal work of the Spirit often affects us in a physical sense. People become lame and unable to walk or are overwhelmed by joy. They experience various tangible phenomena of the Spirit (Ac.2:13–15; 8:39).

In Isaiah's promise of the kingdom, the outpouring of the Spirit in the last days is associated with the joy of the *eschatos*. Joy was one of the manifestations of the outpouring of the Spirit at Pentecost. Such joy is not of this age. It is the joy of the age to come breaking in on us from the future.

This understanding of Pentecost makes one realise just how profound the baptism in the Holy Spirit really is. It is an empowering for service, enabling believers to witness to the ends of the earth. But it is far more. It is an experience of a future age. This is why the theology of the kingdom is the true basis for understanding phenomena that take place during times of renewal or revival. The experience of the Spirit is a kingdom experience.

The day of Pentecost was the result of the ascension of Christ. The coming of the King in Isaiah and the dominion of the Son of Man in Daniel are events of the end. We know that Jesus will reign when the end finally comes, but by virtue of his ascension he already reigns at the right hand of God. The future Messianic reign has begun in the present through the ascension.

## Conclusion

We can conclude that Jesus and the writers of the New Testament were profoundly influenced by the kingdom expectation of Isaiah. Their language repeatedly draws on the major kingdom themes in Isaiah. There is in fact no single element in Isaiah's expectation that one cannot find fulfilled in the ministry of Jesus.

This means that the life and ministry of Jesus did not have to find an interpretation because the interpretation had already been provided by the expectation. His pre-history in the Old Testament provided a ready-made interpretative framework. In terms of its universalism, comprehensiveness and sheer breadth of vision, there is nothing in the Old Testament to exceed Isaiah. The life and ministry of Jesus takes as its starting point the highest peak of Old Testament expectation. It is not surprising, therefore, that Jesus' contemporaries found it difficult to grasp his understanding of Messiahship.

We have also learned that even the highest point of Old Testament expectation was insufficient to express what really occurred in Jesus. The breakthrough of the future kingdom into the present world, before the present world had terminated, was beyond even Isaiah's anticipation. We find that the vision of the kingdom developed progressively through redemptive history with each new picture transcending the previous one. The Exodus event moves to the Davidic monarchy, which then develops into the 'day of the Lord' expectation in the prophets, reaching its highest point in Isaiah. But the coming of Jesus burst beyond everything that had preceded it, and what happened in Jesus is now the basis of what will happen when he comes again. It is not necessary to stress that the next breakthrough of the kingdom will radically transcend everything we have expected. Yet with each development there is a remarkable continuity with what has gone before. This is what makes redemptive history so magnificent. Our only fitting response is to concur with Paul at the end of his survey of redemptive history:

*Oh, the depth of the riches of the wisdom and knowledge of God! How unsearchable his judgements, And his paths beyond tracing out!* (Rom.11.33)

# *The presence of the Future*

## The Implications of the Kingdom

The implications of the kingdom have already been touched on. They are the test of our understanding and require fuller consideration. At this point we edge towards systematic, rather than biblical theology.

*1. The end has occurred in Jesus. Only God himself can be the end (eschatos). Therefore Jesus is God.*

In the revelation of John, Jesus names himself 'the Alpha and the Omega' (1.8), the 'First and the Last' (2.8). The Greek for last is *eschatos.* As a biblical term *eschatos* refers to the end of this world through the final judgement of God. Only God himself, the ultimate judge, can bring about this final intervention. The 'day of the Lord' can only be just that, the day of the LORD. Jesus is not just one who brought elements of final judgement into history. He is the end. To meet Jesus is to meet the end of the world. Once we grasp this, two related implications follow.

- The divinity of Christ is most profoundly based on eschatology. There are many ways in which we can argue for the divinity of Christ. The method usually used by apologists of the Christian faith is to link his absolute claims about his identity to his prediction of future resurrection. If the latter were fulfilled, then surely the former were as well. Actually all of Christ's claims are related to the end *(eschatos).* If he is the *eschatos,* then he has to be God

79

himself, the final judge.[16]

• To have an encounter with Jesus Christ is to meet one's ultimate destiny. When radical events occur on planet earth, creating the apocalyptic fear, you can honestly tell your friends, 'I know about the end of the world. I have encountered it (actually him).' To know Jesus is to know one's eternal destiny.

*2. The last days began with Jesus and in Pentecost. Since then we have been living in the last days.*

One hears Christians quoting texts about the special conditions that apply during the last days as though they only refer to the last seven years of world history, or perhaps to our times. This is to miss the point completely. The last days began with the coming of Jesus. Since then they have just been edging closer and closer to the ultimate 'last' day. When Jesus came it was already the end. Perhaps we can speak of the end, the end of the end, and the end of the end of the end. New Testament texts are absolutely clear on this. Hebrews 1 can say, 'in these last days he has spoken to us by his Son' (1:2). Peter can say, concerning Jesus, 'He was chosen before the foundation of the world, but was revealed in these last times for your sake' (1 Pet.1: 20).

This has crucial implications.

• The last days are one, unbroken continuum, from the first coming of Christ, to the Second Coming of Christ, coexisting in tension with this present world. There is no period of church history that has not been a time of the last days. The last few minutes before the Second Coming will not be some different time, only the climax of the same mysterious dimension Christians have experienced since Jesus first came. This is not to say that history cannot 'hot up' or become more dramatic. Revelation shows that it will, but there is no other dispensation waiting to arrive, other than the very end of the end.

• To grasp this is to understand that all dispensational and cessationist theories and schemes have no substance. Cessationists want to tear the time of the apostles away from the remainder of church history and dispensationalists want to do the same with the last seven years. But there is only one, continued dispensation of the last days. The Bible knows of only two dispensations, or ages: this age and the age to come. The age to come arrived when Jesus came.

*3. Every intervention of God since the end came is a breakthrough of the powers of the future age, or eschatological.*

This point is actually an implication of the previous points. If the powers of the coming age have been present since Jesus came, and are inherent in Pentecost; and if the dimension of the Christian life for the whole history of the church is to live 'between the times', or in the interim; it follows that every intervention of God is eschatological. To grasp this is to re-orientate our perspective. Christians tend to look back to the apostolic age. However, Jesus and the apostles lived with a completely future orientation, in the immediacy of the future breaking in on the present. Every Christian is supposed to live like this, from that time to the Second Coming.

The implications of this are as follows:

- Every revival is an intervention of God. Therefore every revival is eschatological. This helps one understand many of the phenomena that occur during revivals.

- They often heighten the sense of expectation about the Second Coming. People sense that it is very near. This is because the powers of the future are coming upon them. They are entering into the end. In fact one should doubt the genuineness of a revival that does not include this dimension.

- Just as with Pentecost, revivals produce startling physical phenomena, affecting the bodily experience of participants. Phenomena such as ecstasy, tongues, prophecy, healing, shaking, falling, weeping, etc. are evidence that our mortal frame cannot absorb the power capable of transforming our bodies into immortality. We are having a foretaste of the final resurrection and the redemption of our bodies.

- Revivals heighten the sense of church unity. This is because the spiritual sense of the New Jerusalem is coming upon people.

*4. Every element of the end is present, or available, in every breakthrough of the kingdom.*

We have learnt that the end is present in fulfilment but not in consummation. All the promises of Isaiah and Daniel were fulfilled in Jesus and are yet to be fulfilled in Jesus. Jesus is risen, but the resurrection is still to occur at the end. The Day of Judgement occurred in the cross, but will still occur. To experience the powers of the kingdom is to partake in the down-payment of our future redemption. It is important that we do not have a fragmented view of the kingdom, picking off this element fulfilled in the first coming of Christ and that element to be fulfilled at the second coming. Actually, 'first coming' and 'second coming' is not biblical language. There is only one kingdom, undivided, that has come, is coming and will come. Think of one big chocolate cake, which you eat in stages. Do not think of two different cakes, or of different ingredients.

This has the following implications:

- Every element is present every time the kingdom draws near. To use the language of Isaiah, the revelation of the glory of God, the presence of the Messianic king, the outpouring of the Spirit, the coming salvation, the forgiveness of sins, the healing of the sick, the resurrection of the dead, eternal joy, the liberation of the captives, the judgement of sin, and the new people of God in a new Jerusalem, are all present with every in-breaking of the kingdom.

- Understanding the kingdom has to change our sense of expectation. Therefore, whenever revival is in the air, comprehensive kingdom expectation must fill our hearts. Of course, by virtue of the sovereign rule of God, we never know the day nor the hour, nor the extent to which a given revival partakes of the powers of the age to come. Nevertheless, we know what can happen, at any moment, in every revival. We live with great expectations!

- We learn that every foretaste we have is just that, a foretaste. The future will be more, much, much more, of the same. The joy you have experienced now is like the joy you will experience, but you will have much more. Everything we experience in Christ has over it the word 'more'.

5. *The age to come and this age are now separated by a thin veil, in fact a veil that has been torn from top to bottom.* Through Jesus, and in Pentecost, the powers of the future age have broken into the present and remain, coexisting with this present age. Christians live permanently caught between the two. We live in a truly mysterious dimension. The kingdom is always here, almost here, delayed, and future. The barrier between two time zones has been ruptured for us. The event that occurred as Jesus said, 'It is finished!' gives graphic representation to this reality. The Greek word used for 'finished' is *telelestai* (Jn.19:30), from *teleios*, the end, fulfilment, full realisation, ultimate destiny, full accomplishment, to consummate. One could paraphrase Jesus as saying, 'This is the final end,' or 'The end is here.' As he died on the cross he announced the presence of the end of the world, the final eschaton.

At that moment the veil of the temple was rent from top to bottom. The significance of the position of the veil is implied in the language of Hebrews 9:8–9. The RSV translation gives the sense I wish to utilise. Speaking of the outer tent (holy place) and the inner tent (holy of holies) it reads, 'By this the Holy Spirit indicates that the way into the sanctuary [inner] is not yet opened as long as the outer tent is still standing (which is symbolic for the present age).' If the outer tent symbolises the present age then the inner tent symbolises the future age.

The symbolism is not difficult to follow. It was in the inner sanctuary that Moses spoke with God face to face. In the outer tent priests worshipped through symbols as intermediaries: the bread on the table, the incense to signify worship, and the candle to signify God's presence, much as we break bread 'till he comes' in foretaste of the marriage supper of the lamb.

The tearing of this veil therefore has the following implications:

- The barrier between this age and the future age is now torn. People worshipping through outward symbols will find themselves carried by the Holy Spirit into an immediacy of God's presence that will be true of the age to come. The manifest presence of God in the future age pours out of the inner sanctuary and covers those who still live in this age. It is a permeable membrane. Christians who understand the kingdom live hovering between two worlds, never knowing when a very ordinary, 'this-worldly' church service will be transformed into an ultimate encounter, or when a private devotional moment will be injected by the powers of the future resurrection.

- Understanding the kingdom therefore becomes a world view, a permanent orientation, a moment-by-moment expectation. Literally, every moment has within it the potential of being the last moment. The kingdom world view makes us continually open to signs and wonders and overwhelming interventions of God.

- Understanding the kingdom also makes us patient with what fails to happen. It is always here, almost here, delayed, and future. Every promise of God, every prophetic word, every calling, every ministry we engage in, has the mysterious sense of being continually delayed by God and yet just around the corner. We live tasting, yet with our mouths watering; filled and yet hungry; satisfied and yet longing; having all, yet needing all. Get used to it! It will not go away until the very end.

*6. The kingdom of God is the proper framework for one's view of church history, which bears witness to an accelerating phenomenon of kingdom interventions.*

If the end was already present in Jesus and in Pentecost, then as we move forward in church history we move more and more into the end of the end, the end of the end of the end. Instead of a graph that peaks during the times of Jesus and the apostles, then bottoms out, and then climbs suddenly at the second coming, we should conceive of a graph that rises sharply at the apostolic period, then undulates on an upward curve. Understanding the kingdom creates in us a new perspective, which views the future as breaking in upon us in ever-increasing waves of intensity.

If one examines church history one notices that the gaps between great movements of revival are becoming narrower and narrower. This will become evident if we simply mention some of the well-known cases and figures.

Assisi
The Reformation
The awakening with Wesley, Whitfield and Edwards
The awakening with Moody and Finney
The Pentecostal Revival
The Jesus People Revival
The Charismatic Renewal
The Renewal of 1994 onwards

Where centuries came between revivals, only decades seem to come between them now. Further, if one examines missions statistics of world populations and the numbers affected each time, the upward curve of the graph is substantiated.

*7. The kingdom is the proper framework for understanding world missions.*

The church lives between victory and triumph. The resurrection of Jesus signified a major breakthrough of the kingdom. The disciples therefore asked if this was the time for its complete manifestation (Ac.1:6). Jesus' reply sets the context for world missions. Pentecost would bring the power of the Spirit onto the church and the church would proclaim the coming of the kingdom in Jerusalem and Judea (indigenous missions), in Samaria (neighbour-culture missions), and to the ends of the earth (cross-culture missions). Their question was about the coming of the kingdom. His answer is about the coming of the kingdom. It came through his ministry and Pentecost. It would continue to come through the mission of the church, and it will come at the very end. The interim period in which the church engages in world missions is the interim of the kingdom being present yet not consummated, with all the realities of the previous points. To use the metaphor of World War II once more, world missions take place between D-Day and V-Day. By proclaiming the kingdom we bring in its presence and speed the day of the ultimate end. We live between the ascension and the return of Christ. By virtue of the ascension he is Lord and Christ, with full authority over every power. By virtue of his return he will be King of kings and Lord of lords, manifesting what he already is.

This has the following implications:

- The proclamation of the kingdom moves from a position of strength and absolute confidence. We have bowed to him and we proclaim him in the knowledge that every knee will finally bow. We may appear to be subject to politicians, dictators and world powers, but we have access to one who is already over them.

- What we preach has an inherent power to transform communities, nations and societies. The total renewal of the planet is here, almost here, delayed and future. Cosmic events took place while Jesus died. Our mission continues to have cosmic significance. The kingdom we preach incorporates a new people in a new city in a new heaven and a new earth. We must never reduce the ability of the gospel to transform society.

## 8. *The Christian life is truly understood in this context.*

The kingdom is something mysterious – here, almost here, delayed and future. Not only is the Christian life placed within this context, but the very nature of the Christian life finds its meaning within this context. We are here, almost here, delayed, future people. We are saved, being saved, and will be saved. We are holy, being made holy and will be holy. We live between the times. We are already-not yet people. Two ages co-exist within us and we live simultaneously in two ages. The world around us lives in one age, one dimension. We are much more mysterious. We live in two ages. We are becoming what we already are. We are born out of the powers of the future age. We have eternal life, the life of the future ages.

This is not simply a theological construct, but a lived experience.

The Christian is aware of an inner contradiction. The 'old man' and the 'new man' oppose one another from within. The flesh and the spirit work against each other. We are not schizophrenic people, just kingdom people. We do not need counselling; we just need to understand the kingdom. We are victorious and broken, winners and losers, dead and yet alive. Sometimes we feel a sense of victory and despair on the same day.

Understanding this has implications.

- The dimension of the interim is not a passing phase for the Christian. It is always with us. We live permanently in the already and the not yet. This is the air we breathe and the context of our lives. Trying to escape this eschatological tension is like trying to jump out of one's skin. This is it, for the Christian life.

- If we overstate the present reality of the kingdom (realised eschatology) we run the danger of triumphalism and conceive of the Christian life as an experience with no suffering, no pain, and no failure.

- If we overstate the future reality of the kingdom (consistent eschatology) we run the danger of defeatism. It can take many shapes:

escaping from society and waiting for the rapture, social resignation, 'remnantitis', and defeatism. People in such a state do not believe in healing, expect few to be saved, and settle for defeat against sin.

## 9. *The kingdom is the proper context for the ministry of healing.*

Why are some healed while others are not? Why does healing happen some of the time but not all the time? Those who lack the kingdom as a model for healing will tend to lack the sense of the mysterious. They will place too much emphasis on the role of the believing or unbelieving subject, or on the role of the believing or unbelieving prayer. The truth is that whenever someone is healed it bears witness to the fact that the kingdom is here. Whenever someone is not healed it bears witness to the fact that the kingdom is not yet here. Sure, we can grow in the gifts of the Holy Spirit, in faith, in expectation and in availability to God. Some are more used than others. But ultimately, the only way to explain what does and does not happen is to understand the already and not yet of the kingdom.

This means the following:

- Every time you pray for the sick you should be full of expectation. The veil has been rent. Anything is possible at any moment, including the freedom of the captives, the healing of the sick and the raising of the dead.

- Every time you pray for the sick you should 'hang loose' in the mystery. When nothing happens do not be 'fazed' at all. After all, this is the 'not yet' dimension in which we live. Delayed answers to prayer, and things that are not yet here, are all part of the kingdom.

## 10. *This is the perspective for understanding the relationship between the church and society.*

If we fail to grasp the tension between the already and the not yet we will drift off into withdrawal or idealism. Because the kingdom is here, God has given us a mission to transform individuals, families, communities and nations. Because the kingdom is not yet here, no society prior to the return of Christ will ever become totally just, free and godly. Jerusalem and Babylon will struggle against each other continually. The bride and the harlot will win the affections of men's hearts. We have no doubt as to the final outcome, but we must hold the tension.

This has the following implications:

- No 'this-worldly' cause, movement, philosophy or ideology can ever capture us. We have a healthy sense of scepticism about all idealistic endeavours, be they an overly 'social gospel', liberation theology, or reconstructionism.

- We can never give up on the world and withdraw into an evangelical ghetto where we cluster together into our saved remnant and wait for the rapture, because it will all burn anyway. The enormity of knowing that the kingdom is here makes us the most optimistic, prophetic, visionary people on earth. This must transform our attitude towards social issues.

These implications are so significant that we will need to explore some of them in much more detail in subsequent chapters.

*Live expectantly*
*The future is present*

*Good Chapt.*

# Bringing in the Kingdom

The nature of the kingdom, as the breakthrough of the future into the present and the implications we have just examined in the last chapter leads to the fundamental question: What unleashes those future age powers into this present age? Is there a trigger mechanism? Granted that while ultimately it remains in the sovereignty of God, is there nevertheless a way of seeking the kingdom that will make its appearance more likely? Can we penetrate the mystery?

A second question emerges from these questions. We have seen that the coming of the kingdom took place in Jesus and in Pentecost. To say 'Jesus is present' is to say, 'The kingdom is here.' How does this relate to the proclamation of the kingdom by the church? Do the same trigger mechanisms apply when Jesus is physically present and when he is present through the Holy Spirit?

## Jesus, the Personification of the Kingdom

The coming of the kingdom is the 'becoming present' of the rule of God. God's ultimate rule, which will take place at the end of the age, breaks through into this present age. The witness of the New Testament is that Jesus is the personification of that coming. That is why Jesus is God with us. To say 'kingdom come' is to say, 'Come Lord Jesus.' He is the epicentre, the focus, and the essence of the coming kingdom. He is the eschaton!

The witness of the New Testament to Jesus as the essence of the kingdom is twofold.

## Jesus the Messiah

The term 'Messiah' or 'Christ' is the Jewish title for king. Much has been written about the so-called 'Messianic consciousness' of Jesus and many scholars have attempted to deny that Jesus saw himself as the Messiah. This view cannot be supported from the New Testament. It is true that Jesus rejected the political Messianism of his day and therefore seldom identified with the title, but this does not mean that he rejected the Messianic role. The two greatest kings of Israel were David and Solomon. Jesus knew that he was greater than either of them (Mk.12:35–37; Matt.12:42).

Jesus entered Jerusalem as the triumphant king. Each Gospel highlights a particular aspect of this event (Matt.21:1–11; Mk.11:1–10; Lk.19:28–44; Jn.12:12–19). Matthew makes the fullest use of the Old Testament passage: 'See, your king comes to you.' Mark records the Messianic content of the public acclamation: 'Blessed is the coming kingdom of our father David.' Luke records Jesus' comment when the Pharisees wanted him to stop the disciples' praise: 'I tell you, if they keep quiet, the stones will cry out.' This was Jerusalem's hour of divine 'visitation'. John quotes the public acclamation: 'Blessed is he who comes in the name of the Lord! Blessed is the king of Israel!' He mentions how 'the world has gone after him'.

Jesus was tried for his Messianic claims. Caiaphas adjured him to confess whether he was the Christ or not (Matt.26:63). His reply was: 'Yes, it is as you said' (26:64). Mark records Jesus' reply as a clear affirmative (Mk.14:62). Clearly Jesus accepted the Messianic title. However, he immediately connected this title with that of the 'Son of Man' which suited his understanding of his role far better than the current political expectations of the Messiah. As we learned from Daniel, it represented an even greater claim. The Son of Man is the one who is seated at the right hand of God who will come on the clouds of heaven to judge the world.

When Jesus was taken to Pilate, he was asked basically the same question: 'Are you the King of the Jews?' Again he gave an affirmative reply (Matt.27:11). John adds that Jesus explained the nature of his kingdom to Pilate (Jn.18:37). When Jesus was eventually brought before the people, Pilate tried to have him released. He had been disturbed by a dream his wife had had the night before. From all accounts, Pilate was not a forceful character. The Jews put political pressure on him to condemn Jesus on the charge of treason (19:12). His claim to be the Messiah directly confronted Caesar's claim.

It was customary to place a notice above those who were publicly executed stating what crime they had committed. Accordingly Pilate had a notice placed above Jesus' cross: 'JESUS OF NAZARETH, THE KING OF THE JEWS.' It was written in Aramaic, Latin and Greek (19:19–20). The Jews resented this, but Pilate would not reverse his decision. This determination by a weak pagan ruler reveals God's sovereign will. Jesus is the King of the nations, even as he hangs on the cross.

## Jesus, the Announcer of the Kingdom

In Israel kings were elected by public announcement. The people would shout, 'Long live the king!' (1 Sam.10:24) In the New Testament one also finds a connection between kingship and public announcement. The word *kerygma*, translated 'proclamation' comes from *kerysso*, which means 'to announce'.

The Roman Empire did not have a television network to announce imperial edicts to the population. They employed special heralds to do this. The *keryx* (herald or announcer) was a man commissioned by his ruler or the state to call out with a clear voice an item of news and so to make it known. Heralds carried important news items from town to town. They would enter each town, find a prominent public venue, make their proclamation, and pass on to the next town. The *keryx* was always under the authority of someone else, whose spokesman he was. He himself was immune. He conveyed the message and intention of his master. His office had an official character and he was therefore the announcer of judicial verdicts. As the official edict or verdict was spoken, it became binding. The word became an event.

The New Testament writers used this word to describe what occurred in the ministry of Jesus. He heralded in the powers of the age to come by a clear, public proclamation. In fact, it was his word or announcement that caused things to happen. When he spoke, eschatological events began to take place. The very announcement of the nearness of the kingdom resulted in its powers being unleashed. The answer to our question: 'How do the powers of the age to come break into this age?' is therefore: 'By the proclaimed word of Jesus.'

Jesus began his ministry with the announcement of the nearness of the kingdom (Mk.1:14–15). This was immediately followed by an act demonstrating that the announcement was actually in effect. A demonised man was set free by the authoritative word of Jesus (1:27). Like a herald, Jesus had an urgent commission to preach in all the towns (1:38–39). As he did so proclamation became synonymous with healing and deliverance: the leper was healed because Jesus said 'I am willing' (1:41). The lame man walked because he said 'Arise' (2:11). The centurion knew that Jesus had only to 'speak a word' (Matt.8:8). When Jesus said 'Go!' the demons went (8:32). One can view the entire public ministry of Jesus in two ways: *the words of Jesus* and the *works of Jesus*. The works were always the result of the words, and the works were always proclaiming a word. They announced the kingdom.

The scary thing for the disciples, and for us, is that Jesus expected the disciples to make the same announcement. Herein lies the connection between the coming of the kingdom then and now. The trigger mechanism, of announcement, remains the same.

## The Great Announcement

One normally speaks of the 'Great Commission'. We now learn that the essence of the commission is announcement, or heralding the *kerygma*.

The breakthrough of the kingdom occurred through the coming of Jesus and through Pentecost. Pentecost occurred because Jesus ascended. It is therefore, in a sense, an aspect of the coming of Jesus. Jesus' words and works were the trigger mechanism of the kingdom. Jesus' works had their climax in his death, burial, resurrection and ascension. All these works unleashed the breakthrough of the powers of the age to come. The astonishing reality for the church is that Jesus expected the coming of the kingdom to continue, after this departure, through Pentecostal power and the 'great announcement' of the church.

This is such an important subject that we need to delve a little deeper.

Perhaps I should digress into some personal reflection. Since I am a Vineyard pastor it will be helpful to contextualise what we are talking about. This really is a major issue for the Vineyard. I had been a pastor for about five years, in a Pentecostal denomination. I had witnessed Pentecostal phenomena for some time. The university where I studied theology happened to be the context for the beginning of the charismatic renewal amongst Anglicans in South Africa. Then, in the late seventies, I encountered the ministry of Vineyard leaders for the first time and in particular, the prayer, 'Come Holy Spirit.' After worship, or preaching or both, there was always a time of 'waiting to see what God will do', or 'waiting on the Holy Spirit'. I recall how John Wimber would pray a prayer, often using language about the kingdom of God in his prayer, then fold his arms and stand there, eyes open, literally looking to see what would happen. Invariably a great deal would happen, with manifestations of Pentecostal phenomena more intense than I had ever seen in my pastoral experience to that time. It fascinated, intimidated and frustrated me. I would go back to my church and try the same thing, to no effect. They seemed to have some kind of secret, or key. Could I ever move in the same dimension? I now realise that what looked so easy, to an observer, and so simple, was the result of a much wider context. This included the kingdom theology of George Ladd, who had influenced Wimber; the experience of the Jesus People revival; and the particular move of the Holy Spirit that launched the Vineyard movement.[17] I should add that although I grasped the theological basis of what was happening during that period it was only when the 1994 renewal occurred in our church that I was privileged to experience, in my own ministry, the dynamics of the kingdom we are examining in this chapter. What follows therefore is my theological and experiential reflection looking back over about 25 years.

The key to bringing in the kingdom is to engage in the 'Great Announcement'. The announcement takes place in the context of two other vital components. These three components are expectation, prayer and announcement. The kingdom announcement must be made after the prayer of the kingdom. The prayer of the kingdom must take place within the framework of kingdom expectation.

## 1. Kingdom Expectation

If the announcement of the kingdom is the 'Great Announcement' then the expectation of the kingdom amounts to 'Great Expectations'!

Jesus taught his disciples to pray: 'Our Father in heaven, hallowed be your name, your kingdom come, your will be done on earth as it is in heaven' (Matt.6:9–10). When Jesus taught on such prayer his language was expressing the total vision of the kingdom. It is not just about prayer, but about a certain kind of prayer, a prayer that is focused on a great expectation. The greater our expectation, or the more 'kingdom' our expectation, the more 'kingdom' will be our prayer. There are two things that can inspire such prayer: biblical revelation and experience.

## Biblical Revelation

We need to saturate our minds in the prophetic promise of scripture regarding the kingdom. The coming of the kingdom in the exodus event, the Davidic monarchy, and the promises of Isaiah, Daniel and other prophets amount to a massive expectation, all of which was in mind when Jesus told us to pray, 'Your kingdom come.' 'Our Father in heaven, hallowed be your name,' reminds us of the profound connection between the name of God and the coming of the kingdom. Moses first encountered the 'I Am Who I Am', then announced the kingdom to Pharaoh, and then saw the spiritual and military manifestation of the kingdom. David exalted in the name of Yahweh as he responded to Nathan's prophetic word and then saw the victory manifest. When Jesus spoke of his Father he did so in the context of his relationship with the Father, which John's gospel describes and reflects on. To know the name of God is to have the expectation of his becoming present.

Such a total kingdom expectation must be placed in contrast to various forms of reductionism that have plagued the church. Dispensationalism and cessationism combine to reduce what people expect today when they pray, 'Your kingdom come.' If signs and wonders ceased with the apostles, then we do not expect them to happen in answer to this prayer. If the church is going to escape from the world, then we have a reduced expectation of world evangelism when we pray that prayer. We need to allow the full revelation of scripture to enlarge our expectation until it is a truly kingdom expectation. _pray_

## Holy Spirit Experiences

Until one has witnessed what happens during great moves of the Holy Spirit one does not know what to expect. The more you see, the more you expect when you pray the kingdom prayer. In fact, once you have seen it, you can never settle for less. If not much was happening in his meetings, John Wesley used to pray, 'Lord, where are the tokens and signs?'[18] As I reflect on the last decades of pastoral ministry I look back over a gradual enlargement of expectation. The journey is marked by seasons of special enlargement of expectation: my conversion experience, the beginnings of the charismatic renewal in South Africa and my first encounter with Pentecostals, the Jesus People movement in Cape Town, the early visits of Lonnie Frisbee and John Wimber to South Africa, the 1994 renewal and the years that have followed. Each Christian can review his experience of encounter with God. I have found that such seasons have been linked to periods of intense interest in church history and the stories of similar phenomena. The more we see, the more we expect to see.

## 2. Kingdom Prayer

It is not just about prayer per se, or about how much we pray. It is about a certain kind of praying, a specific prayer: 'Your kingdom come.' The theology of the kingdom should be required for groups of intercessors. Once they have been equipped with the full kingdom expectation, intercessors can be informed 'pray-ers'.

The kingdom prayer occurs in the secret place. The kingdom announcement occurs in the public place. What happens in the secret place is the foundation of what occurs in the public place. Even here, there is a sense of mystery. It is certainly not the case that the amount of praying we do is proportional to the amount of breakthrough we see. There are times when one has prayed very little but after announcing the kingdom more takes place than other times when one has prayed much more. It is really about a certain dynamic that takes place in a certain kind of prayer. When our minds and hearts are enlarged with the expectation of the kingdom, the way we pray changes. The early church entered into this dimension when they prayed, 'Now Lord … Stretch out your hand to heal and perform miraculous signs and wonders through the name of your holy servant Jesus' (Ac.4:29–30). The more we expect, the more we pray with expectation. Such prayer then works on our expectation. It quickens it, enlarges it and sharpens it. Prayer and expectation are reciprocal with each other. The Holy Spirit becomes present and one becomes more and more expansive in what one prays for. One begins to feel that it is a small thing for God to act. The long history of his mighty acts in biblical times and through church history, the great revivals one has read about, and the things one has seen all fuse into a focal point as one considers the immediate situation: the meeting ahead, the mission at hand, the time and place. One walks out of such a prayer meeting believing that anything can happen.

### 3. Kingdom Announcement

The commission to the disciples mirrors the prior activity of Jesus. Having watched him role-model kingdom ministry through words and deeds, Jesus told the disciples to go and do the same. They were to announce the presence of the kingdom and to demonstrate its power. 'As you go, preach, saying: "The kingdom of heaven is at hand." Heal the sick, raise the dead, cleanse those who have leprosy, drive out demons' (Matt. 10:7–8). Notice the connection between word and event. The word or announcement ('the kingdom is near') creates or unleashes the events that demonstrate it (heal, raise, cleanse, drive out). Word leads to deed. Announcement, or proclamation, leads to demonstration. The power of the demonstration lay in the announcement. A modern paraphrase of Jesus' words would be:

*Announce that the personal, ultimate reign of God at the end of world history has broken into this present world.*

The significant texts for the commissions are as follows:

- Mark 1:14–15 and Luke 4:16–21 record the inaugural words of Jesus, announcing the nature of his future ministry.

- Matthew 10:1–10 and Luke 9:1–6 record Jesus placing the same ministry on the twelve. Two key terms used here are 'power and authority'. Power *(dunamis)* refers to the ability, or empowering to make the announcement, what we today call anointing. Authority *(exousia)* refers to delegated authority to act in the name of Jesus. When we know under whose authority we act, we have authority. It relates to our sense of confidence and affirmation by God.

- Luke 10:1–9 records the giving of the commission to the seventy (or seventy-two). The fact that there is no difference between the two commissions shows that it was not meant to be restricted to the twelve apostles.

- Matthew 28:16–20 and Luke 24.45–49 with Acts 1:1–11 and John 20:19–23 record the reiteration of the commission to the disciples after the crucifixion and resurrection.

This is still the commission of the church.

How does this work in practice? We return to some personal reflections and lessons from the dynamics of Vineyard ministry. Expectation leads to prayer and prayer leads to announcement. How exactly does one make the announcement? Do we go into the streets shouting, 'The end is nigh!' and find ourselves institutionalised?

I believe the gifts of the Holy Spirit have been given specifically to operate as the means of making the announcement. The word of knowledge, prophecy and healing are particularly helpful. During the time of prayer prior to a given meeting, the Holy Spirit will often give some indication of what the Father intends to do. Particulars of conditions, needs, names and life situations may come to mind. There may be a prophetic sense that God wants to move in a particular way.

Once one is in a meeting one should become sensitive to the sense of God's arrival. Here is where we draw a distinction between the omnipresence of God and his manifest presence. This point should be clear by now. There are church meetings where we 'do church' in a very normal, 'this-worldly' manner, giving worship, teaching the word and having fellowship. Then there are times when, often without warning, an intangible change takes place. Previous experiences of great moves of the Spirit can help us pick up the change more easily. Though intangible to many, some people have physical sensations indicating the shift. It is time to stop whatever we are doing when 'doing church' – and to wait on God.

The worship or the preaching may heighten the sense of God 'becoming present'. Certain kinds of preaching draw closer to the pure act of kingdom announcement than others. Certain ministry gifts have the same effect. Those with the gift of evangelism or prophetic ministry tend to move in a dimension of announcement. Sometimes words of knowledge will come, not during the prayer beforehand, but there and then, at a particular point in the meeting.

Whatever the exact nature of the 'trigger mechanism', announcement means that declaration whereby the people are told that God is about to intervene, manifestly. If a word of knowledge is accurate the recipients cannot but believe that God knows about their private cry, cares about them, and has made this known at this very moment for a purpose. It heightens the sense of expectation. Preaching that carries a sense of penetration into the heart of man has the same effect. Intimate worship can bring people to a state of prostration and transparency before God and will have the same result.

There is ample precedent in church history for this dynamic. The revival that broke out under the leadership of Andrew Murray in Wellington, South Africa, occurred when a young woman read a certain verse from the Psalms after a youth meeting had been in prayer. Suddenly the Holy Spirit fell on the whole group and Andrew Murray was summoned to observe the seeming 'chaos' that followed. The Holy Spirit can use all sorts of moments and mechanisms to release the sense of God's manifest presence. Yes Lord !!!!

The *moment critique* comes in the interface between announcement, prayer and waiting. The announcement has to be made before anything actually happens, even though it may be in response to a subjective sense of God drawing near. Quite often the announcement, 'God is about to move in this meeting, right now ...' will be linked to a prayer for God to do so. This is what we call the 'Come Holy Spirit' prayer. Critics often ask for biblical references for such a prayer. However, the kingdom prayer, 'Let your kingdom come,' understood against the background of Pentecost as a moment of kingdom intervention should reveal the ineptitude of such questions. To pray, 'Let your kingdom come,' or to pray, 'Come Holy Spirit,' amounts to exactly the same thing.

All of this is done through obedience to the commission of Jesus. We are to do it because he said so, not because we claim any particular results for ourselves. To pray such a prayer, or to make such an announcement is therefore to place all the pressure on God and to take all the pressure off us. He told us to do it to the end of time. He is sovereign. It is his business to either endorse our obedience or not.

What does one do after that? The temptation is to try to make something happen. Failure to understand the nature of the kingdom will lead to manipulation. We are not called to press certain emotional buttons and manipulate people into responses. If God is sovereign it is better to 'dial down' into quietness and hang suspended on the raw obedience to the commission. It is time to wait, and if necessary, to wait and wait. Sometimes such times of waiting lead to nothing and it is time to drink coffee. Other times, the longer one waits the greater the sense of pregnant expectation and the greater the sense of intervention by God. For those up front, the time following the announcement and prior to the intervention of God is rather like the experience of a bungee jumper, in free fall. At this point faith is spelt r-i-s-k.

Those who are called to preach the gospel are called to live in this dimension, from Pentecost to the very end. This leads us to the next chapter. Such proclamation is to be the focus of the church, for the entire age of the church, 'between the times'.

# Acts of Intervention

The Old Testament promised that the kingdom would come. The New Testament records the fulfilment of this promise in Jesus and the expectation of the final culmination of the promise in the return of Christ. The church lives between the coming and the consummation of the kingdom, between the times. This does not mean that the church lives in a vacuum, caught between memory and expectation. The Pentecostal outpouring of the Holy Spirit fills the church period. The ministry of the Spirit links what began in Jesus with what continues in the church as one extended event, undivided and yet manifest in repeated waves of divine intervention. No portion of Scripture explains this better than the book of Acts.

## Acts

### *The Act of God*

We have seen that the kingdom is not a static truth or a universal principle but a dynamic event. God breaks into human history and interrupts it. The Word becomes flesh. God's rule collides with the powers of this age. There is confrontation, invasion, warfare and power. The stone falls from heaven and pulverises the image. Satan is vanquished. Death is defeated. People are transformed by God. Society is revolutionised. All this is the *act of God*. The act of God, which is the intervention of his kingdom, is expressed and embodied in his Son, Jesus Christ. To speak of the act of God is therefore to speak of the coming of Jesus Christ. Acts helps us to follow the way in which the act of God is the event of the kingdom in Jesus. It is manifest in the acts of the Holy Spirit and becomes, in turn, the acts of the apostles, which in practice becomes the acts of the church.

## The Acts of Jesus Christ

Luke introduces the book of Acts as the record of the continued acts of Jesus. He reminds Theophilus that his Gospel was the record of what 'Jesus began to do and to teach' (Acts 1:1). His second volume is the record of what Jesus continued to do and teach, how 'God anointed Jesus of Nazareth with the Holy Spirit and power, and how he went about doing good and healing all who were under the power of the devil' (10:38). Jesus is God's anointed king. The presence of the kingdom is personified and manifested in him. This means that the coming of the kingdom is the act of Jesus Christ. This is illustrated time and again.

Pentecost happened because Jesus ascended and poured out the gift of the Holy Spirit. The lame man was healed through faith in Jesus' name. The early church prayed for signs and wonders to be done through the name of Jesus, and this is exactly what happened. Crowds gathered as people were healed. While Stephen was being stoned, he saw the Son of Man standing at the right hand of God. Paul was converted because Jesus appeared to him in blinding light and called him to his service. The Spirit of Jesus guided Paul in his missionary strategy. Acts is therefore a record of the continued presence of the risen Lord in his church.

## The Acts of the Holy Spirit

In reply to the disciples' question about when the kingdom would be restored to Israel, Jesus said that they would receive power when the Holy Spirit came (1:6–8). Henceforth the kingdom would come through the Holy Spirit. When Jesus sat down at the right hand of God, the Holy Spirit brought his kingly rule to earth. Henceforth he would be present through the Holy Spirit. The book of Acts is therefore filled with references to the *acts of the Holy Spirit.*

The Spirit came upon the disciples and they spoke with tongues. The apostles preached and testified in the power of the Spirit. The Holy Spirit was poured out on the Samaritans, on Paul, on the Gentiles and on the Ephesians. It was the Spirit who directed Peter to preach to Cornelius. As he did, the Spirit came on the household, taking Peter by surprise and forcing him to accept them into the family of God. The Spirit directed the church at Antioch to launch its mission to the Gentiles. So closely is the presence of the Spirit associated with the rule of Jesus, that Paul's leading by the Spirit of Jesus is the same as being led by the Holy Spirit.

## The Acts of the Apostles

We can also say that this book records the *acts of the Apostles.* The Spirit works through anointed individuals. Jesus promised: 'But you will receive power when the Holy Spirit comes on you; and you will be my witnesses in Jerusalem, and in all Judea and Samaria, and to the ends of the earth' (1:8). From the moment that they were filled with the Spirit at Pentecost, everything God had done through Jesus continued through the apostles. The result was that when they preached Jesus as King, they turned the world upside down. Wherever they went they caused a social upheaval. Cities like Ephesus were drastically altered. They could no longer obey the Sanhedrin because of their obedience to a higher power. They no longer feared the Roman authorities but called these authorities to account for their administration of justice. Just as Jesus' proclamation of the kingdom caused it to break through, when the apostles proclaimed the kingship of Jesus, the kingdom came.

## The Acts of the Church

The book of Acts also records the *acts of the church*. The apostles were the leaders and representatives of a kingdom people. Believers filled Jerusalem with the teaching of Jesus and went to Antioch to preach the gospel when they were scattered from Judea. Widows like Tabitha and young women like Philip's daughters prophesied. Prophets like Agabus and evangelists like Philip testified to the kingdom, bringing the power of the kingdom to villages, towns and cities. Young men saw visions and old men dreamed dreams, all of them together receiving the prophetic anointing of the Spirit.

The church announces the kingdom in the continual expectation that it will come, finally, at any time. God has fixed a day when he will judge the world through Jesus Christ. The church does not announce a probable hope but an accomplished fact: Jesus is King. The kingdom has come, Satan is defeated and Jesus is Lord of all. Because all this has already been accomplished, the church can heal the sick and drive out demons by the power of the Holy Spirit. Wherever the Holy Spirit moves, the kingdom breaks through. This is no vacuum or waiting period. It is a period of Spirit-filled kingdom intervention when the Word is made flesh in countless individuals.

The spreading of the gospel in this period of history takes place through the missionary strategy of the church. The kingdom is not a vague universal principle. It breaks through as believers proclaim Jesus as King. Jesus gave a clear set of priorities:

- Jerusalem,
- Judea and Samaria,
- the ends of the earth.

The book of Acts records the fulfilment of this strategy. One can describe the latter part of Acts as the biography of the apostle Paul. The destiny of the gospel is tied up with his destiny in arrest, betrayal, mistrial and retrial. Particular cities experience the coming of the kingdom: Cyprus,

Pisidian Antioch, Iconium, Lystra and Derbe, Philippi, Thessalonica, Berea, Athens, Corinth, etc. The record of the coming of the kingdom becomes a travel narrative. Where the apostles go, the kingdom comes.

Because the kingdom is an event, not a principle or a social system, it can only be followed as a series of acts. Kingdom events are acts of the Holy Spirit, in and through the acts of apostolic testimony, in and through an apostolic church.

The nature of the kingdom has not changed; therefore the break through of the kingdom cannot change. Where the word is proclaimed, light collides with darkness, people bow to Jesus the King, their lives are transformed, cities and villages are turned upside down, communities of kingdom people are born, bodies are healed and demons are put to flight, and world rulers are disturbed by the competing claim of the kingdom. The breakthrough has many implications: social, philosophical, economic and political, but the implications are not in themselves the event. The coming of the kingdom has to be a record of acts. Study the history of missions and revivals, and you will be studying the continuation of Acts.

Luke's story is deliberately unfinished. The last verse of Acts says of Paul: 'Boldly and without hindrance he preached the kingdom of God and taught about the Lord Jesus Christ' (28:31). Acts 29 and beyond was to be written by other believers, chapter after chapter of the one, indivisible breakthrough of the kingdom from city to city, from nation to nation and from continent to continent, merging into the history of revivals.

# PART III

## The Theology of the Kingdom

*The title of part three is a little inaccurate because we have been dealing with the theology of the kingdom from the very beginning.*

*However we now move from tracing the overall theme of the kingdom in scripture to probing more of its details and working out more of its implications.*

# The Parables of the Kingdom

Perhaps the most characteristic element in the teaching of Jesus was his parables. Again we find that the kingdom of God is central. Christ often began his explanation of the kingdom (Mark 4:30) with, 'To what shall we liken the kingdom of God? Or with what parable shall we picture it?' A number of themes emerge from the parables that give us a clear picture of how Jesus understood the kingdom.[19]

The overriding theme is the relationship between the present and the future, between the kingdom now and the kingdom to come. In the present the kingdom comes near to men through the preaching of the Word. In the future the kingdom will confront men in final judgement or mercy. This tension brings men to the crisis of response. How they react now to the kingdom will determine how they stand in the future coming of the kingdom. Because the future of the kingdom hovers over men with such nearness, their decision cannot be postponed. They cannot afford the luxury of taking their time to decide. Yet we must not think that men can determine their status in the future kingdom by their behaviour. We enter the kingdom by grace – it breaks through to people who do not deserve it. Our response is merely the receiving of a gift.

We usually speak of 'the present and the future' because we orientate ourselves in the present and look towards the future. But Jesus speaks of the present from the future. He stands with God in the ultimate future of his kingly reign and speaks into the present. This is one of the reasons for saying that Jesus addresses men as God. Only God can speak from the future.

## The Kingdom Comes in the Future

The future orientation appears repeatedly in the parables.

The sower looks to the future harvest (Matthew 13:1–23). Weeds and wheat grow together 'until the harvest' (13:30) at the end of the age, when men will either shine like the sun or be burned in the fire (13:40–42). The mustard seed must not be underestimated because of its future as a great tree (13:31–32). The catch of fish awaits the final moment, when good and bad are separated (13:47–52). It is no use hiding the light in a jar because in the future everything will be disclosed (Luke 8:16–18). One must build on rock, not sand, because the future brings a storm of judgement that will destroy whatever has no foundation (6:46–49). The rich fool was caught because he thought he could live out his days with ease, but the future came upon him unexpectedly (12:13–21).

This theme of the tension between the present and the future is dramatised in two events: the great feast and the return of the Lord. The day will come when God will invite people to a great banquet (14:15–24). The different ways in which men respond is an indication of their position at the Messianic banquet: men are either received or thrown into outer darkness. They find either judgement or mercy.

The future dispensation is initiated by the return of the master. He returns from a wedding banquet (12:35–48). The bad manager is placed in crisis because he is called to account and has little time to find the means to pay. The future has caught him unawares (16:1–13). The servants who were given ten minas face the day when the nobleman will return (19:11–27). Other servants who have been given different talents await the return of their master from his journey (Matthew 25:14–30). In the same way, the tenants of the vineyard face the day of the landowner's return and the virgins face the return of the bridegroom (21:33–46; 25:1–13).

The most dramatic picture of the future is presented in the story of Lazarus and the rich man. The point it makes is that once the future arrives, it is too late to change. He has crossed the river and there is no turning back (Luke 16:19–31).

## The Future Impinges on the Present

This future impinges on the present with such force that the 'now' is filled with significance. Right now the Son of Man is preaching the word of the kingdom (Matthew 13:37); good and bad seed are sown together; the mustard seed looks insignificant; the fish are encircled by the great net, and seed is being scattered abroad (Mark 4:26–29). We are to decide now, in the light of the future, not to hide the lamp in the jar, to build on rock, not on sand. The fool, who lives only for the present age, makes a choice to build a bigger barn but will never be able to complete it. We have to be ready at all times because we do not know when the thief will come (Luke 12:35–40).

We cannot be idle about the present. Already invitations are being sent out for the great banquet and the bad manager is being given notice to draw up his accounts. Those who received money from the master must be making it work for them. The owner of the vineyard is sending out his representatives prior to his coming. The oil in the virgins' lamps is burning down.

We should be aware that we live in a pregnant present overshadowed by an ultimate future. The danger is that we will be mystified by the hidden way in which the future is being manifest now and miss its overpowering significance. How does the little bit of leaven affect all the meal (Matthew 13:33)? How can the mustard seed become a great tree?

How can a Galilean carpenter be the Messiah of the age to come? Why is there a delay before the bridegroom appears? If we conclude that the urgency has passed, we are seriously mistaken. There is no time to allow a tree to fail to bear fruit. If it does not bear within one more season, chop it down (Luke 13:6–9)!

Becoming snagged on the exact relationship between the present and the future will do us no good. We have to accept that it is a mystery. The farmer scatters the seed and goes to sleep. Suddenly, one thing has become another. The seemingly indiscriminate scattering of seed has become a great harvest while he was asleep. He was actually blind to the way in which the one became the other.

## The Kingdom Creates a Crisis of Decision

The way the future impinges on the present has already revealed the priority of decision. The future kingdom has become present in Jesus. A choice is therefore forced upon men and women. Their reactions, attitudes and responses come under the spotlight. Some cannot even understand the message. Others do, but their interest is shallow. Then there are those who respond but allow the pressures of this age to choke the word. Some respond with depth (Matthew 13:18–23). If people could see how their response to the presence of the kingdom determines their ultimate position, they would be like the man who sold all his possessions to buy just one pearl of great value (13:45–46). They would not be so foolish as to make excuses about attending the banquet (Luke 14:15–24). They would rush around putting things right, like the bad but shrewd manager (16:1–13). They would not live in ease and luxury like the rich man and ignore the Lazarus at the gate.

The response to the present challenge of the kingdom must be deeper than mere words. In the parable of the two sons, the one son who said yes to the kingdom actually meant no, while the one who said no actually meant yes. It is the reality of our response that counts (Matthew 21:28–32).

114

We could summarise the mood of Jesus' parables in the words of Paul:

> *We implore you … be reconciled to God … We urge you not to receive God's grace in vain. For he says, "At the time of my favour I heard you, and on the day of salvation I helped you." I tell you, now is the time of God's favour; now is the day of salvation.* (2 Corinthians 5:20–6:2)

Rudolf Bultmann was a European biblical scholar who had difficulty with the 'supernatural' elements in the New Testament. He believed we should strip away the 'mythological' husk that covered the inner kernel of biblical truth. This made him rather unpopular with evangelical believers. Yet despite this he did provide an insight that made a valid contribution. He was strongly influenced by a European philosophy called existentialism which sharpened his perception of how the kingdom message of Jesus brought about a 'crisis of response' in those who heard it. The kingdom preaching of Jesus includes the idea of an event that can take place at any moment. In fact, the event is so near that it is actually here. This event is nothing less than the end of the world. What would you do right now if you knew that this world would end tomorrow? Your priorities would change immediately. Nonessentials would be dropped. Essentials would take their rightful place as you prepared to meet your God. The preaching of Jesus brought about just such a crisis of decision. This note is evident in statements such as: 'Follow Me, and let the dead bury their own dead' (Matthew 8:22). Don't wait for ordinary life to take its course. You don't have the time. Make up your mind now!

But, you may ask, did the end of the world actually take place? Surely the sense of urgency was misplaced? 'Wrong!' says the New Testament. Everything we have looked at so far confirms that the end of the world came in Jesus Christ. Whenever the powers of the age to come break into this world, we experience the end of the world. When you accept Jesus, you encounter the end of the world because he is the end of the world. This is why a confrontation with Jesus is the ultimate confrontation. Once this has happened, death, and the end of the world are no longer foreboding prospects. You have broken through already because the end of the age has come upon you. Since that breakthrough occurred in Jesus Christ, we have continued to live in this mysterious situation where the present world coexists with the last days. In this age of grace any moment can be the last and, for every individual, each moment has the potential to be the breakthrough of that last moment. An oft-quoted sentence from Bultmann is that 'Every instant has the possibility of being an eschatological instant and in Christian faith this possibility is realised.'[20]

As we have seen, this has profound implications for an understanding of signs and wonders, an implication Bultmann certainly did not entertain.

## Vehicles of Grace

Our response to the breakthrough of the kingdom is not what brings us acceptance. We do not share in that future glory because of anything we have done. In this sense we cannot work for our future place. There was no logical connection between how long the labourers worked and what they were paid (Matthew 20:1–16). The farmer paid what he wanted to pay. Those who obtained entrance to the Messianic banquet were those who had no merit in society. All they did was to accept the invitation (22:1–14). They were clothed by the king. Those who are secure in their place in the kingdom are the lost sheep who have been found by the shepherd (Luke 15:1–7). They did not find the kingdom. The kingdom found them, like the woman who searched through her house for one lost coin (15:8–10). The lost son must decide to return to his Father's house, but his acceptance is the result of the forgiving love and mercy of his Father (15:11–32). The crisis of response may be vital, but grace is ultimately significant in our discovering the kingdom.

## Parables of Jesus

Here is a list of Jesus' parables.

| Description | Matthew | Mark | Luke | John |
|---|---|---|---|---|
| Candle and candlestick | 5:14–16 | | | |
| House on Rock/Sand | 7:24–27 | | | |
| New piece/old cloth | 9:16 | | 2:21 | 5:36 |
| New wine/old bottles | 9:17 | | 2:22 | 5:37–39 |
| Evil Spirit/Empty house | | | | |
| Loving because forgiven | | | 7:36–50 | |
| The sower | 13:1–23 | 4:1–20 | 8:4–15 | |
| How seed grows | | | 4:26–29 | |
| Tares among the wheat | 13:24–30, 36–43 | | | |
| The mustard seed | 13:31–32 | 4:30–32 | 13:18–19 | |
| The leaven | 13:33 | | | |
| Treasure in the field | 13:44 | | | |
| The pearl of great price | 13:45–46 | | | |
| The net | 13:47–50 | | | |
| The wicked servant | 18:21–35 | | | |
| The good Samaritan | | | 10:25–37 | |
| The importunate friend | | | 11:5–8 | |
| The rich fool | | | 12:16–21 | |
| Watchful servants | | | 12.35–40 | |
| The unfaithful servant | 24:45–51 | | 12:41–48 | |
| The unfruitful fig tree | | | 13:6–9 | |
| The narrow gate | 7:13–14,21–23 | | 13:22–30 | |
| Taking the humble place | | | 14:7–11 | |
| The great supper | | | 14:15–24 | |

| Description | Matthew | Mark | Luke | John |
|---|---|---|---|---|
| Counting the cost | | | 14:25–33 | |
| The lost sheep | 18:10–14 | | 15:1–7 | |
| The lost coin | | | 15:8–10 | |
| The lost son | | | 15:11–32 | |
| The shrewd steward | | | 16:1–13 | |
| The rich man & Lazarus | | | 16:19–31 | |
| Attitude in service | | | 17:7–10 | |
| The unjust judge | | | 8:1–8 | |
| The Pharisee and sinner | | | 18:9–14 | |
| Workers in the Vineyard | 2:1–16 | | | |
| Investing wisely | | | 19:11–27 | |
| The good shepherd | | | | 10:1–16 |
| The two sons | 21:28–32 | | | |
| The Vineyard | 21:33–46 | 12:1–12 | 20:9–19 | |
| The wedding of the Son | 22:1–14 | | | |
| The sign of the fig tree | 24:32–35 | 13:28–31 | 21:29–33 | |
| The ten virgins | 25:1–13 | | | |
| The talents | 25:14–30 | | | |
| The sheep and the goats | 25:31–46 | | | |
| The vine and branches | | | 15:1–8 | |

# Kingdom Lifestyle

We may describe those who have discovered the kingdom as citizens of the kingdom. Jesus referred to the 'sons of the kingdom' (Matthew 13:38). Being a son of the kingdom involves entering the kingdom and living a kingdom lifestyle. Before we discuss entering the kingdom, we need to make three introductory statements.

Firstly, being in the kingdom is synonymous with being saved or having eternal life. A rich young man asked Jesus what he had to do to find eternal life (19:16). Having answered the man's question, Jesus promptly told his disciples: 'I tell you the truth, it is hard for a rich man to enter the kingdom of heaven' (19:23). The disciples were amazed at this statement and asked: 'Who then can be saved?' (19:25). The terms are used interchangeably.

Secondly, the phrase 'kingdom of heaven' is synonymous with 'kingdom of God'. Matthew tends to use the former while the other Gospel writers tend to use the latter. In Jewish speech 'heaven' was a customary circumlocution for God. Since Matthew wrote in and for a Jewish environment, he used the Jewish idiom. A comparison between Matthew and the other two synoptic Gospels will show that parallel passages virtually say 'kingdom of heaven' in Matthew and 'kingdom of God' in the others.

Thirdly, in terms of New Testament teaching, one is either in the kingdom or not. Certain people will inherit the kingdom while others will be consigned to eternal punishment (25:46). Christ's words about eternal punishment are usually found in texts that describe eternal life. The duration of hell is therefore as eternal as that of heaven. As most of the statements in the New Testament about hell come from Jesus himself, we are in no position to question this awful reality if we wish to submit to his teaching.

## Entering the Kingdom

As we look at our entrance into the kingdom, we come to an issue that has led to a great deal of disagreement amongst Christians, and especially theologians, namely the relationship between divine grace and human responsibility. This issue will certainly not be solved in this book, but the message of the kingdom brings a certain clarity to bear.

The kingdom of God or New Testament eschatology is the true context of most New Testament doctrines. Because Jesus had his focus primarily on the kingdom, and because the kingdom is firstly about eschatology, every major New Testament doctrine has to take eschatology as its starting point. This must include issues of divine initiative and human responsibility. If we take the issue back to its foundations, we may find that the problem loses some of its intensity.

The crucial statement in this regard is found in Christ's first proclamation: 'The kingdom of God is at hand. Repent, and believe in the gospel' (Mark 1:15). Matthew says: 'Repent, for the kingdom of heaven is at hand' (Matthew 4:17). The nearness or presence of the kingdom is a proclamation of divine grace. Repentance is a human responsibility. Should stress be laid on divine grace or on human responsibility? The answer should be obvious. Both statements move logically from the intervention of the kingdom to the response of repentance and faith. Even in Matthew, where repentance is mentioned first, the reason for repentance is stated: 'for the kingdom of heaven is at hand'.

# *Repentance*

This leads to one of the most fundamental principles in kingdom theology. The call to repentance is uttered in the context of kingdom intervention. The kingdom is here, therefore repent! Repentance is part of our response to the good news that the kingdom is near. The presence of the kingdom must initiate repentance and not vice versa. Only when the powers of the age to come are present in the announcement of the gospel can one anticipate true repentance. To say 'the kingdom is near' or 'present' is to announce the fulfilment of Isaiah's expectations:God has come to save his people, to set the captives free, to forgive sinners, raise the dead, pour out the Spirit, renew the covenant, reveal his glory, etc. In response to this wonderful fact, man must turn around and believe the good news. ✱

In this sense Jesus' understanding of repentance and kingdom presence is radically different from the understanding of rabbinical Judaism. In the latter, repentance – obedience to the requirements of the law and the traditions of the rabbis – was the condition that had to be fulfilled by the nation before the Messiah could come. The rabbinical concept of repentance placed the initiative with man and his responsibility to repent. Jesus placed the initiative with God and the dynamic intervention of his reign. When Jesus preached repentance, the offer of grace was no mere verbal promise. When Jesus spoke, things happened. His words were events. When he announced liberty, people were set free. It was in this context, with the power of the Holy Spirit evident amongst the people, that Jesus demanded the most uncompromising repentance. This suggests that the greater the evidence of the power of God, the greater the possibility of deep repentance. When God's power is not evident, a powerful call to repentance only produces legalism.

The rabbinical idea that repentance should initiate kingdom presence has often reappeared in the history of the church. The theology of Charles Finney and his concept of man's role in initiating revival comes close to the rabbinical view. Some traditions within Evangelicalism have also been deeply influenced by this idea. The following remarks are admittedly generalisations, but it seems to me that many Evangelicals and

Pentecostals preach repentance in a manner that places the initiative primarily in the hands of man. In some churches this idea is one of the only subjects that is ever preached. And as one would expect, it does not lead to revival or usher in the presence of the kingdom. It is most gratifying to notice how the emphasis in the Renewal movement is clearly on divine initiative. Renewal preachers are usually preoccupied with what God is doing or what they believe he wants to do in his church. While they do not always conceive of their preaching as an announcement of the kingdom, the content of their preaching often makes this clear. The teaching of Jesus strongly emphasises divine grace and, as a result, human responsibility. This is evident in the parables.

## Divine Grace

Christ's teaching in the parables regarding those who are fit for the kingdom amounted to a complete reversal of current expectations. Tax collectors and harlots entered the kingdom before the Pharisees (Matthew 21:31). To the question: 'Who then is the greatest in the kingdom of heaven?' Jesus answered: '... whoever humbles himself as this little child is the greatest in the kingdom of heaven' (18:1–4). He stated repeatedly that the first would be last, and the last first (19:30; 20:16). The rich, who are first in this world, are the last to be included in the kingdom (19:23–24). The poor, who are last in this world, are the beneficiaries of the kingdom (Luke 6:20). The sinner who beat upon his breast went home justified rather than the Pharisee who fasted twice a week and performed many ritual duties (18:9–14). Jesus said to the Pharisees: 'You are those who justify yourselves before men, but God knows your hearts. For what is highly esteemed among men is an abomination in the sight of God' (16:15).

Jesus came not to call the righteous, but sinners (Mark 2:17). When the Pharisees complained that Jesus received sinners and ate with them, Jesus told them the three parables of the lost sheep, the lost coin and the lost son (Luke 15:1–32). The very people who were generally believed to be beyond help were the ones singled out by Jesus as candidates for the kingdom of God, while those who believed themselves to be acceptable to God had a rude awakening. This radically different choice of people is based on an understanding of grace instead of merit. The only appropriate way to respond to divine grace is like a little child. A child knows how to receive in simple trust (Matthew 18:1–5). A child symbolises humility and receptivity. Human effort and accomplishments are certainly not appropriate in the presence of divine grace. Those who respond like children become the little flock to whom the Father gives the kingdom (Luke 12:32). The contrast between religious pride and childlike humility indicates the radical change of attitude that needs to take place in the heart of man before he can enter the kingdom. Even this change occurs by a work of divine grace. Man must be born again of the Spirit in order to enter the kingdom (John 3:3–6). Notice the emphasis on the sovereignty of the Spirit, blowing where he wills (John 3:8). This is an emphasis on divine grace.

## Repentance and Faith

We have emphasised divine grace because Christ's understanding of repentance must be seen in the context of kingdom proclamation. However, precisely because Jesus ushered in the powers of the kingdom and all the wonders of that saving event, he demanded the most uncompromising form of repentance. No one has ever demanded of men what Jesus does. His demands are so radical that later church history has usually witnessed a watering down of these elements in his teaching.

The need for repentance is usually stated in terms of self-denial and allegiance to Jesus as Lord. On the negative side is self-denial, on the positive is following Jesus. To repent is to leave home, brothers, sisters, mother, father, children and lands for the sake of the kingdom of God (Luke 18:29). Jesus expected men to deny or renounce themselves and take up the cross (14:25–33). The cross was no mere symbol of

Christianity: it meant death at the gallows. The man going to the cross was bidding farewell to his future, career, position in society, family, and wealth – his very life. Christ's disciples must be prepared to 'hate' the dearest things in their lives. Failure to do this will result in a complete inability to follow him. Accordingly, men were advised to count the cost before they decided to follow Jesus. If some part of their lives held them from the kingdom, they were to 'cut it off' (Mark 9:43–48).

Yet the call of Jesus to 'follow me' is not a decision men can spend time on. If they want time, they must forget about following him (Luke 9:57–62). Once the commitment has been made, there can be no looking back. It involves total obedience to Jesus as Lord. Those who say 'Lord, Lord' but do not obey, will not be received into the kingdom (Matthew 7:21–23). Those who serve Jesus as Lord obey the will of the Father. Obedience results in a true righteousness that must exceed that of the scribes and the Pharisees (5:20). Those who have fed the hungry, welcomed the stranger, clothed the naked and cared for the prisoner will inherit the kingdom (25:34–36). Such people are prepared to suffer for righteousness' sake (5:10).

This section brings us face to face with the intervention of the kingdom in our lives. Have we heard the announcement of the kingdom in such a way that we know and hear for ourselves the gracious offer and invitation of God? If this is the case, have we heard and faced the uncompromising claim of Jesus the king? Have we come to terms with the uncompromising call to discipleship?

## Living in the Kingdom

The teachings of Jesus in the Sermon on the Mount were not given in the context of entering the kingdom for the first time. They focus on the quality of life demonstrated by those who have entered the kingdom, responded to the gracious intervention of God and experienced the new birth. The beatitudes are usually regarded as the most significant part of this teaching (Matthew 5:1–12; Luke 6:20–23). It is vital to understand that the essence of Christ's teaching relates to the kingdom. The beatitudes summarise in single, pithy statements fundamental truths that appear in many varied contexts in the remainder of Jesus' teaching. They are really a key that opens the door to his wider teaching.

We have seen how the coming of the kingdom has brought a new age that transcends the age of the law and the prophets. The radical difference between the old era and the new is emphasised in Matthew 5:17–48. The refrain in this passage is: 'You have heard that it was said … But I say to you …' Jesus takes upon himself an authority greater than that of Moses.

Jesus lived and taught a revolutionary concept of ethics because he embodied a totally new age. Those who are in the kingdom do such unheard of things as turning the other cheek, going the second mile and loving their enemies. This new standard does not allow men to harbour anger, lust or insincerity in their hearts (5:21–37). This is not an abolition of the law and the prophets, but an elevation of these to a level beyond the capability of man. The kingdom transcends the law. The new age is so much more glorious than the old that the glory of the old seems to fade by comparison (2 Corinthians 3:7–11).

The new age has come, transcending the old, and yet the old is still here, standing in radical contrast to the new. The beatitudes are placed in the context of 'now' and 'then'. Those who hunger now will be filled then (Luke 6:21). Those who are full now will hunger then (6:25). Those who weep now will laugh then (6:21). Those who laugh now will mourn and weep then (6:25). The contrast is between the present evil age and the glory of the age to come when the standards of this world will be inverted. Those who have entered the kingdom already live by these radical standards.

The beatitudes can only be understood against the background of the presence of the future. Christians are people who have met Jesus, and to meet Jesus is to meet the end. We have been taken out of this present world and already live by the powers of the age to come. Yet at the same

125

time we live in this world. We are caught in the tension between two worlds, but the power, reality and values of the kingdom determine our lives rather than the standards of this world.

Central to the world we live in is the emphasis on public respectability and accomplishment. Men practise their piety before men: they like to be seen when they give to the poor, to be heard when they pray, and to be noticed when they fast (Matthew 6:1–8). Those who have entered the world to come know that the real emphasis is the condition of the heart before God. The former are taken up with material things or the cares of this life. The latter trust in the provision of their heavenly Father (6:19–34; 7:7–12).

If the Sermon on the Mount were taken as the moral standard men have to attain, no one could ever hope to enter the kingdom of God. Jesus is not prescribing a new set of rules. He is describing what happens to those who pass out of this age and begin to live in the age to come. A revolutionary change takes place in our lives when we are overtaken by the powers of the age to come. Jesus does not say, 'Do this and don't do that and you will enter the kingdom.' He refers to those who are the salt of the earth and the light of the world (5:13–14). These are the sons of the kingdom, the last who have become the first, the little children who have been given the kingdom, and the regenerate who have repented and followed Jesus. It is a description of the lifestyle of the new man in Christ, the new creature for whom the old has passed away and everything has become new (2 Corinthians 5:17).

## The Beatitudes

A beatitude is a supreme blessedness or happiness. The actual word means 'to be happy' or 'to be congratulated'. To the Hebrew mind, blessedness involved far more than just feeling happy. It included total wellbeing. The Hebrew concepts of *shalom* and salvation can be summed up in blessedness.

The concept of the blessedness of the age to come developed in the eschatological and apocalyptic writings. References in the Old Testament reflect the beginning of what had developed by the time of Jesus. For Jesus 'blessedness' was specifically linked to the life of the age to come, the bliss of the Messianic era. This is also reflected in the way the term is used in the Revelation of John (Revelation 19:9). In the beatitudes Jesus describes the kind of people who will share in this bliss. Each beatitude could be translated 'Oh the bliss of ...' We should remember Isaiah's concept of a special kind of joy that is only to be found in the future age (Matthew 5:1–12; Luke 6:20–23).

## The Poor in Spirit

In the Psalms a number of Hebrew words are used with similar connotations to 'the poor in spirit'. These include the needy, the weak, the humble, the oppressed and the impoverished. Israel was 'poor' when God delivered her from bondage. Being poor also meant trusting in God and fearing him. Hence the poor were also the godly and the righteous.

While being poor could mean being materially poor, this was never the total concept. The Hebrew concept is holistic, inclusive, the poor in the widest sense including socio-political oppression. The concept in Liberation Theology tends to be reductionistic. It selects one element in the biblical definition and elevates it to the whole. Material poverty is never regarded as a blessing from God. His blessing causes people to prosper. The idea here is that the materially poor and needy have no power and influence of their own. They are often downtrodden by the oppressor. This causes them to trust completely in God rather than in their own resources so that God takes their side against the oppressor.

The context of Christ's pronouncement is eschatological: the poor are blessed when the kingdom comes. In Isaiah the Messianic age meant the salvation of the poor and contrite in heart. In Christ's teaching the abundance of the final banquet must be offered to the poor (Luke 14:13, 21). This is why the good news is preached to them.

If the age to come will bring salvation to the poor, it will also bring devastation to those who are rich and ungodly in their wealth. It will completely overturn the value system of this age. The pronouncement of blessing on the poor is balanced by the pronouncement of woe upon the rich (6:24). God is not against wealth – his blessing brings prosperity and wealth – but against those who are rich at the expense of the poor and who trust in their wealth.

The 'poor' and the 'rich' in the beatitudes are therefore those in circumstances which usually apply to the materially poor and rich. However, because poor people can be proud and rich people can be rich through the blessing of God, it refers to an attitude to life. The 'poor in spirit' are those who know that they need God. Without him they are destitute, weak and impoverished. They do not trust in the righteousness of works but in the grace of God. The most graphic illustration of such a person is given in the parable of the Pharisee and the tax collector (18:9–14). Ironically, this man must have been wealthy as most tax collectors were masters of embezzlement. Though materially wealthy, he was poor in spirit.

When Jesus says, 'For yours is the kingdom of God' (6:20), he means that everything promised in Isaiah is theirs. The poor in spirit have the bliss, happiness and abundance of the kingdom of God and all that it entails.

In Church Growth terminology one encounters the idea of 'redemption and lift'. There is evidence to suggest that the power of the gospel often has more effect in the long-term upward mobility of social groups than state and social welfare programmes. The same can be said for the evidence that is provided through church history. The history of the expansion of Christianity shows time and time again how the church has leavened society. Similar factors emerge from the analysis of the relationship between evangelical Christianity and industrialised nations. The gospel therefore provides real hope for the poor of this world. Nations that are stagnating in poverty are offered more than future bliss when they are evangelised. The kingdom can radically influence the very fabric of society.

We can say then that while this bliss will surely come in the future age, it already works now. While the world thinks that the rich are happy and the poor have no hope, Jesus makes an authoritative pronouncement to the contrary. The poor are blessed both in the future kingdom and in the present. The rich may seem to be blessed, but the day of reckoning can come at any moment and the wealth they trust in will fail them. This beatitude is a profound promise to the poor and a serious warning to the rich.

## Those Who Mourn

The mourning referred to here is the special kind of mourning which the godly experience when they see the devastation of God's people and the horror of human rebellion and its consequences. The man who mourns is either the sinner who is deeply convicted of his own sin or the believer who is deeply disturbed by the depravity of the world he lives in and especially by the bondage of God's people when they turn their backs on him. This mourning amounts to a cry to God for deliverance and redemption. These will be comforted. The kingdom of God will overturn the value system of this present evil age.

## The Meek

The meek man trusts in God for his cause and does not struggle in his own strength. Moses is the classic example of meekness (Numbers 12:3). David possessed the same quality. Psalm 37 is the clearest exposition of meekness in the Old Testament. Jesus quoted verse 11 in this beatitude: 'But the meek shall inherit the earth.' Parallel to this is the statement: 'But those who wait on the Lord, They shall inherit the earth' (37:9). To be meek is to wait for God to vindicate you, not to fret because of the wicked (37:1, 5, 7).

As with the other beatitudes, the promises to the meek are Messianic and come basically from Isaiah. The idea of inheriting the land is a prominent biblical theme. The basic idea originated from the way in which the Promised Land was subdivided by lot among the families in Israel. In the New Testament the 'land' became the symbol of far more than physical Israel. Now God's people inherit eternal life in the kingdom (Matthew 25:34). To say that the meek will inherit the land is another way of saying that the meek will inherit the kingdom. Those who have nothing in this world but who trust completely in God will have everything in the age to come. As the age to come breaks into this age, the children of the kingdom enter into their inheritance.

## Those Who Hunger and Thirst

While Matthew speaks of those who hunger and thirst for righteousness, Luke places the beatitude in the context of material poverty and hunger. As with the poor, the basic idea begins in the Psalms. The abundance given to the poor and hungry is very much part of the Messianic promise that will be fulfilled in the coming kingdom, particularly in the Messianic banquet (Luke 22:16, 30). Jesus demonstrated the presence of the kingdom when he fed the poor and hungry (9:17). Now the rich are sated with food (6:25), but when God comes to his people, the hungry are filled with good things and the rich are sent away empty (1:53). The account of the rich man and Lazarus tells the story in graphic detail (16:19–31).

The fact that Matthew adds the phrase 'for righteousness' (Matthew 5:6) is proof of the fact that the kingdom of God is not mere food and drink but righteousness and peace and joy in the Holy Spirit. Hungry people can be absolutely closed to God while rich people are sometimes deeply hungry for the things of God. The material situation is a powerful symbol of the spiritual values of men and it may be regarded as more than symbolic because more frequently materially hungry people are spiritually hungry as well, while those who never experience material want feel no need for God in their lives.

The righteousness for which men hunger is far more than the external righteousness sought by the Pharisees. True righteousness revolves around relationships. John the Baptist came 'in the way of righteousness' (21:32). This way involved the ethics of human relationships (Luke 3:10–14). The standard of righteousness that Christ will apply when he judges the world will involve human relationships (Matthew 25:37). Sanctification is not a list of external laws about food and clothing but a way of relating to God and man. This hunger for righteousness includes the deep desire of men to be acquitted by God.

This beatitude is both a promise of acquittal to those who long for it and a promise of reversal to the poor of the earth whose hope is in the coming of God's kingdom. In the Messianic banquet they shall be filled.

## The Merciful

Mercy was closely linked to steadfast love, covenant love, or divine faithfulness. The Messianic promise concerning God's covenant and the revelation of his love includes the promise of mercy. Luke shows how the dawning of the new age was regarded as a fulfilment of God's promises of mercy to his covenant people (Luke 1:50, 54, 72, 78). The fulfilment of this promise is apparent in Christ's healing ministry. The 'Son of David' was often called on for mercy.

Only those who are prepared to show mercy can expect to receive the mercy promised in the kingdom of God. If we forgive, the Father will forgive us (Matthew 6:14–15). With the measure we judge, we will be judged (7:2). The man who was forgiven his debt and yet refused to forgive others their debt was cast into jail (18:23–35). The rich man who cried out in hell for mercy had shown no mercy in his life (Luke 16:24). Jesus judged the Pharisees as having misinterpreted the law because they neglected the weightier matters of the law: justice and mercy and faith (Matthew 23:23).

It has often been noted by commentators that this beatitude would come naturally to one who has come to terms with the previous ones. Someone who acknowledges his poverty before God, weeps for his sin and the sins of mankind, does not fret for his own vindication and hungers for God's fullness, will be unlikely to look down on the needy. Such a man will not find it difficult to forgive. A true estimation of ourselves before God ensures a right attitude towards the needs and failures of others.

## The Pure in Heart

This beatitude can only be understood against the religious background of Rabbinic Judaism and the traditions of the Pharisees. In the holiness laws of the Old Testament most objects were categorised as clean or unclean: clothes, animals, food, plants, days, people, etc. By the time of Jesus this tradition had been taken to ridiculous lengths. The Pharisees regarded themselves as defiled if they sat on the clothes of one of the 'people of the land'. Elaborate methods of hand washing were developed. The Essenes had to bathe every day to maintain their ritual purity. The emphasis was on externals. The Pharisees would have agreed with the statement: 'Blessed are the ritually pure, for they shall see God.'

Jesus taught something that was diametrically opposed to the teaching of the Pharisees:

> *Woe to you, teachers of the law and Pharisees, you hypocrites! You clean the outside of the cup and dish, but inside they are full of greed and self-indulgence. Blind Pharisee! First clean the inside of the cup and dish, and then the outside also will be clean.* (Matthew 23:25–26)

It is not what goes into a man that renders him unclean but what comes out of his heart (15:10–20). By saying this, Jesus declared all food clean (Mark 7:14–23).

Jesus not only taught internal purity but also demonstrated by his actions that he could see through facades. He scandalised the Pharisees by eating with tax collectors and sinners (2:13–17). He ministered to 'unclean' Gentiles and even touched lepers. Accordingly, the writers of the New Testament emphasise the purity of the conscience rather than ritual cleansing. This beatitude inverts the value system of the religious world. The kingdom of God brings a spiritual revolution. Purity is a matter of the heart and Jesus pronounces the bliss of the age to come on those who have a pure heart.

The promise that 'they shall see God' is made in the context of eschatological bliss. One may see the face of God in the experience of worship, but this experience will finally be manifest in the world to come. Isaiah saw the future age bringing a revelation of the full glory of God. Luke records that the dawning of the new age was marked by the shepherds and Simeon seeing the salvation of God (Luke 2:20, 30). Jesus told the disciples that many prophets had desired to see the things that they saw.

## The Peacemakers

We have looked at the Jewish concept of peace as manifested in the kingdom under David and Solomon. While peace denoted the absence of war to the Greek mind, in Hebrew thinking it denoted wholeness, well-being, perfection and prosperity. To have all this was another way of saying that you were experiencing salvation as an all-embracing reality. Blessedness, peace and salvation were all closely linked as the experience of the Messianic age. Peace, defined in this way, is the very essence of the kingdom.

Who then are the peacemakers and how does this relate to the coming of the kingdom? A peacemaker is one who has within him the peace or wholeness of the kingdom and imparts it to others. While the thought of bringing peace between estranged parties is not absent, the emphasis is on the ability to bring this peace into the lives of others, to impart something that you have experienced. As the disciples entered a house they could let their peace come to it (Matthew 10:12–13). They carried within themselves the distinctive presence of the kingdom. Jesus said: 'And if a son of peace is there, your peace will rest on it' (Luke 10:6). This peace actually comes upon people through the in-breaking of the kingdom. It is like the presence and outpouring of the Holy Spirit. When others receive the kingdom, they receive its peace and consequently begin to live at peace with each other. Blessed are those who, as sons of God, both contain and impart the Messianic peace.

In the Western world people are accustomed to concepts rather than practice. To the Hebrew mind, thinking, doing and being are part of one indivisible whole. Words are deeds and teachings are practices. Jesus taught within the framework of rabbinical techniques of discipleship. In this context understanding, experiencing and transmitting peace into the lives of others were all part of one reality. When the beatitudes are approached in this way, involvement with the principle must lead to the transformation of our lives.

## The Persecuted

Few human needs are as deep as the need for acceptance. Our egotism causes us to place popularity and prestige as one of the highest goals. In Classical thought, fame was regarded as one of the noblest values in life. In Rabbinic Judaism, those who were considered holy were given much acclaim. They took the best places in the synagogues (Luke 20:46–47). Those who were rejected or cast out of the synagogues – tax collectors and harlots – were regarded as the scum of the earth. They certainly had no chance of being touched by God. No Pharisee could have regarded such a state as being blessed, but Jesus inverts the value system of men. What is exalted among men is an abomination in the sight of God (16:15).

The language of the beatitude has links with a passage in Isaiah about socially rejected people becoming God's accepted people. The wording is so similar to the beatitude that it is difficult not to assume that Jesus saw this as being fulfilled in his disciples. The sons of the kingdom become a counterculture to this world, an alternative people where social popularity has no value but where identity with the Son of Man and his heavenly rule is paramount. When the world rejects such people, they should greatly rejoice: the world rejected the prophets and the Son of Man himself (John 15:18).

## Changing Values

Each beatitude has revealed, in different ways, one recurring theme: the values of the kingdom invert the value system of this present world. The kingdom of God brings a revolution. In the words of the Thessalonians: 'These who have turned the world upside down have come here too, acting contrary to the decrees of Caesar, saying that there is another king – Jesus' (Acts 17:6–7). This is no ordinary revolution based on a temporary political cause. It is brought about by the intervention of the age to come. And because the age to come is so radically different from this age, its intervention can do nothing other than overturn this age. The transition from this age to the age to come can never be evolutionary or tame. While the parables show a secretive, almost invisible presence of the kingdom, the beatitudes show that it is certainly not docile. Nothing less than a total transformation is involved.

Another element in the beatitudes is the total absence of a split between material and spiritual realities. With almost every term, be it the poor, the hungry, those who mourn or the rich, their state is both material and spiritual. This is always the Hebrew way of seeing reality. The split between spiritual and material things is part of the Greek, Western mindset. The coming of the kingdom affects the whole of life: socially, individually, materially, spiritually, in terms of social justice and personal morality. There will be a new heaven and a new earth.

There is something completely sovereign about the breakthrough of the kingdom and its effects. Every attempt to tie the beatitudes down to a list of do's and don'ts will miss the mark. The lifestyle that is being described is beyond our grasp. The moment we think we have finally got it, we are sure to have missed it. We can no more live the beatitudes in our own strength than fly to the moon. They delve so deeply into our inner motives that they can only continually disturb us. If we could escape from this world and live completely in the kingdom, it would be great. If we could forget about the kingdom and live only in this world, things would be safe. But neither is possible. We will continue to be part of both kingdoms at the same time. Our lives are disturbed in a most wonderfully upsetting way so that we can never see anything in quite the same way again.

# The Messianic Banquet

The parables teach us that we have a crisis of decision. The entrance into the kingdom is by divine grace. Once we are in the kingdom we live by its revolutionary values. This has been the subject matter of the last chapter. In the next chapter we will examine the relationship between the kingdom and the church. Before we do that it will be helpful to examine a theme that runs like a thread through much of the biblical teaching on the kingdom and lays the foundation for understanding the church as the community of the kingdom. The Messianic banquet is a predominant concept of the kingdom in Judaism. The theme will emerge as we review the territory we have covered.

The first picture of the kingdom was the exodus event. The land of Egypt had been under plagues of divine judgement, probably for weeks. The devastation was serious enough for Pharaoh to allow a large proportion of his labour force to leave the country. The Israelites were about to embark on a dangerous and frightening journey of escape. What do they do the night before they leave? They have a feast of lamb, bread and salads! Each family is required to have this feast. They are never to forget it for the remainder of their history. It must be celebrated every year for seven days. What would they remember in the generations that followed? Within the text of Exodus 12 is the announcement of Yahweh's judgement on the gods of Egypt (verse 12) and the climax of the final plague (verse 29). This feast would forever be interwoven with the coming of the kingdom.

The next significant moment is the covenant at Mount Sinai, where Israel became 'a kingdom of priests and a holy nation' (Ex.19:6). The climax of the covenant event was the moment when Moses read from the book of the covenant, the people made a confession of obedience, and the sacrificial blood was sprinkled on the people while Moses spoke the dramatic words, 'This is the blood of the covenant that the LORD has made with you in accordance with all these words' (24:8). The next three verses return us to our theme.

> *Moses and Aaron, Nadab and Abihu, and the seventy elders of Israel went up and saw the God of Israel. Under his feet was something like a pavement made of sapphire, clear as the sky itself. But God did not raise his hand against these leaders of the Israelites; they saw God, and they ate and drank* (24:9–11).

Three elements are found in this text.

- Moses had erected twelve stones on Mount Sinai to represent the twelve tribes (24:4). The number seventy shows that the elders were the representatives of the whole kingdom community. The numbers twelve and seventy[21] were to be used again by Jesus as he commissioned his disciples to announce the kingdom. Through their representatives the whole nation was involved in this covenant moment.

- The language used describes a theophany, a direct manifestation of the glory of God.[22] Similar language would be used again and again as prophets and apostles were taken up into the glory of God. The naked presence of God should consume humanity. Yet because of the profound covenantal moment the leaders of Israel are not consumed. John would describe the whole incarnate presence of the Christ as God being present with man in glory (Jn.1:14, 18).

- The sign of this great moment was that they 'ate and drank'. No ordinary or simple meal can be imagined here. Where did the food come from? Yahweh was the host. He had invited the leaders into his awesome presence. They were at *his* table! Once again, the kingdom event was interwoven with a feast.

The next picture of the kingdom was the Davidic monarchy, reaching its climax in Solomon's table. Between the covenant on Sinai and the table of Solomon was the history of a nation required by the covenant to hold feasts of various kinds, filling the annual calendar with moments of table fellowship between Yahweh and his people (Ex.23:14–19; Lev.23). The annual calendar of feasts was closely related to the various harvests. A feast was a way of celebrating Yahweh's blessing on the produce of the land given by covenant promise. Living in the kingdom meant that every man could live under his own vine and fig tree and live in abundance. The blessing of obedience to the covenant created abundance and the curse of disobedience created famine. To keep the feast was to celebrate the kingdom and the covenant. The calendar was arranged into feasts of seven days, seven weeks, seven years and seventy-year cycles (Lev.23:15, 23, 39; 25:4, 8). The year of Jubilee was therefore the crowning example of the whole festive relationship between Yahweh and his people. He was the sovereign and they were his vassal nation. This sovereign demanded continual celebration of the relationship and provided continual blessing to make such celebration possible. At least that was the intention of the relationship.

Solomon's table exemplified the golden age of Israel where, under the Davidic monarchy, the nation actually lived for a season in the abundance of the kingdom. The king's table and the table of every citizen exemplified the presence of the rule of God and all that it entailed. The continual feast of Solomon's table bore witness of the kingdom to the world outside Israel. It was when the queen of Sheba saw 'all the wisdom of Solomon and the palace he had built, the food on his table, the seating of his officials, the attending servants and their robes, his cupbearers, and the burnt offerings he made at the temple of the Lord, she was overwhelmed' (1 Kgs.10:4–5). The image of the kingdom, or of *shalom*, was expressed in food and drink at the royal table. With the collapse of the kingdom and the long night of exile one can imagine that the vision of Solomon's table grew in the minds of the people. The return of the kingdom would be synonymous with the restoration of the feast.

Once the linkage between kingdom and feast was established it became the epitome of the prophetic vision. Two prophetic visions of the coming kingdom place the feast in contexts of final triumph, namely Isaiah 24–27 and Zechariah 9.

## The Lord's Feast in Isaiah

The context of Isaiah 25:6–9 shows how the feast is the expression or symbol of the coming kingdom. It comes in a narrative unit 24:1–27:13, which has the theme of God's final triumph.[23] This unit in turn follows a longer section where Yahweh's triumph over all the nations is revealed (chapters 13–23). Now, instead of particular nations, the whole earth comes into view.[24] The 'city' earth (24:10) comes under Yahweh's devastating judgement, where the party is over (verse 11). This elicits a song of rejoicing from God's people (24:14–16a), which is followed in turn by another description of divine judgement upon all the kings of the earth (16b–22). The climax of the chapter is the announcement of the coming kingdom, where God's glory will outshine the sun and moon and 'the LORD Almighty will reign on Mount Zion and in Jerusalem and before its elders, gloriously' (verse 23). The language is reminiscent of the Sinai experience. The announcement of the coming rule of God is followed by another song of praise (25:1–5). Then comes the feast of the kingdom, where the party truly begins. Yahweh will host the feast (25:6–9). It will have the best meat and the best matured wine. The feast takes place in the context of the banishing of death, the end to all tears and the confession of salvation by his people (verse 9). Another prediction of divine judgement (10–12) is then followed by another song of the redeemed (chapter 26) in which the resurrection of the dead is again anticipated (26:19). Chapter 27 builds to the final climax by repeated references to 'that day' (27:1, 2, 6, 12), the final eschatological day of the Lord. The two verses that conclude the narrative speak of the great trumpet that will gather God's people from all nations (12–13).

As the expectation of the kingdom developed, the feast in the middle of such a narrative became a way of referring to the whole cluster of ideas: the final day, the coming of God, judgement, glory, salvation, resurrection, and praise.

## The Messiah's Feast in Zechariah

Jesus deliberately drew attention to Zechariah 9 by his staged entry into Jerusalem on an ass (Mt.21:1–11, 5). My own attention was drawn to this passage during the renewal of the Holy Spirit in 1994–5. We were witnessing remarkable manifestations of the Holy Spirit in our church meetings in a manner I had never witnessed before. Such times lead one to examine church history for a point of reference. I was particularly helped by the works of Jonathan Edwards. I was fascinated to see how he used Ephesians 5:18 ('do not be drunk with wine, but be filled with the Spirit') with Zechariah 9:15–17 to defend the 'strong affections' occurring during the New England revival.[25] Edwards was not simply 'proof-texting'. He placed the passage in its broader context, which led me to explore the larger narrative.

Zechariah has four sections, relating to the second and fourth years of Darius (1:1–6:15 & 7:1–8:23) and two oracles (9:1–11:17 & 12:1–14:21). The section immediately previous to chapter nine deals with the time of restoration when fasting will be replaced by feasting. Already in that section the theme of restoration from exile is expanded into eschatological proportions where people from all nations will be included in Zion's festivities (8:18–23). Zechariah has a repeated emphasis on the coming of God to Zion (2:10; 8:3; 9:9). The epitome of the coming of God to Zion is the time when the festive calendar is restored and there will be 'joyful and glad occasions and happy festivals for Judah' (8:19).

This prepares us for the oracle that begins with 9:1–10:1, the triumphal entry of the king. After marching triumphantly from the north (9:1–8), the king arrives in Zion (9:9). His arrival brings peace to the nations, the extension of his rule, and the liberation of the captives (10–13). This causes his people to greet him with ecstatic joy. The 'daughter of Zion' theme introduces us to the relationship of father to daughter and bridegroom to bride (Zeph:3:14; Zech.2:10; 8:19). Continued language about the warrior God then leads to the description Edwards referred to where the joy of God's people in festive celebration is compared to the drink offerings at the altar being filled to the brim. Using this picture Zechariah describes the people roaring as with wine (9:15). Edwards pointed out that far from God being offended by such behaviour, he finds it 'attractive and beautiful', like 'jewels in a crown', when his people are overcome with festivity because the Messianic king has visited them (9:16–17).[26]

The Old Testament theme of kingdom festivity is not to be understood as a crass preoccupation with full bellies and the drinking of wine. Descriptions of drunkenness and excess are reserved for pagan festivity. The feast is a vehicle to express the celebration of God the king being present with his people. Neither is the Old Testament emphasis to be understood as a spiritual metaphor alone, as though feasting had no literal dimension. For the Old Testament writers, the physical and the spiritual were inseparable. Literal eating and drinking and spiritual celebration were one and the same thing.

## Jesus the Bridegroom

Although John is not the one to use the language of the kingdom, he is certainly the writer to portray the Messianic age as a time of festivity. The whole gospel is structured around Jesus attending various feasts,[27] performing a series of signs,[28] and teaching through a series of discourses. The first Passover he attended was immediately preceded by a family feast, where he did his first sign and revealed his glory (2:11).

Feasts and signs are therefore woven together from the beginning of his ministry. The feast/sign of the marriage in Cana inaugurates his ministry on earth just as Revelation shows his heavenly reign beginning with the marriage feast (Rev.19:6–10). The whole of his ministry is therefore encapsulated in Johannine literature within kingdom feasts. The future becomes present as the ultimate bridegroom brings joy to a village wedding. Just as John introduces Jesus with the marriage feast the synoptics introduce the ministry of Jesus with the announcement of the year of Jubilee (Lk.4:18–19) and the saying about the inappropriateness of fasting because the bridegroom is present (Mk:2:18–20).

We should not miss the note of extravagance struck with the wedding in Cana. 'Twenty to thirty gallons' (Jn.2:6) equates to about 75–115 litres, or about twelve cases of wine by today's standard. It was the best wine, and Jesus produced it after the guests had already finished the wine supplied by the host. One wonders how many people attended village weddings of that nature. The text seems to indicate that Jesus created a great supply! One also wonders whether contemporary evangelical piety would have ever described such an act as the first and vital revelation of the glory of God? The Jewish lack of a dualism of spiritual and physical festivity continues. The eternal word, being present amongst men, chooses to begin the revelation of the future kingdom in a very normal, human, romantic context.

## Kingdom Meals with Jesus

The way Jesus' ministry is introduced is then followed in the synoptics by the theme of kingdom meals in the company of Jesus. There are three ways in which Jesus relates festivity to the kingdom:

- He gives table fellowship to sinners and thereby invites them to the Messianic banquet.

- He miraculously multiplies food and thereby reveals that the Messianic age is present.

- He dedicates his last meal to the memory of his sacrificial body and blood and then fills that memory with his risen presence.

## *Table fellowship with Jesus*

The saying about the suitability of fasting or feasting in Mark's gospel is immediately preceded by Jesus eating with Levi the tax collector, an event loaded with significance. Apart from the fact that tax collectors were social outcasts, they were also regarded as ritually unclean, because they did not abide by the ceremonial acts of purification. Not only does Jesus eat with Levi but he feasts with him.

The expression used in Ch.2:15, "they reclined at table together with Jesus," suggests that Jesus – the Messiah – and not Levi, was the host at this festive meal – the entire pericope centers on the significance of Messiah eating with sinners. The specific reference in verse 17 to Jesus' call of sinners to the Kingdom suggests that the basis of table-fellowship was messianic forgiveness, and the meal itself was an anticipation of the messianic banquet. When Jesus broke bread with the outcasts, Messiah ate with them at his table and extended to them fellowship with God.'[29]

Luke catches the same idea when he says that Levi 'held a great banquet for Jesus at his home' (Lk.5:29). The teaching of Jesus matches his actions. While dining at a Pharisee's house he describes the kind of people who should be invited to banquets: 'the poor, the crippled, the lame, the blind.' The banquet we give in this age will be repaid at the resurrection of the righteous (14:13–14). Feasts in this age provide a foretaste, or determine the nature of one's place, at feasts in the age to come. This prompts a guest to exclaim about the blessedness of the feast in the kingdom of God. This prompts Jesus to tell the parable of the great feast and the socially acceptable guests who ignore or refuse the invitation to the feast. Street people are invited and welcomed to the feast, but those who turn down the invitation are excluded from 'my banquet' (14:16–24). The climax of the words of Jesus on the Messianic banquet must surely be the parable of the prodigal son. The epitome of the homecoming of the lost son is the fact that the Father throws a banquet for him. For Jesus, to experience the salvation of the kingdom is to feast.

*'Bring the fatted calf and kill it. Let's have a feast and celebrate. For this son of mine was dead and is alive again; he was lost and is found.' So they began to celebrate.* (15:23–24)

Clearly Jesus used meals as vehicles of kingdom nearness, where the Messianic banquet could be experienced in advance by those to whom Jesus extended grace.

### *Miracle feasts with Jesus*

The breakthrough of the powers of the age to come into this age was focused, embodied and personified in Jesus. When the future age becomes present anything is possible. Everything that will occur at the end becomes available in the present when Jesus is there. The vehicle to convey the miraculous, overpowering nature of the future age is the extravagant multiplication of food. Mark links two events, showing a contrast of worldly feast and kingdom feast. Herod, a false 'king of Israel' throws a banquet where he gets caught in his own egotism and ends up beheading John the Baptist (Mk.6:14–29). This is immediately followed by Jesus throwing a banquet in the wilderness, where a few loaves and fish feed five thousand. Later four thousand are similarly fed. The story is rich in symbolism. The green grass indicates that the wilderness is beginning to blossom and the groups of hundreds and fifties recalls the time when Moses led Israel through the wilderness and they were miraculously sustained. There is similarity and contrast. As John would teach, when Moses fed them they would hunger again. When Jesus feeds you, you will never hunger again. There are three gripping images: Moses leading Israel out of bondage, Herod beheading the prophet of God at his worldly banquet and Jesus the Messiah bringing the eschatological banquet to the masses. Both comparisons point to the profound presence of the kingdom in Jesus.

## The ordaining of the kingdom meal

Once one has understood the previous practice and teaching of Jesus the meaning of the last supper has already been interpreted! Here there is a cluster of sayings about eating and drinking in the kingdom. While the Passover meal looked back to the coming of the kingdom in the Exodus event, Jesus transformed its meaning in two ways. He replaced the Passover sacrifice with the giving of his own body and blood, thereby instituting a New Covenant, and he linked the wine they shared in their Passover with the next time he would drink it with them in the kingdom of God (Mk.14:25). Luke's language links the 'kingdom now' to the 'kingdom coming' more explicitly. Jesus will not partake again 'until it finds fulfilment in the kingdom of God' (Lk.22:16). The future feast is the time when 'Abraham, Isaac, and Jacob and all the prophets in the kingdom of God' will be gathered with God's people from all quarters of the earth 'at the feast in the kingdom of God' (13:28–30). In the mind of Jesus future kingdom and future feast were synonymous.

The mysterious nature of the kingdom is particularly evident from the festive theme. The fact that Jesus saw the kingdom as present in his ministry is revealed by the fellowship meals extended to sinners and the miraculous multiplication of food. The fact that Jesus saw the kingdom as still coming is evident from the last supper which he sets up as a provisional meal 'until the kingdom of God comes' (22:18). His behaviour during the forty days of his resurrection appearances shows that the kingdom has now come, fulfilling the 'until' articulated at the last supper, and yet still to come, as he continues to point to a future fulfilment. It is here, not yet here, then again here and not yet here.

There is a deliberate theme of eating and drinking during the resurrection presence of Jesus. It is while Jesus is breaking bread with the two in Emmaus that they suddenly recognise him. He then appears to the disciples in Jerusalem and demonstrates by sharing in their meal that he is not a ghost. John records the encounter between Peter and his fishing friends on the Sea of Galilee where Jesus has prepared a meal beforehand. In Acts his instructions about the coming Holy Spirit were given 'while they were eating with him' (Ac.1:4–5). In fact the apostolic witness to the resurrection is given a generic description. The 'witnesses whom God has already chosen' are 'we who ate and drank with him after he rose from the dead' (10:41). The cryptic 'ate and drank' here carries the same connotations as the 'ate and drank' of the seventy elders on Mount Sinai. It is in the shared meal that the whole meaning of the kingdom event is epitomised and expressed.

In the shared meals of the risen Christ the expectation of the coming kingdom is fulfilled, but not exhaustively. Once again the future has become present but awaits a future fulfilment. There is fulfilment on the way to fulfilment.

Now we must consider two implications.

- The fresh understanding of the kingdom has had a profound effect on some sections of the evangelical Christian community. The Vineyard is one part of the wider community particularly influenced by kingdom theology. We have adopted new models of the healing ministry and have sought to create an environment where the breakthrough of the kingdom in power is expected and endorsed. Have we thought through the implications for our practice of breaking bread, or having communion, to the same extent? It seems to me that the 'eucharist' is one area of church practice that remains peculiarly resistant to reform. How did we get from the feast of the kingdom to the 'nip and sip' of the church today? How did we get from the meal where sinners have the grace of the kingdom extended to them to the exclusive sacramental ceremony that only those within the community can ever comprehend? One wonders if any contemporary evangelical church would ever require an apostolic warning to not get drunk or eat too much at the Lord's Supper (1 Cor.11:21).

An examination of the practice of the early church will show that the eucharist remained a full meal, usually shared in a house church, until well after the New Testament documents were written. My attempt to reform our practice is reflected in the appendix on 'The way we break bread.'

- How does the kingdom relate to the church? The festive theme teaches us that the coming of the kingdom creates a celebrating community. The people of the kingdom are therefore those who are living in the good of the coming God. The obedience placed on Israel through the covenant is to be a joyful obedience, where the annual calendar is filled with times of celebration. Each celebration is to reflect with gratitude on the blessing of living under Yahweh as king. In the New Testament, *koinonia* is the life of the kingdom community who 'broke bread in their homes and ate together with glad and sincere hearts, praising God and enjoying the favour of all the people' (Ac.2:46). The favour of the people and the overwhelmed Queen of Sheba describe the witness communicated by a celebrating community. When we stop celebrating we show that we have lost the sense of visitation inherent in the kingdom. Before any kind of mission or service to the world, the church is to be the celebrating community.

# The Kingdom and the Church

We saw in chapter five that the Old Testament expectation was that the arrival of the age to come would terminate this present age. The mystery proclaimed by Jesus was that the end of the world could break through before this world actually ended. This intervention of the age to come occurred primarily in the birth of Christ, his ministry, death, resurrection, ascension and the outpouring of the Holy Spirit. The last major event in the breakthrough of the age to come, the ascension of Christ and the outpouring of the Spirit, established the nature of the period of delay in which the age to come and this age coexist in tension.

When Jesus was about to ascend, the disciples asked (Acts 1:6): 'Lord, will you at this time restore the kingdom to Israel?' One could paraphrase their question: 'Lord, will you now overthrow the Roman Empire?' They believed that the kingdom of this world would be destroyed and replaced by the kingdom of God. In this kingdom, with Israel as the capital of the world, the Messiah would be the universal king.

Christ's answer affirms that there will be a delay and explains what we ought to be doing in the interim: 'But you shall receive power when the Holy Spirit has come upon you; and you shall be witnesses to me in Jerusalem, and in all Judea and Samaria, and to the end of the earth' (1:8). The interim period is therefore the time of the Holy Spirit in the church. Believers are those who must be faithful to the end, preaching the kingdom until the close of the age.

This leads to a closer examination of the relationship between the kingdom and the church.

## Which is Which?

Two extremes must be noted in the way the relationship between the kingdom and the church has been viewed. The traditional view, associated with both Roman and Protestant traditions, is to identify the church with the kingdom. This error is very easy to make because there are so many points of continuity between the two. The more recent view, associated with dispensationalism, is to make a radical separation between the church and the kingdom. This view is usually based on the assumption that the kingdom refers to the Davidic monarchy and applies to the nation of Israel, while the church is the body of Christ and has a completely separate destiny to the nation of Israel. In terms of biblical support, it has less excuse and is not usually taken seriously by reputable biblical scholars.

In following chapters there will be further references to dispensationalism. This is a theory of particular segments of time, qualitatively different from one another, imposed on biblical revelation. The different forms of the theory share the fundamental problem that they fail to grasp the biblical understanding of two ages. Each kind will be explained in greater detail.

We can summarise the biblical view of the relationship between the kingdom and the church in a number of statements.[30]

- *The church is not the kingdom.* By most definitions, the church is a people or gathering of those who serve Jesus as Lord. The kingdom is the personal, dynamic reign of God. God reigns over his people. They might reign with him in the sense that they share his triumph, but the dominion and the Lordship belong to God.

Furthermore, God's reign is over all: the whole universe, the stars, angels and the redeemed of the earth. The kingdom is therefore much wider than the church.

- *The kingdom creates the church.* The inseparable link between the church and the kingdom is shown in Matthew 18:18–20. The building of the church is discussed in terms of the keys of the kingdom of God. Those who enter the kingdom automatically enter the church. As the reign of God breaks into this world, men are confronted with the demands of God the king. They are called to give their allegiance to Jesus. The moment they accept his Lordship, they become part of the company that has already accepted his Lordship, the church.

- *The church is a structure of human relationships:* brothers and sisters, shepherds and sheep, teachers and pupils, servants, exhorters, leaders and followers. This structure is created wherever the kingdom breaks into society. The life of the kingdom brings the church into being; the resulting network of human relationships must seek to contain, express and transmit the presence of the kingdom. However, sometimes the structure impedes and even resists the power of the kingdom.

The kingdom is illustrated by the analogy of the snail and its shell. The secretions of the snail create the shell which the snail inhabits. Many shells lie empty and lifeless. As church history has progressed, God has given successive interventions of his kingdom. Each time, a shell has been created appropriate to the life of the church. But church history is strewn with empty shells where the structure remains but the life has disappeared. The kingdom perspective should cure us of a preoccupation with shells. Different outpourings of God's presence take on various modes of expression. Our eye should be fixed on the event of the kingdom. Where is God intervening? Where are his mighty deeds being performed? Where can we see the power of the age to come? Our interest in the shells should be functional. The shell is holy while the snail is there. The shape of the shell is not holy and neither is the shell once the snail has disappeared.

- *The church has been entrusted with the proclamation of the kingdom.* One of the most dangerous doctrines found in dispensationalism is the separation of the gospel of the kingdom from the gospel of the church. The result is that the gospel of the church becomes something less than the gospel of the kingdom. The former is usually limited to the Pauline concept of justification while the latter includes the miraculous powers of the kingdom. We must stress that the New Testament knows only one gospel. The gospel of the church is the gospel of the kingdom.

According to the Great Commission, the gospel – the message of the cross and the resurrection, the offer of forgiveness and the call to discipleship – will be preached to all nations by the power of the Holy Spirit, with signs and wonders. All these elements constitute different parts of one commission which is effective for the entire period of church history. Discipleship must involve conveying all that Jesus taught and commanded throughout the entire course of his ministry: the message of the kingdom. The church is to preach the full kingdom message right to the end.

Jesus chose twelve disciples. Most commentators agree that this figure was deliberately chosen to indicate that the new people of God supersedes the twelve tribes of Israel. Christ's disciples are now the 'Israel of God' (Galatians 6:16). Jesus also chose seventy men to proclaim the kingdom. In Jewish tradition the number seventy represented all the nations of the world. This figure therefore symbolises the universal scope of the proclamation of the kingdom. Some details are limited to the situation, for instance, the reference to the bag and sandals – modern preachers drive cars and may carry credit cards – but the principles have permanent application. The fundamental commission of Jesus to the twelve and to the seventy is the same as the commission given to the church of all ages.

- *The church has been entrusted with certain powers and prerogatives* as the proclaimer of the kingdom. The church has the following powers: the right of representation; the keys of proclamation and revelation; the power of excommunication and reconciliation; and the impartation of peace or judgement.

- *The church must demonstrate the presence of the kingdom.* The church is the people who live simultaneously in two ages, experiencing the age to come, yet living out that experience in this age. In the age to come God will have his way in all things. It will therefore be an age of total order, wholeness and peace. The church's witness is that the age to come has become real here and now. The church must therefore demonstrate now the quality of life that will be expressed in the future kingdom. The world must be able to look at the church and see something of God's eternal future. This is why Jesus said that we must be perfect as our heavenly Father is perfect. When the church rejoices, men must catch a glimpse of the eschatological banquet. As disciples love one another, the world must see what eternal relationships are like. The inclusiveness of the church must express something of that great multitude from every nation, tribe, people and tongue. The order of a disciple's life as Christ reigns over every part of it must express the wholeness of the world to come, where faith, hope and love will abide.

## Caught Between the Times

The age to come and this age coexist in tension. This is the environment into which the church is born. Paul's teaching in Galatians shows how this reality is worked out in the Christian life. The old age/new age tension is manifest at various levels where similar tensions are experienced in the Christian life. The various levels are as follows:

| | |
|---|---|
| Old age (1:4; 5:21) | New age (5:21) |
| Law (5:18; 2:21; 5:4) | Grace |
| Bondage (4:22,23,25–26; 5:1) | Freedom |
| Works (2:16) | Faith |
| Condemnation (3:8–10) | Acquittal |
| Death (5:24–25) | Life (5:25) |
| Old man (Eph.4:22–24) | New man |
| Flesh (5:16–23) | Spirit |

Let us look at each of these opposites.

Paul uses both 'age', *aion,* and 'world', *kosmos,* to express the fundamental opposition of the old age and the new. Most of the references are to this present evil world which stands in contrast to the age to come. The experience of the believer in Christ is to be taken out of this present evil age.

Whereas Jesus spoke of the law and the prophets being transcended by the kingdom of God, Paul uses the terminology of *law and grace.* The basic idea is the same. The one breaks through and supersedes the other. Grace abounds over law, yet the law still has an influence, like a divorced person and a previous partner. We live in the tension between the wonder of grace and the legalistic bondage of the law. For Paul the law brings the knowledge of sin, God's wrath and the curse. In Christ we are not under law but under grace. The old has gone and the new has come. The grace of God is often mentioned in conjunction with peace. By grace we are justified and brought into the era of salvation.

It is not difficult to relate the opposition between *bondage and freedom* to the kingdom if we remember Isaiah's promise of freedom and the liberating ministry of Jesus. The most important element of freedom for Paul is the freedom from sin. To live in the new age is to experience freedom from sin; to live in this age is to be a slave to sin.

The concepts of *faith versus works* and *acquittal versus condemnation* are an outworking of being either under grace or under law. The only way to receive the grace of God is by faith; the law demands a system of works or righteousness based on human merit. Those who exercise faith in Jesus Christ are immediately justified or acquitted, while those who continue to trust in works or the law remain under condemnation.

The ultimate difference between the old age and the new age is in *life or death*. For the Christian the transition from this age to the age to come is through death and resurrection. The believer has already been buried and raised with Christ. He looks back at the grave. The sting of death is past. Believers do not die; they only sleep.

It is common to find the opposition between *the old man and the new man* being understood in psychological terms, as if the old man were a part of the human personality and the new man a better part of the same personality. Paul's language is not psychological but eschatological. The old man is the past life of the Christian before he experienced death and resurrection with Christ. It includes anything that still ties him to this present age. The old man was crucified in Christ because he was sentenced to death under the law. The new man is the life of the believer in the new age.

The Christian is someone who is caught between two ages. Two ages compete within us for supremacy: the lifestyle of the old man seeks to re-establish itself through the works of the flesh; the Spirit draws us into the lifestyle of the new man. Our assurance that the new man will triumph over the old man does not lie in a subjective, psychological experience, but in the fact that the new age has invaded the old in Christ and the power of the age to come now influences our life. Even though much about us is weak, we may be sure that the new world will triumph over the old and the new person Christ has made us will prevail over the person we used to be.

The *flesh/Spirit* opposition is closely associated with the old man/new man opposition. The word 'flesh' is used in a number of different ways, none of which involves a rejection of the human body. The flesh applies to fallen human nature which continues to be present in the believer. The 'flesh' in this sense will only cease to exist when Jesus comes again.

While sinless perfection is not possible until then, the Spirit brings the believer the powers of the age to come. This means that we can never settle into this present evil age. A proper understanding of the flesh/Spirit opposition will prevent us from falling prey to perfectionist doctrines or defeatist resignation. Both triumphalism, as it is usually termed, and defeatism can only exist if one loses the sense of eschatological tension.

Christians are mysterious contradictions. We are living in a new world while we exist in the present world. We are new people, transformed by grace, yet we wrestle with the flesh and have to beware that our old nature does not reassert itself. We are victorious failures and broken winners. We do not merely understand the mystery of the kingdom in theory; we experience the mystery within ourselves. The next chapter will examine this subject in more detail.

# 'Already-Not Yet' People

Inherent in understanding the relationship between the kingdom and the church is an understanding of the Christian life. The end of the last chapter began to work towards the implications for the Christian life. This is the area where the theology of the kingdom affects us all personally and where our understanding or lack of understanding will have a profound effect on the everyday Christian experience. Many pastoral and counselling problems are the result of a distortion of the kingdom or an ignorance of the kingdom.

Two kinds of texts express the 'already-not yet' Christian experience.

> *Therefore, if anyone is in Christ, he is a new creation; the old has gone; the new has come!* (2 Corinthians 5:17)

> *Now thanks be to God who always leads us in triumphal procession in Christ.* (2 Corinthians 2:14)

Such statements underline the completeness and the triumph of God's work in us. These are 'kingdom now' statements. Regenerate Christians already live in the kingdom. In Jesus we have eternal life. We have already passed from death to life. To become a Christian is to become a new person, with a new nature, living a new life.

> *Meanwhile we groan, longing to be clothed with our heavenly dwelling. For while we are in this tent we groan and are burdened.* (2 Corinthians 5:2, 4)

> *Conflicts on the outside, fears within.* (2 Corinthians 7:5)

> *We despaired even of life.* (2 Corinthians 1:8)

> *For we are always being given over to death for Jesus' sake.* (2 Corinthians 4:11)

> *Put to death whatever belongs to your earthly nature: sexual immorality, impurity, lust, evil desires and greed.* (Colossians 3:5)

From these and many other texts we can conclude that the kingdom event has only taken place in the Christian in an anticipatory sense. Much still needs to be done. We are still linked to this present world, with its frailty, sin and defeat.

Do these texts contradict one another? Is the man who lives with conflict outside and fear within the man who always walks in triumph wherever he goes? Why do 'new creations' require warnings about lust and greed? If we look a little closer, we find that these texts often appear in the same context. Many passages deliberately place both realities side by side. Listen to the triumphant defeat or the defeated triumph of these statements:

> *We are hard pressed on every side, yet not crushed; we are perplexed, but not in despair; persecuted, but not forsaken; struck down, but not destroyed.* (2 Corinthians 4:8–9)

> *... by honour and dishonour, by evil report and good report; as deceivers, and yet true; as unknown, and yet well known; as dying, and behold we live; as chastened, and yet not killed; as sorrowful, yet always rejoicing; as poor, yet making many rich; as having nothing, and yet possessing all things.* (2 Corinthians 6:8–10)

What a contradiction! These are possibly the most eloquent expressions of the mystery of the kingdom in the Christian life that have ever been written.

The same tension is found in passages about how perfect or imperfect a Christian can be. If we want to find a text about sinless perfection we turn to 1 John 3:6: 'Whoever abides in him does not sin.' Yet if we want a text that totally denies sinless perfection, we turn to 1 John 1:8: 'If we say that we have no sin, we deceive ourselves, and the truth is not in us.'

At the point of repentance and faith, the moment of justification, God imputes his righteousness to us. This is followed by sanctification. We are transformed from one degree of glory to another as we are moulded into the image of God's Son. Justification and sanctification must not be confused. Being born again does not transform us instantaneously into sinless individuals. The history of the Christian church is full of confusion resulting from the failure to understand these issues.

The tension between the 'already' and the 'not yet' does not apply just to history or to the mystery of healing. It exists within us. It is not only the church as a corporate body that lives between the times. The individual Christian experiences this too. The texts we have referred to bear witness to the fact that the Christian life has a duality about it. We live with an inner contradiction. It is important to understand what this does and does not mean.

- The duality we experience is eschatological. Two ages coexist within us. It is not a dualism of different inner parts. The spirit/flesh language of Paul is expressing the 'already' and 'not yet' of the kingdom, not a division of the human person into inherently holy and sinful inner parts. The 'flesh' is about the continuity one still has with one's old life. The 'spirit' is about the continuity one has with one's new life. In the wisdom of God this is the environment into which we were born as Christians. We cannot extricate ourselves from this environment any more than we can jump out of our skin. It is the air we breathe and the reality we live. It is the experience of all Christians. There has never been a Christian who has not been frustrated and troubled by the duality he experi-

159

ences. Sometimes we experience it on the same day. We walk out of a worship service where God was present and we feel a sense of total victory and pleasure. We are truly a part of the celebrating community. Later the same day we get into a family quarrel and we manifest attitudes that make us feel ashamed. Is this the same person? We do not need to see a counsellor about this experience and we do not need to go on a journey of inner exploration. We are just ordinary, typical Christians.

- We should get used to it. It will not go away. The entire age of grace, from the coming of the kingdom to the final consummation of the kingdom is lived 'between the times'. That means the expanse of your entire life is incorporated. Not only should we not be surprised by it, but we should not panic either. As a pastor I know that most Christians live with feelings of lack of self-worth more than a sense of arrogance and triumph. In fact the closer we get to God and the more we experience the in-breaking of the kingdom, the more disturbed we become by the 'not yet' within us. In a strange, contradictory way the more we get from God the more we groan. We should settle for the reality. This experiential dimension is just the way it is.

- There is no doubt about the final outcome. In the metaphor of Daniel, the stone falls from heaven and pulverises the image. The age to come will utterly triumph over the present evil age. The new man in you is beating up the old man in you. As you apply yourself to the means of grace, to Bible study, prayer, worship, fellowship, witness and service you will continue to partake of the powers of the coming age. Inherent in such power is the ability to say no to sin. That is why the New Testament has statements about final triumph. 'He who began the good work in you will carry it on to completion' (Phil.1:6). God will 'present you before his glorious presence without fault and with great joy' (Jude 24).

As with so many of these truths, people who lose sight of the mystery of the kingdom emphasise one side of the tension to the exclusion of the other. There are those who choose all the 'new creature', 'walking in triumph' texts, while others choose all the 'groaning' and 'despairing' texts, and then each group develops a doctrine or lifestyle based on a one-sided understanding of Scripture.

## The 'Groaning' Tradition

An emphasis on poverty, chastity and humility developed in the monastic movement. While Scripture is clear about God's love for the poor, this tradition conveys the idea that poverty has a positive spiritual value. Poverty is a curse. God loves the poor because his mercy is towards them as they suffer under this curse. His will is to deliver them. The tradition suggests that one gains a special sanctity by deliberately embracing poverty. Humility is a profound biblical emphasis, but when people lose the biblical balance they begin to glorify a humiliated creeping of the individual. This is the tradition that has included, at different stages, various forms of asceticism to curb the 'flesh', including flagellation. Linked to this is the tendency to want to escape from society to avoid the power of the world and its many temptations. The underlying assumption is that the Christian is too weak to stand up to real temptations in a real world. Protestants are in no position to blame the Roman tradition for all this. One finds in Protestant circles an approach to spirituality that focuses on introspection, denial, mortification and legalism. This is also true of many Pentecostal traditions. If one takes the dispensational denial of the miraculous and a morbid emphasis on sanctification and combines this with 'remnantitis', one arrives at defeatism. Defeatist Christianity sees the kingdom as a future event; in this world we suffer and are defeated.

Remnantitis is a way of rationalising the failure of the church to evangelise the world. One can take texts about all those who will fall away at the end and those about the few that will be saved and develop a whole theory about the church as a small remnant of faithful believers holding on until the rapture. Link this to an approach to worship that denies all emotion or exuberance and has no place for physical expression, add the belief that no instruments should be used in worship, and the result is a scene from 'Babette's Feast'. It is almost as if God has run out of blessing and has adopted 'austerity measures' to prevent the heavenly resources from going bankrupt. The resultant Christian expression is not glorifying to God. It is not surprising that other traditions have reacted in the opposite direction. How widespread is this belief? If the standard portrayal of Christians in the secular media is anything to judge by, this is the concept most of the secular world has of the Christian church.

## The Perfection Tradition

We will discuss three of the more visible traditions that still influence the evangelical church at various points: Methodist, Pentecostal and Baptist. But no single tradition within the church can be labelled with the problem.

### *Methodist Triumphalism*

John Wesley wrote *A Plain Account of Christian Perfection*.[31] Subsequent church leaders have questioned whether Wesley's account was either 'plain' or totally biblical. Wesley explained that the sanctifying experience of the Holy Spirit so fills the Christian with God's love that he never really sins thereafter. He may make mistakes, because he remains a finite human being, but the true intentions of his heart will remain pure. This teaching flourished in various 'holiness' movements. Elements of Wesley's teaching can be found in the Keswick Movement and in the 'holiness' tradition within Pentecostalism.

## Pentecostal Triumphalism

The early Pentecostal movement gave rise to a novel doctrine called 'manifest sons of God', an idea that has surfaced in various places at different times. One of the more extreme cases was the Church of the Living Word led by John Robert Stevens in California. The early Pentecostals who initiated the doctrine misconstrued the text of Romans 8:18–25 where Paul describes the moment when the sons of God will be revealed. At present we have the 'first fruits of the Spirit', but one day we will be adopted as sons and obtain the redemption of our bodies. Paul is clearly describing the final resurrection of the saints at the second coming when our mortal bodies will be transformed into immortality. However, this teaching takes Paul's words to refer to a special generation of believers who will be manifested or revealed before the second coming. This will be part of the 'latter rain' outpouring of the Holy Spirit. The generation that immediately precedes the second coming will receive a special anointing, and those who respond to this will become 'manifested sons'.

One can understand that if someone is convinced that he is living just before the second coming and has some valid charismatic experiences, he can imagine himself as about to be 'manifest'. Stevens predicted that he would not die but would obtain a 'manifest' body. He is now deceased.

More recently there is some indication of a special emphasis on a 'prophetic' or 'Elijah generation' that will emerge out of the church during the final outpouring. This is taken from the passage in Revelation about the return of the two witnesses for the last three and a half years of world history (11:1–13). Just as Elijah returned in 'spirit and power' through John the Baptist to inaugurate the first coming of Christ, so a special generation of Christians will emerge to inaugurate the second coming.

This idea is sometimes explained by a novel dispensational theory that divides church history since Luther into ten ages. Luther is said to represent the time of the pastor, Wesley the time of the evangelist and so on until we emerge in the time of the prophet. Apart from the arbitrary way in which church history is interpreted, all attempts to subdivide the age of grace collide with the fundamentals of kingdom thinking. Dispensational thinking and kingdom theology are not compatible.

The way this idea is articulated is clearly elitist. Only those who are 'into' this insight will have the privilege of the Elijah anointing. A special class of Christians, a type of charismatic illuminati distinct from the ecumenical body, is said to exist. The truth is that the whole church will operate in this Elijah-dimension during the tribulation. All regenerate Christians have equal value before the Father – the value of the blood shed on our behalf. The experiences the church will endure during the tribulation will be universal because the anti-Christ system will persecute the entire people of God. Any special grace of the Holy Spirit given during this time will be equally universal to the people of God. Further, this grace has been operating in the history of the church whenever there has been persecution. It does not have to be understood as a distinct dispensation.

## Baptist Triumphalism

The third kind of triumphalism is found in the writings of E.W. Kenyon. His views have been associated with the 'faith' teachers of the American Bible Belt because they have drawn heavily on his theology. However, Kenyon was not a Pentecostal. He was actually an independent Baptist. This is not the place to examine whether his views are the result of metaphysics or not, the subject of McConnel's *A Different Gospel*.[32] What is relevant to our discussion is Kenyon's emphasis on the 'new creation' texts without the balance of the 'groaning' texts to produce a concept of some special breed of 'super' Christians. For Kenyon the Christian has it all 'already'; there is no need to balance this with the 'not yet'.

'We have never realised,' says Kenyon, 'that the tenses are often ruled by the senses. Most of our popular hymns are in the future or in the past tense.'[33] This, he says, is a mistaken reading of the Bible. 'When I read it, it is His present tense message to my heart, for the Word is always Now. The Father is always Now.'[34] What the believer has now is the new creation. 'We have seen that an actual New Creation takes place within his spirit when he receives Jesus Christ as Saviour and Lord. Spiritual death is eradicated from his spirit, and he is taken completely out of Satan's dominion of death.'[35] For Kenyon the old nature is eradicated and replaced with God's nature to such an extent that the believer knows only victory. 'The new creation man is a partaker of God's nature. He is really an Incarnation. He has received the nature and life of God ... If this doesn't constitute a superman, then I don't know what a superman is.'[36] 'This righteousness makes a man actually one with Christ. It has given to man a creative ability, a dominating spirit. He is an overcomer. He is a master ... He has become an actual Jesus man. He takes Jesus' place on earth.'[37]

Like the manifest sons of God teachers, Kenyon says that a special generation will arise to claim this 'new creation' victorious walk. He teaches that 'The hour is coming before the Lord's return in which a remnant of the body will rise and walk before God the Father in the fullness of the New Creation Life. Disease will not be able to lay hold upon us.' [38]

Kenyon's writings are repetitive and many more examples could be given of such statements. A novel idea he links to this, is that only the Anglo-Saxon races, who have had the gospel for generations, have produced new inventions because the 'super-race' is amongst them.[39] This breed of Christian knows nothing of pain and defeat. 'There need be no more struggles with sin, no more battles with the Adversary, just an acting upon the Word of God.'[40] 'The old things of weakness and failure, of doubt and fear, have passed into forgetfulness. We take our place and enjoy our rights ... I have no sense of guilt or sin.'[41]

It is significant that triumphalist excesses have arisen during times of revival. When the sense of the immediacy of the kingdom is accentuated, people easily misread this as an indication that the 'not yet' has been superseded. On the other hand, times of spiritual dryness tend to emphasise the 'groaning' texts. Men always want to read their own experience into the Scriptures. Sadly these emphases in the history of the church represent a truth that is being overstated because of a previous extreme where this truth was denied. Kenyon was reacting to the deadness he saw in the church around him. Wesley led a revival when moral conditions in England were at an all-time low. If we sift out the overstatement, we find an important truth. But overstating a truth instead of establishing it merely brings it into disrepute. Others react to the triumphalists and embrace introspective monastic tendencies.

## The Kingdom Perspective

The New Testament teaches that there is both 'kingdom now' and kingdom 'not yet'. Our Christian experience takes place within this tension. The Christian is a glorious contradiction. We are simultaneously triumphant and groaning. We are new creatures, with new natures, yet we war against the flesh. God always leads us in triumph, yet our lives seem to be one long battle. As we look within ourselves we sometimes feel victorious, joyful and free, yet these moments are quickly replaced by feelings of great weakness, fear and 'groaning' from which we long to escape.

We do know that the new age is triumphant over the old. The stone falls from heaven and pulverises the image. What we are becoming in Jesus will prevail utterly over what we were. There is every reason to be filled with hope – the confident expectation that we move from the victory Christ has 'already' obtained, to the victory of Christ still to be obtained.

Understanding the tension of the kingdom is essential to measure truth. Any teaching that tries to evade either the 'already' or the 'not yet' runs counter to the balance of Scripture. And doctrine always has an outworking in life. A defeatist emphasis will produce defeated Christians.

A triumphalist approach will produce unreal people who live in a spiritual bubble, or worse, an arrogance and fanaticism that brings the name of Jesus into disrepute.

# The End of Cessationism

'Signs and wonders' is a biblical term for the demonstration of the kingdom in the ministry of Jesus through the power of the Holy Spirit. Jesus evidenced this in healing the sick, casting out demons, raising the dead, multiplying food, having knowledge of the secret thoughts of people and control over natural forces. These signs and wonders continued in the experience of the early church. Acts records healings, people raised from the dead, the casting out of demons, prophetic gifts, dreams and visions, divinely arranged earthquakes and sudden deaths.

Those who are sceptical about the Christian faith have often doubted these things, especially since the rise of modern rationalism, but those who believe in the authenticity of the New Testament accept that they occurred. Yet the moment one begins to speak about the continued manifestation of signs and wonders in the church today, serious objections are raised by those who believe the miraculous was confined to the apostolic age. The age of the church is said to be a different or distinct 'dispensation' from the age of the apostles. This belief is called cessationism.

## What is Cessationism?

In the following chapter we will deal with a form of dispensationalism that arose during the 1860s in Scotland. It separates the last seven years of history from the destiny of the church. In this chapter we will look at an older form of dispensationalism, namely cessationism, which denies the possibility of signs and wonders occurring after the Apostolic age. The two views are similar in the sense that both divide the age of the church into isolated segments. The later form of dispensationalism arose in a circle that was not especially equipped in the area of theological training. The older type, however, was propounded by such renowned theologians as Benjamin Warfield.[42] It was closely associated with certain forms of Reformed theology. The body of Christ needs to be forever grateful to the Pentecostal movement for challenging this doctrine.

The early Pentecostals experienced the miraculous in no uncertain terms. Any reading of their early history makes this plain. The church environment into which Pentecostalism was born was deeply influenced by cessationist teaching, linked to the generally materialistic world view of the Western world. Historical church leaders ruled the Pentecostal experiences out of court and concluded that whatever was taking place had to be either demonic or imaginary because they knew that miracles no longer occurred in this dispensation.

The Pentecostals lacked the theological background to tackle the roots of cessationist teaching, so they fought back with true grit instead. They simply continued to testify – adamantly – that God was moving power-fully in their midst. The proof was there for all to see. After some decades Pentecostalism had become one of the fastest growing movements that the Christian church had ever seen. One prominent church historian has described it as the 'third force' in Christendom, comparable with the great traditions of Catholicism and Protestantism. The Pentecostal conviction won through sheer weight of numbers so that today, with the Charismatic Movement taking the 'charismatic experience' back into the historical churches, fewer and fewer cessationists remain.

What the Pentecostals did not realise was that a true understanding of kingdom teaching completely destroys cessationism. If they had known this they could have fought the battle with a two-edged sword:

the Word and the Spirit. It is important for us to develop this theme because cessationist hard-liners still exist and we need to ground our openness to the supernatural on clear biblical foundations.

Cessationism probably arose as an explanation for the dearth of signs and wonders in the drier periods of church history, aided by fanatics who brought signs and wonders into disrepute during and after the Reformation. This caused more sober Reformed leaders to react in the opposite direction: knowledge of the Word and faith in Jesus Christ was said to be all a Christian must desire. Added to this was an emphasis on the dangers of 'subjectivism'. People were told to be careful about becoming too subjective about their faith as this could lead to all sorts of fanaticism: we must base our faith on the Word, which is objective, not on subjective experiences. Countless wild-eyed believers, fresh from the 'charismatic experience', have run into the solid, unmoving conviction of a Reformed pastor that all such phenomena are impossible. Such pastoral interviews end with the believer's morale shattered and him doubting his own sanity.

Behind the emphasis against the 'subjective' lies a conviction about dispensations. The argument is as follows. The reason the miraculous no longer occurs is that God has ordained it so. When the early church was being formed and the foundation of the apostles and prophets was being laid, God gave the witness of signs and wonders. They testified to the ministry of Jesus and the authority of the apostles. Then the apostles wrote the books of the New Testament. The foundation they themselves represented was replaced by the foundation they left with the church, the canon of the New Testament. Once this was completed, there was no further need of the testimony of the miraculous. It was replaced by the testimony of Scripture and the inner testimony of the Spirit authenticating the message of Scripture. The passing of the apostles and the formation of the New Testament canon therefore marks a transition between two dispensations: the apostolic and the post-apostolic.

Some developed an intricate theory about multiple dispensations in redemptive history based on the idea of a number of different covenants between God and his people: Adam, Noah, Abraham, Moses, David and Ezra/Nehemiah. Based on all these covenants, there were found to be ages with miraculous events and ages with no miraculous events. For instance, the Mosaic era was filled with the miraculous, while the time of Ezra and Nehemiah was not. So, we were told, one cannot assume that every age is destined to include the miraculous.

The Old Testament situation was carried into the New Testament. Dispensations were demarcated within the New Testament era too: the time of Jesus, the time of the apostles and the time of the post-apostolic church. The first two were times of the miraculous while the third is a time without the miraculous because it has the authority of Scriptures. In fact, if we want miracles today we show great arrogance because we think that we should have the same testimony to our confession as Jesus Christ himself. How dare we demand such a thing?

Strange inferences have been drawn from this theory. Some portions of the New Testament are said to be doctrinal while others are experiential. The book of Acts is experiential, while Paul's letters are clearly doctrinal. If we attempt to build doctrine on the book of Acts, we are using the experiences of the early church as our foundation. We must only build doctrine on clearly doctrinal sections such as Romans and Ephesians. This was used to circumvent the testimony of Acts to the 'charismatic' dimension. Underlying the rejection of Acts is the idea that apostolic charismatic experiences are not relevant to later church history. John MacArthur argues for the 'uniqueness' of the charismatic experiences in the book of Acts. They occurred during the period when the gospel was first preached to Jews, Samaritans and Gentiles. These unique events cannot be applied to us today.[43]

The apostolic writings contain a number of references to the laying of a foundation. The church is built on the foundation of the apostles and prophets. Paul has laid a foundation. The foundation is Jesus Christ. Each man must take care how he builds on that foundation. At the end of the New Testament we read about the twelve apostles as the foundation of the New Jerusalem. After the apostolic foundation no more must be added or else the plagues described in the book of Revelation will occur.

Essential to the ability to lay the foundation was the apostolic dimension of revelation through the Holy Spirit. If someone in the post-apostolic era claims supernatural revelation, he therefore claims something reserved for the apostles and the same curse must come upon him. The ministry of apostles and prophets has been discontinued. This means that prophecies today compete with the Scriptures. A person who claims a prophecy is adding to Scripture and undermining the New Testament canon. Did Paul not make it clear that prophecies will cease when perfection comes? This 'perfection' can be found in the fully inspired, authoritative New Testament canon. Since it was established, prophecy and tongues have passed away.

Another novel idea is that there are actually two gospels: the gospel of the kingdom preached by Jesus, which included the miraculous, and the gospel preached by the church as expounded by Paul in Romans 1–8. This is about justification through faith and makes no reference to signs and wonders. The gospel preached by the church cannot include the miraculous because it applies to a later dispensation.

The conclusion is that all Pentecostals and Charismatics are fanatical, disrespectful of biblical authority, subjectivist, arrogant and misguided.

## Kingdom Teaching

A proper understanding of the kingdom destroys the entire theory so that none of its parts retains any viability. I believe that the continued teaching of this theory, even if it is in part, undermines the faith and expectation of the church as to the readiness of God to break through into the affairs of men. It is an extremely unhealthy doctrine. Cessationism, rationalism and materialism have all had their share in devastating the health of the Christian church. Cessationism needs to be rooted out. We will begin with those implications of kingdom teaching that collide with the theory.

## The Last Days

The actual word 'dispensation' does not occur in the New Testament. One can relate Paul's comments about the 'ministry of death' and the 'ministry of the Spirit' in 2 Corinthians 3:7–18 to the word 'dispensation', but his argument will not allow for what cessationists infer. Paul is contrasting the Old Testamental, Mosaic covenant with the new covenant in Jesus Christ. There are just two dispensations in God's dealings with man, represented by the Old and the New Covenants. The New Testament has very definite language to express this: the age of promise has been replaced by the time of fulfilment; the law came through Moses, grace and truth through Jesus Christ; the law and the prophets were until John, since then the kingdom of God has been forcefully advancing.

The new covenant time of fulfilment is known throughout the New Testament as the 'last days'. The last days came with Jesus. From the coming of Christ to the second coming, no further subdivision into dispensations is permissible. There are no more than two dispensations.

Hebrews contrasts the time of the Old Testament prophets with 'these last days' when God has spoken through his Son. Peter is clear that the outpouring of the Spirit on the day of Pentecost fulfils the promise of Joel about the 'last days'. If the last days began with Jesus and the day of Pentecost, we have been living in the last days ever since. The 'last days' cannot get more 'last' than they are. The period in which the early church lived is the same period or dispensation as the one in which we live. Scripture references could be multiplied. The church is that company 'on whom the ends of the ages have come' (1 Corinthians 10:11). John can say that his day was already the 'last hour' (1 John 2:18).

Such statements reflect the underlying kingdom theology of the New Testament as a whole. In Jesus Christ, and through the Holy Spirit, the powers of the age to come have broken into this age. The result is the unexpected coincidence of this age and the age to come. When Paul points to things that are still to happen in 'later times' or the 'last days', he is not pointing to some distant time separate from his own. He is speaking of things that occur in his own time – he also lives in the last days. There is a delay in the last days, but this in no way constitutes a division. Since Jesus came, the two ages exist side by side. When he comes again, this age will cease, and the age to come, which is already present, will be finally manifest. This is the framework for the entire New Testament. To grasp this truth is to understand that there can be no further subdivisions within the New Testament era. It destroys the entire dispensational and cessationist theory.

## Preaching the Gospel

We can be even more specific.

The book of Acts is prefixed with and ends with two key statements about the kingdom. The giving of the Great Commission is recorded in Matthew 28, Mark 16, Luke 24 and Acts 1. This places Matthew 28 and Acts 1 in the same context. In Matthew 28:18 Jesus reveals that he has all authority in heaven and on earth. He commissions his disciples to preach the good news of the kingdom to all nations before the end can come. The commission was first given to the disciples during the ministry of Jesus. The same commission was given to the seventy. Both are inextricably bound to signs and wonders: he gave them authority to preach the kingdom, drive out demons, heal the sick, raise the dead and cleanse those who have leprosy.

Jesus not only demonstrated the kingdom, he explained it in the parables and the beatitudes. His teaching included forgiveness by grace or, as Paul explained it, justification through faith. As Jesus reissued the commission to preach the kingdom to all nations, he specified that it should include 'teaching them to observe all things that I have commanded you'. This must therefore include the full spectrum of kingdom teaching given during the course of his ministry, including the commission to perform signs and wonders. The disciples were to wait for the power of the Spirit, but before he left them, Jesus spent forty days speaking about the kingdom of God.

Jesus' proclamation of the kingdom included signs and wonders. He commissioned the twelve and the seventy to preach the same message. After his resurrection he intensified this commission over forty days. The whole message of the kingdom was to be preached to the end of the age. This sets the stage for the book of Acts. There is no doubt that the dimension of signs and wonders is part of the gospel.

The last verse in Acts tells us that Paul boldly preached the kingdom of God. There was no diminishing of the commission nor is there a change from the kingdom message to the message of the church. Any talk about 'another gospel' is heresy. Far from the proclamation of signs and wonders throughout the church age bringing forth the curses of the book of Revelation, it is the reduction of the gospel that is anathema. There is one gospel, the full gospel of the kingdom – including signs and wonders to the very end.

## Expectation

Understanding the kingdom means that we understand the nearness of the powers of the age to come. Jesus himself is the end, the first and the last. To encounter him is to encounter the end. When someone experiences the gift of the Holy Spirit, he partakes of the powers of the coming age. Whenever someone is healed, a kingdom event has taken place, and the age to come has broken through. Jesus described the casting out of demons as a sign of the presence of the kingdom. The demons complained that this was happening before the time – they understood that an end of the world event was happening in this world. When people speak in tongues, they speak in the language of men and of angels – a foretaste of the communication that will only really make sense in the age to come.

When the end finally arrives, our bodies will be transformed into glorified, heavenly bodies, no longer bound by space or time but like Jesus' resurrected body. He could pass through walls and appear and disappear; yet he was a real, tangible person. He had flesh and bones, and could eat and be touched. This remarkable body was the first fruit of the future harvest. Even now, when people come under the power of God, their bodies are often overcome. The Pentecostal disciples appeared to be drunk. Philip was taken up and found himself miles from where he had been. These phenomena demonstrate that the barrier between this age and the age to come has been ruptured. We do not know exactly when the end will come, but the breakthrough of the end hangs over us as an ever-present cloud of glorious promise.

The term 'supernatural' is not a biblical one, and strictly speaking it should be avoided. It conveys the idea of two kinds of reality, the natural and the supernatural. This idea is more Greek than Hebrew. The biblical understanding is of two ages, one of bondage and one of deliverance. In Jesus and through the Holy Spirit, the age to come is continually available, immediate, and often present. The book of Hebrews gives a helpful illustration.

The Old Testament tabernacle is a picture of man's relationship with God. The barrier between the sanctuary and the Holy Place represents the barrier between God and man. When Jesus died, the veil in the temple was rent from top to bottom, indicating that his atoning blood had removed the dividing wall of hostility between God and man. The other barrier in the temple was between Jew and Gentile. The blood of Jesus tore down this dividing wall too. Both vertical and horizontal relationships were reversed through the cross.

This is fairly well-known symbolism, but Hebrews adds another factor. The distinction between the sanctuary and the Holy Place is not only symbolic of the barrier between man and God but of the separation between this age and the age to come. The outer tent was symbolic of the present age, implying that the inner tent is symbolic of the future age. Other biblical statements explain this symbolism. In this present age we worship God through symbols. The seven-branched candelabrum or menorah, the table of showbread and the various offerings speak of indirect contact with God. Even in the New Testament the symbolism of bread and wine in the context of congregational worship is a form of indirect contact with God. In this age we see in a mirror, 'dimly'; in the age to come when we are united to Jesus, we will see 'face to face' (1 Corinthians 13:12) as Moses saw God in the inner tent. If the outer tent represents the indirect presence of God through symbols and the inner tent represents the direct presence of God appropriate to the age to come, the tearing of the veil means that the barrier between this age and the age to come has been removed.

Since the coming of Jesus, people worshipping God find themselves carried by the Holy Spirit into experiences that really belong to the next world. The immediacy of God's presence that we will know in the world to come, breaks into this age in mysterious and unpredictable ways, disregarding the normal distinctions between this age and the next. The wind blows back and forth between the two chambers, now drawing someone in this chamber into the next, now revealing the glory of the inner tent to the outer tent. This perception makes kingdom theology, with its understanding of the breakthrough of the ages, the basis for an understanding of signs and wonders.

## Refutation

What then of the various cessationist arguments? The neat subdivision of the Old Testament into a multiplicity of covenants and dispensations is almost as problematic as such subdivisions within the New Testament. There is good reason to argue that the Old Testament knows of only one covenant. Prior to the beginning of redemptive history with Abraham, God's relationship with man cannot really be described as covenantal – one can only find anticipations. Sin had broken contact between God and man. With Abraham God initiated the relationship of grace, and this is where covenant truly begins. The covenant with Abraham has its first outworking in the Exodus: God promised the Patriarchs that he would deliver Israel from bondage. Moses knew that he was dealing with the fulfilment of promises made by the God of Abraham, Isaac and Jacob. The Mosaic covenant was a covenant of grace and the whole Exodus event was an act of grace. The conquest was similarly a fulfilment of God's promises to Abraham. David's ministry was to restore the land conquered by Joshua but subsequently lost to Israel. The covenant with David was a reiteration of the covenant with Abraham and Moses. So was the renewal of the covenant under Ezra and Nehemiah. All these covenant events go back to God's promise to Abraham. The rise and fall of the miraculous was a measure of Israel's faith or unbelief, covenant faithfulness or covenant disloyalty. When good kings ruled, the covenant was renewed. When evil kings ruled, the covenant was threatened. The miraculous was usually associated with the prophets: prophets meant God was speaking. The absence of prophets meant God was silent because the nation was under judgement. This had nothing to do with special periods when signs and wonders were in the plan of God and everything to do with revival or backsliding.

The neat division between apostolic and sub-apostolic is not supported by the New Testament, despite the confident tradition to the contrary. Traditionally it was believed that when Judas was replaced, although the apostles chose Matthias, God actually chose Paul. This places Paul amongst the twelve, after which all apostleship was terminated. This argument does not hold water. Apart from the fact that there is absolutely no support in the New Testament for the idea that Paul replaced Judas, a number of references make it clear that the twelve were not the only apostles. Paul indicates that he was not an apostle like the twelve. He was not with Jesus from the baptism of John until the ascension (Acts 1:21–22). He describes himself as one 'born out of due time' (1 Corinthians 15:8). But neither can he be placed on the same level as subsequent apostles. He did have an experience of Christ which was so unique that it could almost be placed alongside the meeting of the twelve with the resurrected Christ (15:6–7). This places him in a unique category.

A number of individuals were called apostles although they were not one of the twelve: Barnabas, James the Lord's brother, Timothy, Andronicus and Junias. No amount of explaining the use of the word *apostello,* 'messenger', can remove the apostolic ministry from these individuals. Apart from James, the others were part of the apostolic ministry alongside Paul. If their apostleship is that of some vague messenger, so was Paul's, which is palpably false.

Paul places apostles and prophets alongside evangelists and pastor/teachers without any indication that these ministries are divided between different dispensations. These, along with the charismatic gifts, are what God has appointed in the church. As long as the body is required to function in its many parts and the church needs to be brought to full maturity, these ministries will be required. The church certainly did not reach full maturity during the first century. Finalising the canon is one thing. The church attaining the 'measure of the stature of the fullness of Christ' is another. Apostolic and prophetic ministries will be necessary 'till we all come to the unity of the faith and the knowledge of the Son of God' (Ephesians 4:13). 'Till' settles the time for the termination of these gifts, not the formulation of the canon. The perfection described in 1 Corinthians 13 is the perfection of the age to come, when we see God face to face. Rather than an argument for the cessation of the charismatic gifts, this chapter shows quite clearly that tongues and prophecies will only cease when we see God face to face and understand all things fully.

The New Testament does make a distinction between two levels of apostleship. The twelve, who were witnesses to the historical Christ, are an unrepeatable and unique company. Those who Paul describes as having their commission in the Ascension of Christ, which led to Pentecost, do not have that unique distinction. They were not the authors of the New Testament canonical writings. However, the New Testament never formulates this distinction as a distinction of dispensations, but as a distinction of testimony to the historical Christ.

The attempts to evade the testimony of Acts to the charismatic element are examples of confused thinking. The whole biblical revelation is grounded in history. Throughout the Bible the deeds of God in history are interpreted by prophetic and apostolic writers. The Judaeo-Christian faith is unique precisely because it records God's revelation of himself in history. The Gospels are both history and interpretation. They are not merely chronicles of Jesus' life but inspired interpretations of his life, death and resurrection. The fact that they are Gospels means that they are evangelistic books, written to proclaim faith in Jesus Christ. Acts is the second volume of a two-volume work by Luke. If Acts is not a basis for doctrine, then neither is Luke. Acts is both history and inspired interpretation in exactly the same way as Luke. Historical narrative is as much doctrinal material as any New Testament letter. Luke is about the acts of Jesus. Acts is about the acts of Jesus through the Holy Spirit. Both are the basis of New Testament doctrine about salvation.

The subdivision of each stage of the in-breaking of the kingdom of God cannot be supported from the New Testament. The explanation that each record of people being filled with the Spirit is unique and cannot be applied to the Christian church merely evades the evidence. The kingdom of God began to break through from before the birth of Jesus. From that moment, event after event was evidence that the age to come was breaking through into this age. This is true of the birth and baptism of Jesus, the ministry of John, the preaching and miraculous ministry of Jesus, his death and resurrection, Pentecost, and the signs and wonders recorded in Acts. Since that time the history of revivals through the centuries is all part of one dispensation, the dispensation of the future age.

Having accepted this fundamental truth, one can look at details. Were the disciples Spirit-filled before Pentecost in the same way that they were after Pentecost? Certainly the cross and resurrection was a decisive turning point. Yet even here the ministry of Jesus prior to his death placed his disciples within the framework of the kingdom. They had already experienced the new age. There is no neat division of periods into distinct dispensations. The overriding impression of the New

Testament is that the new age has dawned.

What about the danger of fanatical prophets claiming equal authority with Scripture? This problem was dealt with in the New Testament. They had an established canon of inspired books in the Old Testament and a clear sense of the difference between the words of Jesus during his earthly ministry and the subsequent words of New Testament prophets. The apostles gave numerous guidelines about testing prophecy and subjecting it to the foundation of apostolic teaching. When a prophetic word was disturbing the Thessalonians, Paul merely reminded them of his previous teaching, because apostolic teaching was considered to be authoritative over individual prophecy. Paul's command to the very church that was in danger of taking a particular spirit or word too seriously was: 'Do not despise prophecies' (I Thessalonians 5:20).

The so-called dichotomy between scriptural authority and prophetic ministry finds no support in the New Testament. Christians who prophesy in no way undermine the prohibition on adding to the Scriptures. Prophecy must be subjected to the examination of Scripture and given its rightful place in the ongoing life of the church.

The message of the kingdom destroys the cessationist theory. It is the best foundation for faith in the continued manifestation of signs and wonders throughout the history of the Christian church. It is therefore not surprising that John Wimber, who was a specialist on signs and wonders, grounded his approach to the subject on the theology of the kingdom. His thorough research has shown that signs and wonders never died out.[44] They did not cease after the death of the apostles or after the formation of the canon. One has to bury one's head in the sand to evade all traces of the miraculous in the annals of church history.

# Healing

Someone well known for his healing ministry comes to town. A Christian who is overflowing with faith and expectation attends his meetings, but no healing takes place. At the same time someone who is deeply sceptical about healing is prayed for by a few Sunday School children and a remarkable healing takes place.

Why are some people not healed? Is it because the faith of the sick person is insufficient? Is it because the person who prays is not anointed or gifted at the time? Is there sin or unforgiveness in his life? These are some of the questions that are raised when one attempts to grapple with the evident fact that there is no logical relationship between the actual occurrence of healing and the amount of faith, anointing or gifting. In praying for healing, the batting average of some is better than others. Certainly faith is a vital factor. Jesus made this plain. We know that there are gifts of healing. We also know that there are moments when we sense a moving of the Holy Spirit and are not surprised when a healing takes place. The problem is that so many real healings have an unlikely combination of factors, yet so many likely combinations do not produce healing. The mystery of the kingdom is the only biblical explanation that fits the facts. Having understood this, we will see why insisting on other explanations is cruel and shows a lack of spiritual perception.

Let us return to the statement we have made over and over again. In Jesus Christ and through the Pentecostal outpouring of the Holy Spirit, the end broke into the present. The powers of the age to come – the future, universal rule of God – invaded our world. The result is that the church now lives between the times in a unique dimension where the fallenness of this world and the glory of the future kingdom coexist. The implications of this can best be understood if we work from the future towards the present. In the final consummation of the kingdom all sickness will be banished. This was the promise of Isaiah. God will wipe away every tear and there will be no more death or mourning, crying or pain (Revelation 21:3–4). Nothing impure or shameful will be allowed in his kingdom. God will rule supreme and unchallenged, and the devil will be cast into the lake of fire. This settles a question that sick people often agonise over: Is it God's will to heal me? The answer is that when God rules supreme, there will be no sickness. Sickness can never be part of his will. To suggest that it is so dishonours the character of God. The devil comes to steal, kill and destroy. God comes to give life.

In Jesus the future rule of God broke into the present. The presence of Jesus brought the presence of God's perfect will. When people said to Jesus: 'If you are willing, you can make me clean,' Jesus replied: 'I am willing; be cleansed' (Mark 1:41). Wherever Jesus went, healing followed, because wherever Jesus went, God's will broke through. Jesus is what God has to say about himself. Watch the deeds of Jesus and see the will of God!

When the Holy Spirit was poured out, the powers of the age to come broke through. The result was that gifts of healing were seen. The presence of the Holy Spirit is synonymous with the perfect rule of God, which is synonymous with healing. When a person is healed it means that the power of the future kingdom has broken through into the present. Every healing is a kingdom breakthrough.

Why are some people not healed? This is because the kingdom has broken through but has not yet taken over. It is here, but in a provisional sense. The final takeover of the kingdom will occur at the second coming. Until then the present world continues. This means that we live in a world that is filled with sin, disease, violence, depravity and sickness. God does not apply his perfect will at all times and in all places. In fact, *good* many other evil powers have their way: Satan, demonic powers, and fallen human beings.

In this world power corrupts and absolute power corrupts absolutely. When an oppressive ruler violates his people, he does it, not God. One day God will judge him for it. When a rapist violates a woman, he does it. God will judge him for it. Sickness is part and parcel of this fallen world. The kingdom breaks through in an anticipatory sense. If the total power of the kingdom touched any particular human being, he would immediately be transformed into a glorified, immortal body. Being born again would involve instantaneous resurrection. But this is not what happens. When we receive Christ the kingdom is 'now' and also 'not yet', which is why the Bible uses the word 'salvation' in three tenses. We are saved; we are being saved, and we will be saved. If every Christian who was ever sick got healed, it would mean that the second coming had arrived. ✱ *good*

Think of it like this. God loves his children. He does not want any harm to come to them. There are testimonies of Christians suddenly being driven to prayer for someone, only to find later that at that exact time the other person was very nearly involved in a fatal accident. The sudden intercession averted the accident. God's Spirit led the intercessor to pray at that moment, and God intervened and prevented the accident. But if every time a Christian was about to have an accident, God intervened so that Christians never required motor insurance policies, it would involve a total takeover by God of this present world in every detail. God has decided to postpone this until the second coming to give mankind a chance to repent. The special interventions of God are moments when his future total rule over all things breaks through into a particular situation. It does not happen all the time simply because the second coming has not yet arrived.

All healing doctrines that proclaim an exact formula about healing occurring totally every time we pray in real faith reveal a fundamental misunderstanding of the nature of the present kingdom. They confuse the 'already' with the 'not yet'. Equally, all doctrines that remove the continual, any moment likelihood of healing reveal a fundamental misunderstanding of the kingdom. They confuse the 'not yet' with the 'already'. They deny the 'already' by a total postponement into the 'not yet'. The truth is that the kingdom is near all the time. We live in the last days when the powers of the age to come are continually breaking through. The end hovers over us like a rain cloud that is ready to burst at any moment. Our Christian experience is regularly interrupted by thunder, flashes of lightning and torrential downpours. This is the history of revivals – times when the powers of the age to come break through in special intensity.

Is there a formula by which we can predict or explain the how, or why, or when of the breakthrough of the kingdom into this present world? Jesus' answer about the timing of the end must apply to all such questions: 'No one knows about that day or hour, not even the angels of heaven, nor the Son, but only the Father' (Matthew 24:36). During his earthly ministry Jesus was totally dependent on his Father for doing the works of the kingdom. Signs and wonders took place by the moving of the Holy Spirit, who blows when and how he chooses. We can say categorically that healing occurs because the kingdom of God breaks through. We can say equally categorically that healing does not always occur because the kingdom of God has not broken through finally. No one can say what determines how frequently and on what basis this intervention of the powers of the age to come takes place. This is the mystery of the kingdom.

There are many factors that seem to play a part. Prayer certainly plays a major role in the history of revivals. Healing ministries are often praying ministries. Expectation is a factor. When people do not expect God to move, he seems to move less. Gifting is another factor. When someone has a gift of the Spirit for healing, the batting average is higher.

But none of these factors can explain what happens. The only explanation is the nature of the kingdom. This is why watertight doctrines are misleading and cruel. They remove healing from the context of mystery and place all the responsibility on the shoulders of a person, either the one who prays or the one being prayed for. How can we burden a finite human being with such a profound responsibility?

# Israel

There seem to be two kinds of attitude towards Israel today. The most common attitude is one of general sympathy and concern expressed in the following ideas: Anti-Semitism is a bad thing. The holocaust was one of the most gruesome events in human history. The Jewish people deserve a place of their own in Israel. When Jews become Christians, they are usually a great blessing because they rediscover so much that Gentile Christians do not have. The restoration of Hebrew thought and culture to the church is a very positive development, be it in dance, music, or holistic Hebrew thought. Christians should witness to Jews sensitively and lovingly, and the emergence of the Messianic Christian movement is an exciting development.

This group does not place too much weight on every political development in Israel as a sign of the end times, wants to have equal sympathy for the cause of Palestinian Arabs who have suffered as a result of the Middle East conflict, and believes that Jewish Christians are merely part of the church of Jesus Christ. They do not constitute another people of God.

The other less common but usually highly motivated group consists of those who believe that Israel is key to the purposes of God in the world and in the church. They believe that the return to Israel in 1948 was the sign of the last generation before the second coming. They believe that it is a serious error to teach that the church has replaced Israel as the people of God. In a given domestic situation they will organise special prayer meetings for Israel, hold Feast of Tabernacles celebrations and motivate tours to the Holy Land. They tend to think that the former group is a little blind and needs to be helped to see how important these things really are. The second group tends to use the term 'replacement theology' pejoratively. Those who cannot see the things they see have been blinded by the Reformers who established replacement theology. This group sometimes stoops to a rather negative estimation of the motives of the former and makes accusations, the insinuation being that whoever supports replacement theology is likely to be guilty of an underlying anti-Semitism. They sometimes come across with the attitude that those who have understood the place of Israel in the last days are the elite. This tends to irritate the former group, and so 'feelings' have built up.

The general shift towards kingdom theology in the church has led to a reaction against the 'Israel message' and one condescending attitude has been replaced with another. All this does not contribute towards Christian unity. It is therefore vital to deal with the issue on a theological basis, to search the Scriptures and take the debate out of the environment of innuendoes, hidden motives and elitism.

It should be understood at the outset that the general unhappiness with 'Israel theology' is not based on anti-Semitism. To use the anti-Semitism lever is manipulative: 'Don't rethink your theology; it will make you guilty of anti-Semitism.' Surely our attitude towards the Jewish people should not be founded on guilt but on the truth of God's Word. The real problem is that the whole superstructure of 'Israel theology' has been built on dispensationalism, and dispensationalism is a shaky foundation, to say the least. David Stern, one of the most theologically competent Messianic Jews to have written on the subject, comments that dispensationalism 'in its more extreme form, says that the Jewish people have promises only on earth, while the Church has promises in heaven'.[45] As we shall see in the next chapter, this is the problem with Dave Hunt's dispensationalism.

## What is Dispensationalism?

The origins of modern dispensationalism go back to the Charismatic
Movement that took place in Scotland led by Edward Irving, founder
of the Catholic Apostolic Church. Margaret MacDonald, who was sick
at the time, had a special 'revelation' one evening. She was later filled
with the Holy Spirit, spoke in tongues and was healed. Her revelation
was that Christ was to come secretly before the second coming to rapture to heaven a special group of believers who had been 'sealed'. This
is known as the 'partial rapture theory'.

News of her revelation and subsequent charismatic experience spread
and began to influence the founders of the Plymouth Brethren. J.N.
Darby, founding father of the movement, 'borrowed from her, modi-
fied her views, and then popularised them under his own name without
giving her credit'.[46]

Darby dropped the partial rapture theory but took over the pretribulation
rapture idea which he spread through various 'prophetic' conferences held
at the time. According to MacPherson, 'Darby introduced into discussion ... the ideas of a secret rapture of the church and of a parenthesis
in prophetic fulfilment between the sixty-ninth and seventieth weeks of
Daniel. These two concepts constituted the basic tenets of the system
of theology since referred to as dispensationalism'.[47] The dispensational
idea is that God deals with man through the dispensation of Israel (up
to the first coming), the dispensation of the church (between the first
coming and the last seven years) and the dispensation of Israel (the
last seven years). Dispensationalism and the secret rapture theory are
therefore inextricably bound. Darby's views were further popularised
through the Scofield Reference Bible. They became so popular that some
denominations in the United States require ministerial candidates to
sign a confession of faith that includes dispensational 'truths'.

There are two significant facts about this theory. First, despite frequent
attempts at denial, it was never heard of in church history before
Margaret MacDonald. It was not part of historic premillennial faith.

Second, the majority of reputable evangelical biblical scholars have never embraced it. As Robert Gundry has shown with devastating clarity in *The Church and the Tribulation,* there are numerous holes in this theory.[48]

The whole system stands or falls on 2 Thessalonians 2. A casual reading of this chapter, based on any reliable translation, will reveal the following: Paul is correcting a false alarm in the Thessalonian church that the coming of the Lord (a sudden secret rapture idea) had arrived. He says that the believers should not be deceived, because the day of the Lord (the rapture) cannot occur until certain events have taken place. There must be a 'rebellion' and the 'man of lawlessness' (the anti-Christ) must be revealed first. Although the secret power of the anti-Christ system is already at work, someone or something is holding it back until the proper time. When the restraining factor is removed, the anti-Christ will be revealed and deceive many with counterfeit signs and wonders. The believers are encouraged that they will not be deceived because they have been chosen by God and will stand firm in the faith.

Dispensational interpreters invert the plain meaning of the text with a mistranslation. Instead of 'gathering together to him' they insert 'catching away' (2:1), a translation which cannot be substantiated. Instead of the text saying that the church cannot be gathered to Jesus until the anti-Christ has been revealed, they make it say that the anti-Christ cannot be revealed until the church has been lifted to Jesus. They suppose that the restraining factor that is removed is the church. Support for this interpretation is totally lacking because comparative expressions tend to suggest an angelic power restraining the final emergence of evil. The text shows that the rapture occurs at the same time as the second coming, the moment when Christ judges the world system. The moment of the church's rescue or 'rest' coincides with the world's demise or 'everlasting destruction' (1:7, 9). The former will happen when the latter happens. This text alone destroys the dispensational system.

Some of the mental gymnastics that dispensationalists have undertaken are quite bizarre. The church is said to be absent from the scene after Revelation 4:1, which makes almost the whole book, written by a Christian to encourage other Christians, irrelevant to Christians. Christ's extensive description of events leading up to the end (Matthew 24–25) is also said to be relevant only to the Jewish elect, not to the church, a remarkable distortion given the fact that the twelve apostles, who founded the church, were the ones he was addressing! It is not surprising that people with a minimum of theological training are unwilling to accept this system. Dispensational interpreters have done such violence to so many passages that one can sympathise with those who overreact and want to deny any eschatological role for ethnic Israel. However, the answer is not another swing of the pendulum to the other extreme. We will need to examine the one systematic treatment of the place and eschatological role of Israel in relation to the church, Romans 9–11. Before we do this, we must understand how dispensationalism forms the basis of Israel theology.

## Israel and Dispensationalism

Based on the idea of neat dispensations, the theory says that the last seven years of world history will focus on Israel and that the church will be absent during this time. It follows that God has two different people, the church and Israel, and that the destiny of the two is distinct.

The restoration of Israel to Jerusalem is for a time when the dispensation of the Gentiles is fulfilled and the church has been removed (Luke 21:24). For dispensationalists, Israel repossessing Jerusalem is therefore a key event. Since this can only occur with Israel back in Palestine, 1948 is absolutely central. In fact, the whole destiny of the church and of mankind hinges on Israel in Jerusalem during the last seven years. Without this special dispensation there can be no second coming. This is why every political development in Israel is so important and why no Christian should ever side with the political grievances of the Palestinians.

What happens to this theory when the dispensational base is removed?

## Israel Without Dispensationalism

We said previously that there is no support for the idea of dispensations within the age of the church. The 'last days' are the last days, from the birth of Christ to the second coming, with no subdivision. Further, if God dealt with Israel and the church in an overlapping period of some seventy years before the fall of Jerusalem, the obvious conclusion is that whatever role Israel plays before the second coming will again take place alongside God's dealings with the church.

What then of the special significance attached to 1948? The fall of Jerusalem (70 AD) brought about a permanent change in its status. Prior to that, everything about the coming of Christ was focused on Jerusalem. Christ's journey to the cross was to Jerusalem. He died in Jerusalem. The gospel went from Jerusalem to the world. Paul took a special offering to the saints in Jerusalem. The early council of the church took place in Jerusalem. The city represented the birth of the gospel and of the church. However, Jesus predicted that it would fall, and even before it did, the church emerged out of the confines of Judaism.

What then is the importance of Jerusalem (post 70 AD) in the New Testament? Are there any references to suggest a future, long-term role for Jerusalem as the holy city? If we read Luke 21:24 without a dispensational assumption it becomes much less complicated. It simply says that the destruction of Jerusalem as the holy city will continue until the second coming. The times of the Gentiles are fulfilled when everything else is fulfilled, at the second coming. The warning about Jerusalem being surrounded by armies was fulfilled in 70 AD by the Roman general Titus. The fall of Jerusalem is seen as a symbol of what will occur when the final anti-Christ system is revealed. This in no way implies that the second fulfilment has to occur in the same place. The earthly Jerusalem can never again be a holy city. It has been replaced by a heavenly Jerusalem. The present city of Jerusalem is in slavery to the law. The 'Jerusalem above is free, which is the mother of us all' (Galatians 4:25–26). This is the Jerusalem that believers experience in worship.

Apart from the statements of Jesus about the fall of Jerusalem in the Gospels, there are few other references in the New Testament to a future role or a theological significance for the physical city. John 4:19–24 repudiates any locality having special significance. Jerusalem will no longer be a special holy place. Believers will worship anywhere, in spirit and in truth. Revelation 11:8 describes the city where Christ was crucified as 'Sodom and Egypt', scarcely a reference to a holy city. This implies that whatever may occur in physical Jerusalem in the last moments of human history will not be occurring in a holy city. Jesus gives the impression that the population of the earthly city of Jerusalem will remain in a spiritually 'desolate' environment until the very moment of his return, when they will eventually say: 'Blessed is he who comes in the name of the Lord!' (Matthew 23:39). As we shall see, Romans 9–11 makes no reference to Jerusalem or Palestine.

All this leads to a rather startling conclusion for dispensationalists. There is actually no New Testament emphasis or clear teaching on the importance of Israel being physically present once more in Jerusalem. One may be able to argue that a few verses assume by implication that Israel will have populated the physical city once more when Jesus comes, but none of these verses can be made into a special emphasis about events that must take place in Jerusalem before Jesus can return. 1948 and the Seven Day War may be of very little significance.

## Israel in New Testament Perspective

How does a Christian interpret the Old Testament? The age-old answer is, through the eyes of the New Testament. We are not at liberty to take our own independent line and claim to submit to the New Testament. A rabbinical scholar can do this because he is not bound by New Testament authority. The way in which Jesus and the apostles looked at the Old Testament is authoritative for us.

This means that the way in which the New Testament interprets Old Testament passages about Israel, the land, Jerusalem, the elect, etc., is normative for us. If an Old Testament passage is never used in a certain way by New Testament writers, we cannot assume that we can use it in that way. The mere accumulation of Old Testament texts to prove an 'Israel theology' point will not do. Many Old Testament texts speak of the people returning to the land and Jerusalem being the centre of the earth, but the crucial question is: how does the New Testament view such texts?

Paul is adamant that all the promises of the Old Testament have found their fulfilment in the person of Jesus Christ. He is the seed of Abraham. Everything about the Old Testament people of God narrows down into one person. From that one person comes the new people of God, the new man in Christ. Paul saw something that no Old Testament prophet ever saw, that Jews and Gentiles who are in Christ together make up the people of God. Gentile Christians are now included in the 'commonwealth of Israel' (Ephesians 2:12), and this gathered people from both sides of the wall are now the temple of God. There is 'one new man from the two' (2:15).

Peter writes to the church as if he were writing to Israel. He addresses himself to 'the elect', the 'Dispersion' (1 Peter 1:1–2), in language that would have been used for Israel. This diaspora of the elect is the very group that once was not a people but is now 'a chosen generation, a royal priesthood, a holy nation, His own special people' (2:9–10). This is not 'replacement' theology but 'addition' theology. Jews who have accepted the Messiah have been added to by Gentiles who have accepted the Messiah. These two together are the true heirs of every Old Testament promise.

The definition of what it means to be a 'Jew' has therefore changed. A real Jew is someone who has experienced a circumcision of the heart. The way to be a child of Abraham is the same for Jews and Gentiles:

repentance and faith. Born-again Gentiles are now more Jews than unbelieving Israelites. The 'Israel after the flesh' (1 Corinthians 10:18) stands in contrast to the 'Israel of God' (Galatians 6:16). Despite all to the contrary, Paul's 'Israel of God' means the people for whom circumcision no longer matters. All that matters is being a new creation. This could never be said of Israel 'after the flesh'.

This new Israel does inherit the Holy Land, but even the land has become new. Just as Joshua led Israel into the land of Canaan, the new Joshua, Jesus, leads his people into the Sabbath rest (Hebrews 4:1–11). The blessing of Abraham, which included the land of Canaan for the Old Testament believers, is now the gift of the Holy Spirit (Galatians 3:14). Where they inherited Canaan, New Testament believers inherit the whole world (Romans 4:13). All nations and all families can now be blessed with Abraham's blessing. David, the king of Israel, is king of all nations. The gathering of God's people to Jerusalem is fulfilled in a great company from every nation, tribe, people and language that will inhabit the heavenly Jerusalem. All the Old Testament prophecies about Israel and the Holy Land are fulfilled in a way that eclipses Palestine. The universalising thrust of Isaiah has been completed and taken to its final form. We must conclude that the New Testament writers laid down very clearly what our understanding of the Old Testament promises should be. There are no gray areas.

## How Many People of God Are There?

Can anyone speak of two people of God? Paul speaks of one olive tree with natural branches and wild engrafted branches. Gentiles who have been justified by faith are now children of Abraham and members of the commonwealth of Israel, not a new Israel but the historic Israel of the Old Testament. They are now as 'Jewish' as any Jew. Paul also speaks of the 'new man' which carries the idea of a totally new species. In this sense we do have to speak of a new Israel, because we are no longer living in the time of expectation but in the time of fulfilment.

The kingdom of God has broken through and there is a new covenant that is much more than a prolonging of the old one.

To return to the olive tree metaphor. The one olive tree, signifying one people of God and one new man in Jesus Christ, has its roots in the Old Testament people of God. It will include many who at present are Israelite branches that lie dead and cut off from the tree. They can only live as true members of the people of God by being a part of the one olive tree. The moment any Jew is justified by faith, he becomes a member of the one church of Jesus Christ. Before this happens he is not a part of the olive tree and therefore not a member of the people of God.

Jewish believers are supposed to be members of local churches that include every type of Christian in that area, Gentiles included. In the early church the membership of most local churches consisted of ex-synagogue members and Gentile converts. Purely Jewish congregations existed when the gospel was confined to Judea amongst a predominantly Jewish population, but in the Gentile cities there was only one local church that included all believers. The idea of separate Jewish Christian congregations around the world today has no biblical foundation. All the arguments in favour of such a practice will be the same arguments that have been used to support apartheid. They will tend to elevate ethnicity and ethnic distinctions. It may be true that from a missiological perspective one can reach people better in homogeneous units – people do feel more comfortable in their own culture – but we should be clear about when we are using sociological arguments and when we are using biblical arguments.

If there is now only one people of God, any arguments about a right to the land of Palestine today would have to apply equally to every member of the church, Jew or Gentile, anywhere in the world. 'Israel, here I come to claim my plot of ground. I would prefer a site overlooking the Sea of Galilee, please! I am of Arab descent!' The moment we say that ethnic Israel still has Old Testament promises that apply to her and not to the church, we have moved back to a two-people idea, and this flatly contradicts Paul's teaching.

This theological issue should be clearly distinguished from matters of political ethics. The fact that Israel deserves a state in Palestine is due to the horrifying way she has been treated by the nations of the world, not because of the validity of a special 'Israel' theology. It may well be that God has ordered the course of human history by determining this particular ethic but we must not imagine that we can deduce this directly from the New Testament.

## Israel's Future

Is there no special role then for ethnic Israel, the Israel 'after the flesh'?

We come to Romans 9–11. The theme of Romans is the righteousness of God. Having shown that God is righteous in condemning and forgiving sin (Romans 1–8), Paul argues that God is righteous in choosing Israel and rejecting Israel, in rejecting the Gentiles and choosing the Gentiles. In all his dealings with man, he is perfectly righteous. This section was prompted by the fact that Israel as a whole had not accepted Christ. It raised difficult questions. Had the Word of God failed? Is there injustice on God's part? Has God rejected his people?

Paul's opening statement makes it plain that he is dealing with Israel, his 'kinsmen according to the flesh' (9:3), whom he loves and to whom God gave all the promises. He argues that Israel has not rejected Jesus, and in that sense the gospel has not failed for Israel, because a remnant, the true Israel, has accepted Jesus. The real Israelites are not simply the physical descendants of Abraham but a smaller group who are the descendants of Isaac. Paul shows how the principle of election occurred again and again, and how no one has a right to question God in his ordering of this process (9:6–23). Real Israel is therefore not made up of every living physical descendant of Abraham, but of a special group elected by God. This group of true Israelites includes those 'whom he called, not of the Jews only, but also of the Gentiles' (9:24).

This raises an uncomfortable question. Are some Gentiles more God's people than many Jews (9:30–31)? Paul affirms that this is the case. The Jews have stumbled over the law while Gentiles have accepted that the only way of justification is by faith (9:32–10:13), through believing the gospel (10:14–17).

Are there excuses for this failure of Israel as a whole to accept Christ? Perhaps they have not all heard the gospel (10:18)? Perhaps they have not understood and things should have been explained to them more clearly (10:19)? Both these excuses will not do. The real problem is that they are a 'disobedient and contrary people' (10:21). Does the disobedience of the majority mean that God has rejected his people (11:1)? There are two answers to this. In the present, the very existence of the remnant demonstrates that God still loves Israel (11:1–10). And in the future there will be a response to the gospel by the main body of the nation. How will this work?

The fact that the main body of the Jewish nation rejected Jesus was the original reason for the apostles turning to the Gentiles (Acts 13:46). The rejection of the gospel by the Jews provided the trigger mechanism for the gospel to go to the Gentiles. This suggests that the same trigger mechanism will occur again. When the full number of the Gentiles has come into the kingdom, God will turn to his ancient people. The 'full inclusion' of the Jews will be the final trigger mechanism that sets off the resurrection (11:12–15). This is consistent with God's dealings in the past, because it has always been the Jew first, then the Gentile. If Gentile believers have been added to a Jewish faith, Jews can be added even more readily (11:16–24). Gentile Christians must never look down on unbelieving Jews.

At present the main body of the Jewish nation has been hardened. During this time the gospel is being spread to the Gentile nations. When this process is complete, the last nation to respond to the gospel will be the main body of the Jewish nation. This will be followed by the second coming and the final resurrection. While Israel has not been faithful to God, God will remain faithful to Israel, 'For the gifts and the calling of God are irrevocable' (11:29). God is wise and righteous. Jews and Gentiles have had equal opportunities to accept or reject his ways (11:30–32). God has been totally fair. The wonder of God's wisdom (11:33–36)!

## Conclusion

Certain deductions can be drawn from this argument. Firstly, the Jewish people have a missiological significance. The gospel must go to all nations before the end can come. Here we learn that the last nation to be reached will be the Jewish nation. This does not mean that Jews cannot be saved now. The remnant principle will always be there, but there will be a final, general turning to Christ amongst the Jews that is part of a linear development: all nations, then the Jews, then the resurrection. If we want to hasten the second coming, we have to hasten the completion of the Great Commission to all nations culminating in the Jewish nation. We will never hasten the day of Christ's return while we leave out the Jews. Consequently the shortest route to Jewish evangelism is through world evangelisation. This, incidentally, means reaching Arabs as well. We cannot love Jews any more or any less than we love all people. Jesus died for all, equally.

Secondly, the Jewish people has an eschatological significance. Their destiny is closely linked to the second coming. This means that they will never disappear as a visible national ethnic group or religious tradition, Hitler and whomsoever notwithstanding. They remain God's people in a shadowy, waiting capacity. They are the olive branch that lies dead on the ground. Although dead, it is nevertheless an olive branch, and God will bring it to life again. When that occurs it will join the existing olive tree. That is why we can never speak of two people of God. The Jews are the people of God only in the sense that they wait to be taken up into the church.

This is 'addition' theology. The apostolic perspective is always addition, subtraction and addition. The Gentiles never replace the Jews and the Jews never replace the Gentiles. God simply uses the one to reach the other. Paul's exposition never depends on a geographical location in Palestine. The final response of the Jewish people can happen throughout the dispersion of the Jews in every nation. It may include a particular concentration of Jewish people in Palestine, but the event does not depend on a particular demographic situation either. There is therefore no reason why the Jews have to return to Palestine to fulfil end time events. There is also no reason why Palestinian Arabs have to be thwarted from gaining a just solution to their aspirations for the sake of some eschatological priority.

In practice, what does this view of the biblical witness mean? Firstly, it repudiates the classic Reformed 'replacement theology'. Neither the Puritans nor more recent Reformed theologians support the eradication of ethnic Israel as the subject of Romans 11:12. The church is placed in a position of continual love and respect for the Jewish people. No Christian can ever support the kind of antagonism expressed by Luther with biblical justification. Secondly, it repudiates a mindless support for the Jewish cause in the current Palestinian conflict. The Christian attitude is one of love for all Jewish people, not support for current Israeli political causes. Thirdly, the Christian attitude is one of equal love for all lost people, including Arabs. Perhaps I should add that regenerate Arab Christians are now more part of true Israel than unregenerate Jews. Fourthly, the whole thrust of the biblical teaching on Israel aims us at world missions.

I have a theory that illustrates the biblical approach. When Paul had the vision of the man of Macedonia, he went west with the Gospel. If one follows the flow of church history, it becomes apparent that the gospel spread most successfully thereafter in Western Europe. Europe became the cradle of Christianity for centuries. Then Christianity spread through the colonies of the European powers into North and South America, Australia, Africa and China. More recently the gospel has been spreading most dramatically in central Asia, Indonesia, South

Korea, India and China. The story of the Chinese underground church has become known. This flow represents the gospel gradually encircling the globe. Once China and India have been reached, the last land mass en route to Israel from the east is the Arab world. The last great missionary thrust will therefore be amongst the Arabs and once this is completed the gospel will have encompassed the globe. Finally, ethnic Israel, in Palestine and throughout the Diaspora, will turn to Christ and this will lead to the second coming and the resurrection of the dead. The mission to Israel will only be ultimately successful when it comes via the Arabs. If you want to win Israel, win the Arabs! God loves mankind everywhere with the same redeeming love.

*Interesting*

# Confusion about the Kingdom

Revelation 21 describes a millennium or thousand-year period of Christ's rule to be shared with him by victorious believers. The interpretation of this passage has always been difficult and differing theories about it have often divided Christians. This is true of our time too. Conflicting views on the millennium have emerged in a debate between dispensationalists such as Dave Hunt and 'kingdom now' teachers such as Earl Paulk.[49]

The issue came into focus in Britain during the seventies when the present leaders of the Restoration Movement were formulating their thinking and has now gained prominence in the United States. The debate is certainly not a purely academic one. Our views on the millennium shape our understanding of the relationship between the church and society, and this in turn determines our Christian behaviour. The enemy is always pleased when the ordinary Christian is unsettled and confused and 'feelings' build up between Christians. It is therefore important that we place this issue in perspective, seek to remove the confusion and understand what is really happening.

## The Debate

We said in the previous chapter that modern dispensationalism arose among the Plymouth Brethren. 'Kingdom now' teaching is Presbyterian. In very simple terms, a shift is taking place from a Brethren to a Presbyterian eschatology. Both these traditions have been accepted for a long time as valid testimonies within the body of Christ. The relevant differences between these two traditions revolve around the millennium. There are basically four views on the millennium.

The oldest view is that the millennium (thousand-year reign of Christ) will take place after the second coming. Christ will come before the millennium. This is known as premillennialism. The second oldest view is that the present age of the church is actually the millennium and that, rather than a literal thousand years, the millennium is a symbolic way of speaking about the present rule of Christ through his church. This is known as amillennialism. These two branches each have a variant form that is more extreme than the parent idea in the sense that it is further removed from the opposite view.

Third in time is postmillennialism. This is a development from within amillennialism that teaches that the age of the church will culminate in a special period of glory, a thousand years when the church will triumph in the world before the second coming. Christ therefore comes after the millennium.

Last in time is a variant of premillennialism called dispensationalism. This view, usually known as the pretribulation rapture theory, holds that the church will be secretly 'raptured' by Christ seven years before the second coming and the millennium. These last seven years of world history will be a time of great tribulation. The church will go before the tribulation and the millennium.

The four views can be pictured as follows, in order of development and in relation to each other.

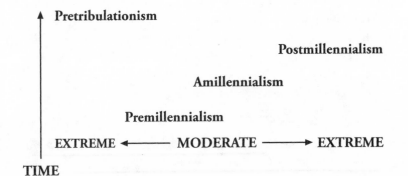

You will notice that pretribulationism and postmillennialism are furthest apart. We have traced the historical development of pretribulation dispensationalism. The Presbyterians and, in fact, most Reformed believers have traditionally been amillennial although postmillennialism has also been popular in Reformed circles. In recent years there has been a resurgence of postmillennialism amongst some conservative Calvinists in America, and this movement has developed a teaching called reconstructionism. Ordinary premillennialists and amillennialists find it fairly easy to have a rational conversation with each other because their views are not very far apart. On the other hand pretribulationists and postmillennialists, who are on opposite sides of the spectrum, find it very difficult to dialogue with one another. It is this meeting of two extremes that is taking place in the current debate, and this is why the feelings are running so high. Before each view is described we will examine how the kingdom teaching we have developed so far relates to these issues.

The basic divide between the two sides revolves around the relationship between the church and the world. Taken to an extreme, one view holds that the church must withdraw from the world because it can never be improved and the Christian should expect persecution and suffering. The world will not improve until Jesus comes, destroys the anti-Christ and sets up his millennial kingdom. The other view is that the church has both the power and the responsibility to take over the present world for Christ. When the church, empowered by the Holy Spirit, has been triumphant in this, Jesus will come to meet his mature, victorious bride. The first view is world denying, the second is world transforming. How does the New Testament message of the kingdom relate to this?

## Kingdom Now Or Then?

We have outlined how New Testament texts can be used selectively to teach that the kingdom is either totally future or totally present. Very few would want to deny either the 'future kingdom' or the 'present kingdom' statements of Jesus. This led us to the understanding of the mystery of the kingdom. The future kingdom has broken through into the present world so that this age and the age to come coexist in a totally unexpected tension. We have called this the 'already' and the 'not yet' or the 'presence of the future'. There is both 'kingdom now' and 'kingdom not now'. Until we have grasped this, confusion about many biblical truths will continue, especially concerning the millennium.

Worked out in terms of the church/world relationship, these two views lead to certain conclusions. A totally future view of the kingdom leads to defeatism, escapism and world denial that makes people negative about this world. A totally present view of the kingdom leads to triumphalism and utopianism so that people confuse worldly developments with the kingdom of God. The human tendency is to deny the validity of the texts that contradict one's position. Premillennialists, and especially pretribulationists, tend to evade texts that speak of the present triumph and involvement of the church in the world. Amillennialists, and especially postmillennialists, evade those texts which state that the present world order is doomed to destruction and that the church should live for the next world.

Both kinds of text are found in abundance in the New Testament and it will not do to evade some texts because of our commitment to others. We must submit to the authority of the whole Bible, rather than to those texts that we have chosen. Let us then examine the two types of text.

## World-denying Texts

The most obvious world-denying texts are found in the apocalyptic sections of Scripture. Daniel and Revelation speak of a cataclysmic destruction of this present world with the coming of the Son of Man. The stone from heaven will pulverise the image of man. In Revelation the kingdom of the anti-Christ, represented by the beast and the harlot, is powerfully destroyed by the rider on the white horse. Linked to these two books is the teaching of Jesus in Mark 13, Luke 21 and Matthew 24 where he describes a period of great tribulation and suffering for the church prior to the second coming.

The letters of the New Testament have their share of the pessimistic view of the present age. Paul encourages the Christians through their persecutions and assures them that Christ will destroy the persecutors of the Church at his second coming. He expects the 'man of lawlessness' to deceive many, but is sure that the believers will be able to withstand his deception (2 Thessalonians 1–2). He warns that in later times men will abandon the faith and follow demonic doctrines (I Timothy 4:1). The last days will bring terrible times (2 Timothy 3:1). He believes that these events are imminent and encourages Christians to hold lightly to worldly things (I Corinthians 7:29–31).

After that glorious passage on all the men of faith who endured persecution and yet lived for the city of God, the writer to the Hebrews tells us that God will shake all things once more. Believers are to receive a kingdom that cannot be shaken (Hebrews 12:26–29).

Peter feels that the end of all things is near. He warns the Christians that judgement must begin with the family of God. The present world order is being reserved for fire and destruction. The day of the Lord will come unexpectedly, therefore Christians must live holy lives as they look forward to the day of God and speed its coming (I Peter 4:7, 16; 3:7–13).

Taken in isolation, these passages create the impression that, because this world is doomed to imminent destruction and Christians should expect persecution, we must not bother too much about social conditions and the hopes and aspirations of the secular world. We are not part of it and it cannot last long. We should be urgent about preaching the gospel, rescuing people from certain damnation and preparing them for the coming of the Lord. Our focus is not on this world but on the coming kingdom which Jesus will bring. Only he can change it into the new society that will follow the second coming. One can describe this as a 'waiting for departure' attitude.

## World-transforming Texts

Jesus made a conscious connection between his ministry and the anticipations of Isaiah. If one gathers together the various elements of Isaiah's total picture of the kingdom one certainly has to conceive of the transformation of the entire world into a just society ruled by the Davidic King. The only way of denying this is to postpone the kingdom entirely to the next world and evade all the 'fulfilment' texts. Jesus commissioned his disciples to disciple the nations through the proclamation of the gospel. The successful fulfilment of this commission would involve the teaching of 'another king, Jesus' in all the world (Acts 17:6–7). The gospel not only transforms people inwardly but also changes their entire lives through sanctification. This is why Christian discipleship includes teaching about husbands and wives, parents and children, rich and poor, slaves and masters, citizens and government, honesty at work, how to relate to those outside the church, and how to appreciate the good things of life – a transformation of the whole of life.

Missionary success means that a new humanity is born, one 'new man' to replace the previous divisions between Jew and Gentile, slave and free, rich and poor, as the grace of God abounds over the power of sin (Ephesians 2:15; Galatians 3:28). As more and more people are transformed, the gospel works like leaven and salt in society. Disciples are like a city on a hill that cannot be hidden (Matthew 5:13–16).

While this age is ultimately doomed to the judgement of God, he nevertheless cares for and protects the world. God's care for the world goes back to creation. This is God's world. He created man to be fruitful, multiply and subdue the earth. He wanted man to have dominion over the natural order. Sin has marred this, but redemption restores God's original intention. There are many passages that show God's sovereign rule over history and nature. This is known as providence. He sends his rain on the just and the unjust (Matthew 5:45). The magistrate is the servant of God for the common good (Romans 13:1–5). Orderly government has been ordained for the protection of mankind (Romans 13:6–7). He controls the allotted periods and boundaries of the nations (Acts 17:26). He raises up some rulers and disposes of others. Despite the fact that this is the history of man outside of Christ, God has ultimate control over the power of evil. Even in the unredeemed world he enlightens every man (John 1:1–9).

If we look at the biblical texts on creation, providence, world mission and Christian discipleship, the net result is world transformation. Such transformation can be denied on the basis of a total failure of world missions but this cannot be supported from the New Testament and still less from church history. In the last century the gospel spread more dramatically than ever before! We can summarise the attitude that results from these passages as 'aggressive gospel takeover'.

### Biblical Balance

Many more biblical references could have been found. I simply wish to establish that it is impossible to wipe out either type of text. This leaves us with a biblical tension. On the one hand this present world is doomed to judgement and on the other Jesus is victorious and has commissioned us to preach his triumph to all nations. Because the kingdom is already here, the triumphal, 'take over the world' texts are true and essential. Because the kingdom is not yet here, the 'wait for departure' texts are equally true.

The Christian has an ambivalent attitude towards this world. He is in it but not of it. He must not be conformed to the world, yet this cannot involve an escape from it. An understanding of the 'wait for departure' texts prevents the Christian from ever being in love with this present world. These texts also teach us to be very wary of all forms of utopianism. No movement, ideology or nation can ever be the kingdom of God. The 'aggressive takeover' texts prevent us from ever becoming defeated pessimists. Even though the final stage of history may see a rise of great evil, we should be confident that there will be, simultaneously, a great triumph of the gospel.

Holding these two truths together gives a view of the end of history as the climax of both the power of God and the power of Satan. The contrast between the two will make the choice for or against Christ very clear. This is precisely where Revelation ends. 'He who is unjust, let him be unjust still; he who is filthy, let him be filthy still; he who is righteous, let him be righteous still; he who is holy, let him be holy still. And behold, I am coming quickly' (Revelation 22:11–12). Such a view is both realistic about fallen human nature and optimistic about the power of the gospel.

## Views of the Millennium

It has been important to look at the broader biblical teaching because there is only one clear passage on the millennium (Rev.20:1–10) – it is always precarious to build a whole system of interpretation on one passage. Each millennial theory runs this danger. Any interpretation of the millennium that has to ignore or evade a whole series of texts is likely to be wrong. Because the Bible is so comprehensive, different emphases within the Word become especially important to different groups within the church at different times and in different circumstances. People select those texts that relate to their situation. A persecuted church will appreciate the 'wait for departure' texts while a church that is experiencing growing social power will appreciate the 'takeover' texts. The problem is that the social situation of the church can blind it to the texts that don't seem to fit. This is exactly what occurred in church history.

## Historic Premillennial Faith

Both before and after John wrote Revelation, there is ample evidence of a belief in a thousand-year period of Messianic rule. There were various Jewish theories about the length of the Messiah's rule, some one thousand, some seven thousand years. Such expectations were based firmly on the idea that the Messiah would rule from Jerusalem. These beliefs arose when Israel was under oppressive foreign rulers. The same can be said for the early Church Fathers. They believed that John spoke of a literal thousand-year reign of Christ over this world after the second coming. The millennium was so literal that some rather exaggerated ideas developed.

Montanus declared himself to be a prophet of the 'Third Testament' (beyond the Old and the New), a special millennial age of the Holy Spirit. Various prophetic individuals associated with Montanus claimed infallible inspiration. They stressed the imminent return of Christ. Tertullian, the North African church leader, became a Montanist. The Montanist concept of the millennium became increasingly materialistic, an extreme that brought premillennialism into disrepute. Premillennialism was known as chiliasm, from the Greek term for one thousand. In later times the chiliasm of the Montanists was regarded as a fanatical excess.

The early Church Fathers, those nearest to the writer of Revelation in time, understood him to refer to a literal millennium after the second coming. Because they lived during times of persecution, they had no difficulty believing that only Jesus could change this world into a just society. They tended to identify with the 'wait for departure' texts. The premillennialism of the early Church Fathers is known as historic premillennialism. This should be distinguished from the fanatical chiliasm of the Montanists and their followers. It is interesting to see how this exaggerated concept of the millennium developed later into revolutionary movements that were very critical of every worldly status quo.

## Fanatical Premillennialism

In the twelfth century, Joachim of Fiore taught that there would be a third age of the Spirit when all normal forms of government would be replaced by a dispensation of total freedom. He was followed by the Taborites, a Hussite movement which sought to establish the kingdom of God by force of arms. During the Reformation Thomas Muntzer began preaching an imminent millennial kingdom. He tried to establish the New Jerusalem in Westphalia, assisted by the radical prophets of Zwickau. This 'New Jerusalem' was ruled with a rod of iron by the fanatical John of Leiden. During the English Civil War in the seventeenth century, the Puritans tried to set up a 'Fifth Monarchy' through revolution. They based this on Daniel, where the fifth kingdom is the kingdom of God that destroys the four kingdoms of man. Strangely, this type of premillennialism is the most radical in its attempt to take over worldly power. Postmillennialism, which is usually associated with world takeover, also emerged within the Puritan Movement. Premillennialism taken to an extreme can develop into its opposite.

Alongside this fanatical breed of premillennialism, the historic premillennialism of the early Church Fathers continued in various groups such as the more responsible Anabaptists of the Reformation and the Moravian Brethren. Many contemporary evangelical Bible teachers hold to this historic, non-fanatical type of premillennialism.

## Augustine and Amillennial Faith

We said that extremes tend to produce a reaction in the opposite direction. The extremes of the Montanists were partly responsible for the spiritualising teaching of Origen, the third-century Christian leader. He reacted to the literal, 'this-worldly' view of the millennium towards the metaphysical, spiritual presence of the kingdom in the soul of the believer.

This set the stage for Augustine of Hippo, the fifth-century North African leader. There was an added factor in his belief. The conversion of Constantine made Christianity the accepted religion of the Empire. With the absence of persecution, there was no compelling need to be pessimistic about this world. Augustine never became optimistic about the world but he did move away from the idea of catastrophe. No imminent dramatic intervention of the kingdom was expected. Instead, he emphasised the present rule of Christ through his church. The spiritual kingdom was the city of God, while the rule of earthly authorities was the city of man. These two cities struggle against one another throughout history, but the city of God is certain to prevail. He derived these ideas from the descriptions of Jerusalem and Babylon in Revelation.

Augustine was the first to establish the idea that the various visions of Revelation do not follow in chronological order but repeat the same story in different ways, each covering the whole period from the first coming to the second coming. If this is the case, Revelation 20 can be regarded as a new section going back to the first coming of Christ when Satan was bound through the victory of the cross. The one thousand years is a symbolic way of speaking of the rule of Christ through his church throughout church history. At the end of history the devil will attempt a final rebellion against God. This will be the time of the great tribulation. It will build up to the battle of Armageddon, also described as Gog and Magog, but Jesus will come and destroy this rebellion and set up his everlasting kingdom.

Augustine's view holds together the two strands of New Testament teaching. It neither hands the world over to the devil in resignation nor imagines that it will ever reach utopia. The Reformers tended to follow Augustine.

## Postmillennial Believers

The Enlightenment was a period of reaction to the control of the medieval church and its dogmas. It was also a time of great discovery. People became optimistic about man's ability to build a new society on earth shaped by his control of nature through scientific progress. Francis Bacon disagreed with Augustine's pessimism about this world and believed that a new world could be created through man's ability to control nature.

This is the context in which postmillennialism arose. The new thinking can be traced back to Joseph Mead (Mede), a seventeenth-century Anglican biblical scholar. He believed that Revelation promised a literal millennium before the second coming. The priority was to study history and the chronology of events related in the book of Revelation and plot when this millennial age was likely to begin. The discoveries of the Enlightenment meant that history did not have to be reversed in a cataclysmic manner. The dark ages could merge gradually into the new world of the millennium through historical progress.

Mead's idea became the dominant view in the Reformed churches in the eighteenth century, replacing the symbolic amillennialism of Augustine. An Anglican commentator called Daniel Whitby (1638–1726) gave strong support to postmillennialism. His views were in turn adopted by Jonathan Edwards, the great American revivalist (1703–58). In his *History of the Word of Redemption,* he saw great significance in the settlement of the New World (America), and believed it would usher in the millennium in about the twentieth century. This belief fed the fires of nationalism in the United States. Samuel Cox, a Presbyterian minister, felt that 'in America, the state of society is without parallel in universal history … I really believe that God has got America within anchorage, and that upon that arena, He intends to display his prodigies for the millennium'.[50]

Essential to the postmillennial view is the idea that most of the prophecies of Christ and the apostles about the beast and the anti-Christ were fulfilled in the fall of Jerusalem. The great tribulation has already occurred. The disasters are past, and the church awaits the second coming. Furthermore, what Revelation promises is an extensive period of successful world missions culminating in a triumphant church bringing in the kingdom of God before the second coming. This is the millennium. It may take thousands of years, but the world has been improved significantly through the gospel and will continue to improve.

While postmillennialism arose out of the Enlightenment, most of those who have been deeply committed to it have been men of great prayer and vision. It was this 'Puritan hope' which led to one of the greatest movements in world missions that the church has ever known. Benjamin Warfield, one of the most respected defenders of biblical authority and inspiration, was a postmillennialist. These men were not at all optimistic about fallen human nature, but they were optimistic about the triumph of the gospel in human history. Although Calvin himself was an amillennialist, postmillennialism has usually been the belief of strong Calvinists. Calvin's actual practice in Geneva amounted to a takeover of secular society which was more in keeping with postmillennialism. This led to some tragic results which showed the darker side of the Reformed order. There were numerous infringements of basic human rights inflicted on those who would not tow the line.

The recent resurgence of postmillennialism in the United States can be traced to two Calvinists, Cornelius van Til and Rusas Rushdoony. Van Til was a professor at Westminster Theological Seminary in Philadephia. His philosophy has been summarised and popularised by Rushdoony, an ex-missionary to the Paiute and Shoshone Indians and a minister of the Orthodox Presbyterian Church. Rushdoony is the founding father of the numerous 'reconstructionists' of today. In line with Calvin, Rushdoony believes strongly that the law of Moses is still relevant. The gospel does not displace the law. Once people have been born again, they are to be discipled in the ethical principles of God's law. This involves an outworking of the principles of the law in every facet of human life, be it art, economics, ecology, geography or physics. All things must be brought under the rule of Christ, and the whole of society must be transformed.[51]

Postmillennialists tend to favour all the 'world takeover' texts, but relegate all the 'wait for departure', 'doom and gloom' texts to the period before the fall of Jerusalem in 70 AD.

## *Dispensational Faith*

All dispensationalists are premillennialists. They appeal to the early Church Fathers and the Anabaptists during the Reformation. They believe that this present world can only be changed into a just society by the return of Christ. This will be followed by the millennium. Dispensationalism not only re-emphasised this older premillennialism but considerably adapted and exaggerated it.

In the previous chapter we traced the origins of dispensationalism in Scotland. Edward Irving, one of the founders of the Catholic Apostolic Church, believed that God wanted to restore the office of the twelve apostles before the second coming. Their denomination spread to various countries, but as most of the original apostles died and the second coming did not take place, the movement began to dwindle. There were no new ordinations after 1901, by which time all the founders had died. The New Apostolic Church arose as a breakaway from this denomination. They have replaced the idea of a last generation of restored apostles with the idea of apostolic succession.

Dispensationalism spread rapidly in the United States during the 1830s and 1840s. It was a time of great excitement. Many believed that the millennial kingdom was about to begin. A New York farmer, William Miller, predicted that it would come before 1843. Many were disappointed when his prediction failed.

This caused people to drop the habit of fixing dates, but the fundamentals of dispensationalism continued. The Niagara Bible Conferences helped to spread dispensationalism amongst Anglicans, Baptists, Presbyterians and Dutch Reformed believers.

## The Lessons of History

The lesson of history is that all theories about the millennium have a particular genesis in time within a particular social context. The only one that can claim to be linked directly to the early church is historic premillennialism. This should help us to distinguish between the authority of the Word of God and the theories that men create to interpret the Word. None of these theories is infallible.

None of these theories is heretical either. One can find many godly, zealous, educated believers in each camp. Each of us will find some of the theories less appealing than others but we should realise that there are many committed Christians who will not agree with us. We should therefore be careful not to be arrogant and dogmatic about our own particular preference. Evangelical Christians have always agreed to disagree on the issue of the millennium.

My own view is that both postmillennialism and dispensationalism have to do an excessive amount of explaining of too many biblical texts. I am sceptical about the idea that all the predictions about the great tribulation and the anti-Christ can be explained by the fall of Jerusalem. One cannot simply evade all the apostolic warnings about the last days. I am equally sceptical about the idea that human society is improving. One of the disturbing things about the current reconstructionist postmillennialism is its tendency to wave the American flag. American society tends to be identified with the millennium, following Jonathan Edwards. The American Republican system is to spread the light of freedom around the world. While I have a great respect for the American political system, I do not believe that it should be equated with the millennial kingdom of God.

Equally, the dispensational idea that the church will be raptured seven years before the end and miss the tribulation has to resort to some amazing manipulations of clear biblical passages to the contrary. This idea encourages a most irresponsible attitude towards human society. Why be concerned about issues of social justice if we are all about to disappear and leave the remainder of the human race to suffer on through the tribulation? More and more thinking Christians are abandoning this theory. The British Restoration Movement moved away from dispensationalism in the 1970s.

Postmillennialism cannot be dismissed as easily as dispensationalism because it has a great deal to teach the church about faith. One can learn from a position without having to agree with all its details.

Both historic premillennialism and amillennialism are able to hold together the balance of New Testament teaching. The differences between them are not as great as most imagine. One can teach either of these views of the millennium in a way that fails or succeeds in holding the balance between the 'already' and the 'not yet'. On the other hand, when postmillennialism and dispensationalism meet, there is bound to be conflict. This is evident in the current American debate.

Dave Hunt is not just a premillennialist, he is a dispensational pre-tribulation rapture theorist. He is appalled by anything that looks like a Christian 'world takeover'. He quotes all the 'prepare for departure' texts but does not do justice to the 'world takeover' texts. He stoops to making a caricature of his opponents and then attacking the caricature. The Calvinist reconstructionists were unmasking the New Age cult long before any of the dispensationalists, yet Hunt attempts to identify them with the New Age because they are optimistic. This is a bad case of mistaken identity.

What should we make of the recent shift by Charismatic leaders such as Rick Godwin and Earl Paulk towards reconstructionism? Hunt attempts to link this to the Manifest Sons of God teaching of some early Pentecostals and the positive confession teaching of E.W. Kenyon. This is a large subject. All I wish to point out is that E.W. Kenyon was a dispensationalist.

If his own teaching did not lead him to become a postmillennialist, one wonders why his followers have to become postmillennialists. Kenyon's teaching is triumphalist in the sense that the new nature of the believer in Christ is said to cause him to walk in triumph. Kenyon emphasises this a great deal. It would not be surprising if those who have followed Kenyon should take this positive emphasis to its logical conclusion and embrace postmillennialism although I am not aware of any shift in this direction to date.

Earl Paulk does not seem to have been influenced by Kenyon but by the Presbyterian reconstructionists. It is therefore illegitimate to link him to the Manifested Sons of God teaching. His views, on the one side of the spectrum, are no more extreme than those of Hunt on the opposite side.

The positive aspect of the American debate is that it seems likely to shake the Bible Belt out of its uncritical and dogmatic commitment to dispensationalism. Elsewhere in the world, where the Charismatic Renewal has rediscovered kingdom teaching, it has led to a rejection of dispensationalism. It is not surprising that this shift should also occur in the United States.

Perhaps the only way to get everyone's attention is to preach the opposite of dispensationalism, namely postmillennialism. If the majority of believers were thoroughly converted to the latter, we would be faced with a swing of the pendulum to another extreme. What is more likely is that the two extremes will cancel each other out and the evangelical church will settle down to either historic premillennialism or amillennialism. The swing of the pendulum is perhaps how the American church undergoes reformation.

# A Final Perspective

In this chapter we will present a final focus on all we have said so far.

When Paul lists the elements of Christian unity he mentions 'one body and one Spirit ... one hope ... one Lord, one faith, one baptism; one God and Father of all' (Ephesians 4:4–6). This is another way of saying 'one kingdom'. The rule of God can have no rivals, and those that exist will perish when the kingdom is consummated and Jesus puts all his enemies under his feet.

## Kingdom or Denomination?

All those who have experienced the end of the times in Jesus have been apprehended by the reign of God. They are subjects of one Lord. We have seen that the church is created by the in-breaking of the kingdom of God. As the power of the age to come breaks through into this world, it creates a community of people who have experienced a transformation of their lives and loyalties. This creates one body and makes nonsense of the idea of divisions and alienations within the body of Christ. Such things can only exist if there is disobedience and resistance to the rule of Christ. This means that if denominations are manifestations of alienation, they have to be regarded as testimonies of disobedience. But there is another way of looking at church history that places denominations in proper context.

Kingdom teaching interprets the history of revivals as eschatological events. From Pentecost to the second coming, every outpouring of the Holy Spirit can be explained in the words of Peter: 'This is what was spoken by the prophet Joel,' in other words, a 'last days' phenomenon. Each such event, as it works through into society and begins to take shape in relational and social structures, produces a new movement. All such movements have leaders, circumstances, places and times in their genesis. The details are different each time, be it Augustine or Francis of Assisi, Luther or Wesley, Jonathan Edwards or Charles Parham. What is really significant is the event of the kingdom that took place. A testimony now exists because the kingdom broke through at such and such a time and at such and such a place. This event is God.

The community that results, its particular shape, the personalities involved and the emphasis that follows is part of the very human history of the church. The new wine is contained in a new wineskin; or to use another metaphor, the living organism has created its own shell. We honour the shell and we respect the wineskin because of the testimony borne to the quality within. We call these human historical shells movements and traditions within the body of Christ. They are tributaries within one river, traditions within one church, different wineskins containing the same vintage throughout. The person who has grasped the kingdom always looks for evidence of the event of the kingdom rather than the details of the shells – the structures and traditions that result.

This perspective immediately 'desacralises' denominations, which are simply the names given to different movements and traditions. Denominations within Protestantism and orders within the Roman tradition mostly date back to such an historical testimony. This perspective makes it impossible for us to give too much loyalty or commitment to them. Our commitment is to the kingdom that created them. This perspective also prevents disrespect for our brothers who hold a different testimony. I may not be able to follow all the details of the now highly developed Roman tradition but I look at Francis of Assisi, for instance, and see him as my own. In his history there is testimony to a kingdom event. I look at Luther and may not be able to follow various elements of the shell that now represents the event that took place in his history, but I am totally committed to the act of God in Jesus that took place.

No matter which denomination it is, if you examine its history you will find the breakthrough of the kingdom. When you relate to someone in that tradition you can drink from the fountain of life that stands at its genesis. By doing this you not only show respect for his faith, but you help recall him to the roots of his own tradition and therefore to the kingdom. One can relate to Methodists in terms of the days of Wesley and immediately focus on the event of the kingdom. Pentecostals have no difficulty discussing the signs and wonders of their history.

We can say what Paul said about the apostles. 'For all things are yours: whether Paul or Apollos or Cephas, or the world or life or death, or things present or things to come – all are yours. And you are Christ's, and Christ is God's' (1 Corinthians 3:21–23). If someone has been used to proclaim the kingdom, he belongs to every son of the kingdom. Why claim only those who stand in our particular tradition? Why allow only this tradition to shape our thinking?

Does this mean that we should not be concerned about theological issues of truth? The kingdom forces its own answer on us. We are orientated on the event of God as it broke through in Jesus and the Holy Spirit. Because Jesus is the embodiment of the kingdom, we will be driven to see his centrality in all things. Any teaching that does not present a clearly Christ-centred focus will fail to testify of the kingdom. Because God's rule broke through in Jesus we have concluded that Jesus is God. Because God's rule broke through in the Pentecostal outpouring, we have concluded that the Holy Spirit is God. Because of these conclusions the church has arrived at the doctrine of the Trinity. This is no theoretical construct created by men. It arose out of the attempt to explain what actually happened. Kingdom theology forces us to be Trinitarian.

A kingdom orientation will drive us to the supremacy of grace. This will

225

shape our understanding of salvation as the act of God. Because of the way in which the kingdom creates the church, we will come to certain conclusions about the nature of the church and its relationship to society. There are in fact no issues of doctrinal truth that do not go back, in some way, to the plumb line of the kingdom. Because the kingdom takes us back to the foundation of the gospel, it lifts our vision from a sectarian preoccupation with certain traditions and places before us the full spectrum of the testimony of the whole ecumenical church. We are called to have the breadth of mind of Solomon. The perspective of the kingdom will destroy our small-mindedness.

## Future Expectation

Most profoundly of all, seeing the kingdom will orientate us towards future expectation. There are two kinds of expectation about the future of the kingdom, one fanatical and one profound. The fanatical kind is adventist. It sends us to the top of the mountain to await the second coming on the day we have appointed for ourselves from our eschatological charts. It leads us to rash predictions about events and times and their exact correspondence with prophetic predictions about the anti-Christ and the beast. It leads us to arrogance and fanaticism so that we are confident that our generation is the very last, moreover that we are the people with the final Elijah anointing. This kind of expectation always leads to a spilling of the new wine of the kingdom, to a chaotic sowing of the seed to the wind and to an abandonment of the real confrontation of the kingdom with the powers of this age. It speaks more of the understanding of Shimei son of Gera, who could not even understand the signs of the moment (2 Samuel 16:5–8), than the men of Issachar, who understood the times and knew what Israel should do (1 Chronicles 12:32).

It is all too easy to react to this adventism and dispense with real expectation. We do this at our peril. There is a definite correlation between expectation and revival. It is not the expectation of dates and charts, but of God's intervention. The future hangs over us like a cloud. The nearness of the kingdom and the presence of the kingdom merge into one another. It is a case of living in the mystery.

The future breaks in on us in ever-increasing waves and the course of church history looks more like a jet fighter preparing for takeoff than an old clock winding down. We do not look back at the golden age of the apostles, nostalgic about what we never experienced. We face an exciting future of the gifts and ministries of the Holy Spirit being restored to the church and world missions moving forward at an unequalled pace. We look to a final breakthrough of the kingdom. Whatever the symbolism of the apocalyptic and prophetic pictures may signify, they point to something cataclysmic, cosmic and final. The second coming of Jesus is always there, just over the horizon. The global village we live in can set the stage for the final scenario more quickly than any of us could imagine. We simply do not know the day or the hour. It could be much closer than we expect. Or we may never live to see it. God alone knows. Whatever the case, the power and presence of the kingdom is all around us.

Maranatha!

# Studying the Theology of the Kingdom

Hopefully this book will have whet your appetite to delve more deeply into this fascinating subject. Your question may be, 'where to from here?' This has not been a critical or academic study of the kingdom, but has sought to communicate with the ordinary church member, not schooled in academic theological study, by drawing on the positive results of such literature. This last chapter will introduce some of the complex terms and ideas found in contemporary scholarship and will make suggestions about further study. It will be relevant to those who are beginning on the journey of theological study in academic environments outside of conservative colleges and faculties.

At the outset it needs to be understood that evangelical writers have not dominated theological study on the kingdom. They have often caught up with the field rather late. They have frequently been reactionary, and the evangelical church has in general awakened slowly to the re-emergence of the centrality of the kingdom.

One cannot follow the history of theology on the kingdom without reading many writers who operate with assumptions and methodologies that are unpalatable to the evangelical. Nevertheless, the work they have done has produced a harvest we are certainly benefiting from today. It will therefore be necessary to introduce, albeit very simply, some of their assumptions and methodologies and to give some general guidelines as to how one can discern the way through a sometimes bewildering world of ideas.

The chapter will be part guided bibliography and part theological dialogue. My aim is to point you to the important works and to briefly discuss their content.

Let me begin at the end of the process and then return to the beginning (rather like the kingdom itself). Mark Saucy, in *The Kingdom of God in The Teaching of Jesus in 20th Century Theology*[52] has written what is probably the most comprehensive history of academic studies on the kingdom by any evangelical writer. There are a number of ways in which he makes an excellent contribution. First, like John Wimber, he is a Fuller man, completing his Ph.D there. Second, he includes, with appreciation, the influence of George Ladd on John Wimber and the focus on the kingdom of God in the Vineyard, with its emphasis on signs and wonders.

Third, his work is comprehensive and up to date. Fourth, he provides a critique of approaches to biblical studies of the kingdom outside of evangelicalism, giving the evangelical student a grid through which the entire field can be assessed. Fifth, his extensive references and his bibliography are a comprehensive guide to further study. It was therefore disappointing to me that I found his own views on the kingdom, which he offers at the end, less than satisfying. He attempts to defend a watered-down version of dispensationalism, which, to my view, is one theology that cannot survive a clear exposition of the biblical teaching on the kingdom.[53] Nevertheless, I would start by reading Saucy's work.

As he shows, the modern study of the kingdom has to start with Johannes Weiss and Albert Schweitzer, who, following a cue from Reimarus, turned the previous century of biblical studies on its head and started a revolution.[54] One should view what followed as a case of thesis, antithesis and synthesis. Schweitzer, following Reimarus and

Weiss, produced the radical thesis (itself an antithesis to the previous century of study). C.H. Dodd produced the antithesis, and a number of subsequent scholars produced the synthesis, particularly W.G. Kummel, Oscar Cullmann, and Joachim Jeremias. This synthesis was then refined and articulated into a more evangelical theological context by Hermann Ridderbos, George Ladd and G.R. Beasley-Murray.

It is really not worth reading too many recent works until one has read these primary sources representing the fundamental theological positions on the kingdom. The last six scholars provide a sane and balanced view of the biblical material and nothing has been written since their works that represents a radically new departure. There are any number of works that attempt to evade either the radical thesis of Schweitzer or the responsible synthesis that these scholars articulated, but none of them have been compelling enough to establish themselves within conservative theological circles. In addition I would recommend one more work, actually unrelated to the study of the kingdom, namely Karl Barth's *Protestant Theology in the Nineteenth Century*.

## The Thesis

In order to understand the bombshell dropped by Schweitzer one has to review the dominant views on the kingdom at the time. Protestant liberalism had defined the kingdom as the fatherhood of God in the heart and the brotherhood of man. Schweitzer, with devastating clarity, surveyed the history of New Testament studies in his book *The Quest of the Historical Jesus: A Critical Study of Its Progress from Reimarus to Wrede*.[55] He showed that the attempt, through historical criticism, to recover the original Jesus behind the extant gospel narratives had merely provided liberal scholars with an opportunity to create a Jesus in their own image, a nineteenth-century liberal Christian gentleman. Then, in his other works he showed how they had completely missed the fundamental eschatological nature of Jesus's message.[56] Because Schweitzer returned to the original lead given by Reimarus, and because his work is fairly brief, one should read Reimarus at the same time.[57]

The conclusion Schweitzer came to was inevitably going to be made. During the nineteenth century the literature of Judaism from the time of Jesus was being discovered and explored, leading to an understanding of Jesus's environment, which had been hidden ever since the first century. It showed how saturated Judaism was with an expectation of the apocalyptic coming of the kingdom of God as the final end of history. As Reimarus had noticed, Jesus never qualified what he meant when he announced the kingdom because its meaning was assumed and understood by his audience. A preacher announcing the imminent end of the world was radically different from a nineteenth-century liberal gentleman.

Barth provides another critique of Protestant liberalism, equally penetrating. Those who have struggled to follow his long ponderous sentences in *Church Dogmatics* will be surprised by the incisive style of *Protestant Theology in the Nineteenth Century.*[58] Writing later in the century and through a critique of a different sort, Barth shows the poverty of any theology that confuses the transcendence of God and the virtues of man. The two works of Schweitzer and Barth will lay a solid foundation for understanding the essential issues of the time.

The history of subsequent studies on the kingdom, and on the historical Jesus, have shown that many have simply failed to face the issues raised by Schweitzer. Many have tried to evade the fully or 'consistently' eschatological nature of Jesus's teaching. Any view of the kingdom that does not begin with this fundamental reality is bound to fail. However we understand the 'already' of the kingdom, we must never view it as a diluting of the 'not yet'.

Since Schweitzer, one can observe three broad tendencies:

- First, there is what I will call the 'synthesis' between Schweitzer and Dodd, which is one that evangelical scholars can happily embrace.

- Second, there is the 'symbolic' view, which cannot be embraced, although some aspects are helpful.

- Third, there is the still ongoing 'third quest' for the historical Jesus. Here it is too soon to derive a definitive consensus view of Jesus, but there are more hopeful signs that the Christ of biblical scholarship and the Christ of the New Testament writers may find one another, in some sense.

While there have been enough voices raised in critical scholarship to keep the eschatological kingdom before us, it has been mostly scholars in the 'third quest' who have pointed to the other evaded lesson of Schweitzer's work, a lesson Schweitzer never intended to give. The problem is with the nature of the critical methods used on the New Testament, or perhaps aspects and assumptions within these methods. The methods themselves have made their contribution: source criticism, form criticism, and more recently redaction and tradition criticism. This is not the place to analyse such methods. Two problems have emerged. The moment the modern scholar believes it is his responsibility to disregard the witness of the gospel writers themselves and to deconstruct the text so as to work backwards towards the historical Jesus, irrespective of which discipline or method he chooses, the scholar has to use criteria of selection to disentangle 'original' or 'Dominical' texts, sayings or traditions from redactional ones. Some texts are attributed to Jesus while others are attributed to the early church community that transmitted the traditions or the editorial tendencies of the evangelists.[59]

The truth is that the century after Schweitzer did no better than the century before him. Scholar after scholar created Jesus in his own image. The disciplines that are supposed to remove the subjective selection of texts in favour of a particular theological interest simply do not work. As Saucy has shown, this problem continues to today. There is Jesus the existentialist philosopher making 'Being' statements and communicating through 'language events', Jesus the preacher of metaphorical tensive symbols, Jesus the linguistic philosopher, Jesus the cynic-sage, Jesus the social revolutionary, and Jesus the political revolutionary, to mention just a few. This introduces the dialogue between the so-called Jesus Seminar and those who have provided the alternative or critique of the seminar.

Generally the criteria of selection require that texts that can be explained as a reflection of Judaism at the time, or the transmission of the tradition by the early church, or the editorial activity of the evangelists, cannot be original to Jesus. This involves the dubious logic of denying that Jesus was influenced by his environment, or became a pivotal influence on his followers. While the idea is at first to discover the irreducible minimum of texts that *must* come from Jesus, the notion of methodological doubt changes on the way to become a method of profound historical scepticism. It has to assume that in its memory of Jesus, the early church is less qualified than the modern critic to tell us what Jesus taught. Methodological doubt evolves into historical scepticism and then into arrogance. But the price is high. Schweitzer's judgement on the century before him must fall equally on the century that followed him.

The lesson for evangelical scholars is obvious. Only a method that submits to the witness of the gospels as they stand can ever hope to grasp the teaching of Jesus on the kingdom of God.[60] To anticipate a later section, this is where James Dunn's *Jesus Remembered* is particularly helpful.[61] This does not mean that we should hide from or evade all the critical issues. Clearly the traditions about Jesus were shaped by the community prior to their use by the evangelists and equally clearly, the evangelists were theologians who shaped the tradition they received. Much of the work done on ancient contemporary documents, contemporary Palestinian socio-political conditions and on the evolution of translation from Aramaic and Hebrew Palestinian sources to the Hellenistic Christian community will continue to make a rich contribution to our knowledge of Jesus in his context. However, after we have assessed all such data, we are still relatively far removed from Jesus in comparison to the writers of the New Testament, no matter how much research we do.[62]

## The Antithesis

Schweitzer overstated his case in various ways, believing that Jesus threw himself on the wheel of history to precipitate the end of the world.[63] He failed to come to terms with the texts that Dodd later used to support his position.[64] Dodd's antithesis was that while Jesus may have used the language of apocalyptic and futurist eschatology he changed its meaning to refer to the realised presence of the kingdom in his ministry. Dodd was able to show that the parables of Jesus prove that he believed the kingdom to be present.[65] However Dodd also overstated his case, insisting that language about the kingdom's nearness referred to the kingdom's presence.

## The Synthesis – The Older Consensus

The older synthesis established by scholars such as Kummel, Cullmann and Jeremias was therefore not a compromise but a true synthesis. They showed that Jesus taught *both* the future, eschatological kingdom and the present, or 'realised' kingdom. Kummel's *Promise and Fulfilment* places the kingdom in its true context, namely Old Testament expectation.[66] While there have been discussions about some aspects of Oscar Cullmann's concept of linear time, his work is still foundational to an understanding of the kingdom.[67] Jeremias is important for his work on the parables. Much of the debate about the future or present nature of the kingdom has tended to hinge on scholarly interpretations of the parables. His thorough knowledge of Rabbinical and Palestinian sources gave authority to his work and lent weight to the synthesis.[68]

While Ridderbos may be placed more within the reformed bracket than conservative evangelical, his scholarship is generally conservative. He and George Ladd were the first conservative scholars to dialogue with the new synthesis and to articulate it clearly. Their work occurred at about the same time.[69] Ladd's *Theology of the New Testament* was the first evangelical work to structure New Testament theology on the new understanding of the kingdom.[70] Also of significance for evangelicalism was Ladd's debate in various journals with J.F. Walvoord, a leading dispensationalist, and the literature that reflected that debate. The debate shows how a proper understanding of the kingdom makes it impossible to defend dispensationalism. Wherever the theology of the kingdom spreads, therefore, dispensationalism retreats.[71] *Jesus and the Kingdom of God* by Beasley-Murray is important because it shows how the consensus held over the succeeding twenty years.[72] Although he seems to have been influenced to some extent by the symbolic consensus, he nevertheless gives due place to an actual eschaton.[73]

## The 'Symbolic' Kingdom – The Later Consensus

Dodd underlined a universally recognised fact. The parables are crucial to one's understanding of Jesus's teaching. To say that the parables use the language of symbol, or metaphor, is obvious. However, it all depends on what one means by 'symbol'.

Norman Perrin is renowned for his description of the kingdom as tensive symbol, and is normally regarded as a formative influence in developing a school of thought in recent scholarship. His definition of symbol effectively evacuates the kingdom of its power and reality. It is not the exposition of metaphor and symbol in Jesus's teaching that is problematic, but what Perrin does with it. For him the category of symbol in the parables must be understood against the background of mythical, apocalyptic Old Testament expectations. Myth in turn is defined from a particular world view. This becomes transparent towards the conclusion of his seminal essay, where he draws attention to the difference between the approaches of Bultmann and Walter Rauschenbusch. The latter 'fully accepted the ancient myth and hence was able to return to a direct and natural use of the symbol. Using the symbol directly and naturally remains a hermeneutical option for those for whom the myth is still valid and meaningful'. By way of contrast, for Bultmann 'the myth is dead and the symbolic language, archaic'.[74] Perrin places himself more with Bultmann than Rauschenbusch. 'Myth' is earlier defined as a mixture of actual events and legends about the way in which Israel came to believe that Yahweh fought against her enemies and intervened in history to be enthroned as their king. The 'myth' itself was borrowed from general pagan sources. Since Jewish apocalyptic makes use of such mythical language, Jesus's use of the myth can be viewed as a symbol which we may find meaningful, but which Perrin cannot adopt in its 'direct and natural' sense. Put very simply, God did not really intervene in the history of Israel and so what Jesus believed about a future, final intervention of God cannot really be believed either.

The pervasive influence of Perrin can be seen in Bruce Chilton. His obvious desire is to derive his theology from careful research. Using redaction and tradition criticism he examines a minimum of texts that he believes contain elements that are original to the historical Jesus.[75] This is the basis of a subsequent and broader study on the kingdom.[76] However, despite the careful and scholarly procedure, his conclusions are shaped by Perrin's concepts.[77] Taking his lead from Perrin, he believes that a new scholarly consensus has been established, replacing the assumptions about apocalyptic language held by Weiss and Schweitzer.[78] With the new consensus apocalyptic language from the Old Testament and other Jewish literature is understood as more symbolical than cataclysmic. They stress that the term 'kingdom of God' refers to God's power to rule, or to his active presence, rather than a timetable leading to the end of the world events. Jesus is therefore understood to have taught a fairly symbolical, or metaphorical concept of God becoming present, without much stress on cosmic end-time events.[79] Technically there is little doubt that Schweitzer misused his pre-Christian sources and overstated the cosmic, cataclysmic elements in apocalyptic language.[80] However, the attempt to strip Old Testament, intertestamentary and New Testament texts of a clear expectation that this world as we know it will end, dramatically, by some kind of final, climactic intervention of God, will not endure. To overstate such language is one thing, to replace it with a symbolical, metaphoric, or mystical idea is equally dubious.

Part of the problem is the vagueness of the notion of symbol. Chilton enlists the support of Howard Marshall, a conservative evangelical scholar, to define the kingdom of God as belief in the fact that 'God is already at work in the world'. Then, to demonstrate the consensus that exists, he enlists the support of Marcus Borg for a similar view. However, Borg describes the kingdom in the teaching of Jesus as similar to another sage, Buddha. The meaning for both Jesus and Buddha is not the 'product of the age; rather, the transformation of perception is the product of their spiritual experience', a 'mystical perception' which is beyond time. Within this framework Borg speaks of dying to the self and re-birth.[81]

This is an obvious case of scholars seeming to hold a similar view but in fact operating from radically different positions. While they might both use the concept of symbol, what they mean by it is very different. For Marshall the acceptance of the definition of the kingdom as God being present does not evaporate a belief in a real eschaton, while for Borg the symbolic and metaphorical nature of the kingdom can blur the differences between biblical faith and Buddhist mysticism. Clearly when scholars talk about the term 'kingdom of God' having symbolic meaning, we must probe into what they actually mean.[82]

This almost brings us to the subject of the "third quest" but we should pause to look at another field of study. While New Testament scholarship has been engaged in these endeavours, developments in systematic theology have been equally significant. I will mention three.

## Systematic Theology

Wolfhart Pannenberg was one of the first to write Christology within the framework of the kingdom and particularly to make the resurrection, as an eschatological event, the fulcrum of his Christology. He also shows how the resurrection is an 'already interpreted' event due to the history of Old Testament kingdom expectation. His view of Old Testament kingdom expectation is similar to Kummel's.[83]

Jurgen Moltmann has constructed his entire *Theology of Hope* on the eschatology of the kingdom. Recommending a reading of Moltmann will raise a number of questions for evangelicals. He belongs within the circle of radical German theologians who are true to the post-Bultmann scepticism about the gospel narratives. Many have wondered about an underlying commitment to Hegelian dialectical philosophy. His influence stands behind much liberation theology. While all this may be true, his significance lies in the way he takes the fundamental understanding of the kingdom as realised and future eschatology and creates a total world view. He shows how the kingdom can and should be the paradigm for an entire theology and praxis of the Christian life. It begs for evangelicals to do a similar work without the troublesome assumptions.[84]

Adrio König is a South African reformed theologian who has also constructed his systematic theology on the kingdom. However, there is nothing that would offend an evangelical reader. He does in fact represent an evangelical theological perspective on the kingdom. His theology helped repudiate cessationism within his own tradition. *The Eclipse of Christ in Eschatology* shows how the whole ministry of Jesus must be understood within an eschatological context.[85] A reading of his *Here Am I!: a Christian reflection on God*, will be equally rewarding.[86]

There is one implication of kingdom theology that is worth special mention. Conservative evangelical theology has generally digested the results of this history but evangelical church life has not. Students study the kingdom, or issues of eschatology, but few make the kingdom the primary model of their preaching. That is why the relationship between Ladd and Wimber and the resulting focus on the kingdom in the Vineyard is so significant. In some ways it mirrors the manner in which the kingdom has slowly become the paradigm of major evangelical mission conferences and structures. Saucy's section on the Lausanne Congress and subsequent events is significant. *Mission Between the Times, Essays on the Kingdom* by Rene Padilla shows how a leading evangelical has absorbed kingdom theology and translated it into his primary language.[87] What has occurred in the Vineyard is therefore not unique and in fact places us within the general context of evangelical theology and practice.

## The Third Quest

One cannot deal adequately with the subject of the kingdom and fail to place it in the context of the various 'quests' for the historical Jesus. The problem for this volume is that the subject is so vast that any attempt to give a brief outline runs the risk of reducing large subjects too much. However, anything like an adequate treatment would make this chapter too long. What follows is highly summarised, but the recent works that will be mentioned have excellent summaries of the 'quest' history.[88]

The three quests roughly cover the following periods:

- the first quest, 1800–1900;[89]
- the second quest, 1900–1980,[90] and
- the third quest, 1980 to the present.

The first quest has been found wanting by so many that all we need do here is list some of the most commonly held views. The first quest failed for the following reasons:

- It operated with a naïve, nineteenth-century view of history, normally described as historical positivism.

- Key assumptions inherent in the historical-critical method, namely the principles of analogy and correlation, have proved to be problematic. The issue here is not the principles themselves, but how they are defined and the world view in which they are formulated.[91]

- A century of books on Jesus was exposed by Schweitzer as a series of Jesus figures that looked more like nineteenth-century European gentlemen than the apocalyptic Jewish prophet of the end times found in the New Testament.

- Their methodology of trying to strip away the mythical layers to get back to the original Jesus is rather like the disappearing onion. If one peels off the layers of an onion to get to some core inside one merely ends with the last layer and nothing left. The embarrassing historical anomaly is that one cannot then explain the origin of the early church or of the New Testament itself.

The second quest, properly called the 'new' quest, was not an actual quest for the historical Jesus, but rather a flight from history followed by a failed attempt to re-engage with history. After Schweitzer, with his devastating criticism of the first quest, New Testament scholarship, largely led by Bultmann, retreated into existentialism. Eventually his followers realised the pendulum had swung too far and began to attempt a return to history. This new beginning is usually credited to Ernst Käsemann.[92] The so-called 'new' quest failed for the following reasons:

- It never really broke away from the escape from history of the Bultmann school.

- The escape from history was into existentialist philosophy, which proved to be little more than a passing fashion.

- The result was a kind of 'faith in faith' similar to the 'word of faith' movement of the American Bible Belt. It is interesting to note that Bultmann emphasised Gnostic elements in the New Testament and perpetuated Kant's dualism. The 'word of faith' movement, founded on the writings of E.W. Kenyon, was similarly a fundamentally dualistic Gnostic phenomenon.[93]

- The retreat into a 'safe' area immune from history came at the price of irrelevance. If Christian faith cannot be sustained in public history, then is it credible?[94]

- The problematic assumptions about historical method in the first quest were never questioned in the 'new' quest.[95]

The third quest is ongoing, but its results are far more hopeful. The third quest has as its foil, or opposing counterpart, the so-called Jesus

Seminar, the popular self-designated term for a group of scholars who have attempted to revive the first quest, but in novel ways, once again making much of Gnostic thought.[96]

There is a growing literature in the third quest, with a growing list of scholars. Here my purpose is to help the prospective student begin with the most important works.

First, as noted, is the work of the Canadian scholar Ben Meyer, who can be credited with the first real critique of the assumptions that bedevilled the previous quests. He laid the essential philosophical foundation by defining critical realism for New Testament scholarship. One can observe all the major third quest scholars referring back to this foundation.[97]

Then, building on Ben Meyer are the works of the Catholic scholar from Notre Dame, John P. Meier. His three volumes on *Jesus the Marginal Jew* indicate that he has placed Jesus firmly in the setting of second temple Judaism.[98] This reflects the other characteristic of the third quest. E.P. Sanders is usually taken to be the pivotal writer who brought the fruits of the growing volume of literature from the period to its obvious conclusion, placing both Jesus and Paul in their true context.[99] There are a number of other features in Meier's work.

- First, following Meyer, is his more sensible definition of the historical method.[100]

- Having been careful to define his method, he then examines the Jesus tradition. He 'recovers' a comprehensive framework of kingdom preaching and teaching, and then, using fairly narrow criteria, still allows many of the miracles and exorcisms of Jesus to stand the test of historical research. While none of the third quest scholars come out and say that the resurrection is clearly verified, they deal with the evidence so as to leave the weight of proof more with those who would deny its historicity.[101]

- Both Meyer and Meier deal adequately and thoroughly with the thesis of the Jesus Seminar. Meier deals in particular with its reworking of the primary sources (in favour of layers of Q and the Gospel of Thomas).[102]

Graham Twelftree, the Regent University scholar and past Vineyard pastor builds further on the work of Paul Meier. True to the third quest, he carefully defines his methodology, or criteria, and adds a thoroughly contemporary discussion on the issues of miracles and presuppositions.[103] As with Meier, having used fairly narrow, or hard criteria, he finds that Jesus was clearly both an exorcist and a miracle worker.

While Meier and Twelftree work within the generally recognised criteria of New Testament criticism,[104] N. T. Wright takes research in a fresh direction of his own. One can describe Wright's work as massive and somewhat magisterial, 'massive' in the sense of being so comprehensive, and 'magisterial' in the confidence of his position.[105] Here are what I view as some of the strengths and weaknesses of his work:

- He takes the method of placing Jesus in the context of second temple Judaism further than Meyer and Meier, by a fresh approach to historical method, dealing with the 'big picture' issues of world view and meta-narrative, and using the idea of comprehensiveness and coherence as the test of historical hypotheses.[106]

- He argues cogently for a replacement of the criteria of dissimilarity for the double criteria of similarity and dissimilarity, something that was a long way in coming. The result is that he can generally come to yet more affirmative results on the Jesus tradition than Meier and Twelftree can.[107]

- As with Meier, while he does not blatantly state the historicity of the resurrection, his exhaustive study leaves the burden of proof with those who would find an alternative explanation.[108] I found his logic concerning the unexpected role of the testimony of women particularly persuasive.

- If Meyer, Meier and Twelftree deal adequately and thoroughly with the Jesus Seminar, Wright's analysis deconstructs their methodology even further. He is particularly helpful in the way he shows that the Jesus Seminar has first decided on the Jesus they want, and has then created a methodology to find such a Jesus.

If space permitted I could go on extolling the virtues of Wright's work. It is therefore unfortunate that I have to discuss some weaknesses:[109]

- The way he places such emphasis on the meta-narrative, or controlling story, leads to debate, but more problematic is the way he elevates one aspect of the controlling story to a kind of hermeneutical principle, namely the theme of the return of Israel from exile. As one reads through his often brilliant analysis of the Jesus tradition, one is almost ready for his conclusion before turning the page: this story, or parable, or feature is once again to be viewed as focusing on the return of Israel from exile. The often forced nature of this habit tends to undermine his overall thesis. (I concur with Dunn's list of kingdom expectations.)[110]

- In order to circumvent the false directions of Jesus research in the post-Schweitzer era, he makes much of the fact that 'apocalyptic' in the second temple period did not convey the idea of the end of the space-time world in a final cataclysm. His basic point, on Schweitzer's misunderstanding of apocalyptic, is probably correct. However, he then so evacuates apocalyptic into the equivalent of theologising language for moments of great historical transformation that one is left wondering if his great confidence is well placed. For instance, if the events of Jesus's life are realised eschatology, what should one make of the 'cosmic' signs that accompanied the cross and resurrection? Did the tradition invent these, and if not, can one think of the eschaton as not somehow involving cosmic, rather than historical, or this worldly transformation? Since the resurrection of Jesus is realised eschatology, how can one conceive of the general resurrection of the dead, with millions of people in trans-physical bodies,[111] as something that does not really end history? I suspect that he would argue that these comments are part of a general tendency to misunderstand him.

James Dunn has only produced the first in his series so far. However, the progress of the third quest takes another step forward with his work.

- Wright had already begun to suggest that New Testament research should take a new look at oral tradition.[112] Dunn, while criticising Wright on the issues just mentioned, tends to build on his conclusions as well. Like Wright, he moves away from the narrow and hard use of the historical criteria applied to the various sources (leaning too heavily on "multiple attestation" and what Wright calls an "atomizing" approach) with his fresh thesis on the fixed nature of the core oral tradition which explains the subtle variations in the differing tellings (performances). This allows him to draw together aggregates, or the general tenor of the various core traditions instead of peeling off layers (peeling the onion).

- He concludes that we can never get behind the 'remembered' Jesus of the gospel writers to some more original Jesus. However, this should not lead to historical scepticism about the remembered Jesus, due to the very nature of the oral tradition.

- As with the other third questers, the Jesus Seminar is thoroughly and critically examined. Most telling is his view that the whole exercise is neo-liberal, in the sense that Jesus is once again being re-cast, this time to look remarkably like a 21st Century intellectual philosopher/theologian.

This then would be the recommended reading list on the third quest. Of course, to really grasp all the issues one would need to read the counter-position of the Jesus Seminar. A short list would include the works of Marcus Borg,[113] Dominic Crossan,[114] Burton Mack,[115] Robert Funk,[116] J. S. Kloppenborg,[117] and Helmut Koester.[118] Alternatively, a student beginning on this journey may want to read a helpful summary of all of these authors by a 'safe' author. Here one should make use of Ben Witherington.[119]

My point here is not to give a full list of authors or to make adequate comments on them, but merely to outline the architecture of a journey of study that would equip evangelical students to further their studies by following some of the major milestones and having some idea of the larger issues involved.

Theological literature on the kingdom will continue to be written and will continue to be important because of the central position this theology holds for the whole biblical narrative. There are certain criteria one needs to be aware of when reading either biblical scholarship or systematic theology.

## Important Criteria

1. One must beware of a selective use of scripture and a resulting reductionism. The portions of scripture a particular scholar either selects or repudiates in some way, or ignores, will work its way through into a reduced understanding of the kingdom. For instance, there is an ongoing debate between the kingdom as reign or realm. Those who tend to wander off into an abstract, unworldly view of the kingdom tend to repudiate the kingdom as a concrete realm, such as the history of national Israel and the promise of a restoration or enlargement of the same. A selection of the Psalms as the major Old Testament paradigm of the kingdom with an evasion of the Davidic monarchy as a primary model of the kingdom will support such an option. Equally a selection of the Exodus event over all other themes by liberation theologians reveals their bias. In the New Testament a focus on the parables alone will tend to go with a symbolic, or metaphorical view of the kingdom that evades the full-blown expectation of the end of history and its concrete, dynamic breaking into the present. As we have already noticed, a selection of 'already' texts or 'not yet' texts will represent a loss of balance in various directions.

I have found four strands of teaching on the kingdom: future, present, near and delayed. A gratifying result of third quest Jesus research is the almost total agreement on the two-fold dimension (present/near and future), often described as inaugurated eschatology. However, none of these scholars takes the delay texts seriously. They either reinterpret the parables to place the listener near the end[120] or attribute them to the early church. I am totally unconvinced that these parables were created by the early church, and am not satisfied by the alteration of the listener position approach either. Did Luke get Jesus totally wrong, since he explicitly says that Jesus told this parable because people supposed the kingdom was going to appear at once (Luke 19:11), or are contemporary scholars assuming they are better placed than Luke to know what Jesus said?

2. The way in which the environment of Palestinian Judaism and intertestamental literature is used should also be noted. Some scholars see Jesus as so different from his context that he could not have lived in the same century. Others see him as a total product of his environment. One does not have to be overly wise to realise that Jesus was a thoroughly contextualised first century Jew, who communicated within the thought patterns of his day. At the same time he must have stood for a radically new departure. Otherwise how did he create such a new beginning in history or get to be crucified? Wright is particularly forthright on these issues.

3. The way in which Jesus is believed to have influenced those who followed him can be as obviously unreal. If an undue emphasis is laid on the creative role of the history of transmission or on the editorial activity of the evangelists, one arrives at an historical anomaly. Where did this remarkably creative and transformative community come from in the first place?

It is not difficult to follow an evolution of thought within the New Testament, from Hebrew to Greek categories and from a Palestinian to a Hellenistic environment. The book of Acts and the epistles show how the message of the kingdom was contextualised and reformulated. Where the primary message of Jesus was the kingdom, the primary message of the apostles was Jesus. New terms and concepts were used to communicate in a new environment. However, many writers represent this as a radical departure from, or a distortion of the original message of Jesus. Once again some fairly obvious anomalies arise. The epistles are not a later literature to the gospels. The same general community that handed us the epistles handed us the gospels.[121] Did they manage to recall the original message of Jesus, or enough for scholars to deconstruct and reconstruct the message of Jesus, only to communicate something totally different themselves? We depend completely on their testimony as our source, yet we find all sorts of inner contradictions and distortions in their theological reflections.

4. Such problems in New Testament studies reveal the role played by presuppositions, particularly those present in post-enlightenment continental Europe. Views of historical causality, of analogy, of miracles versus myth, combined with a particular contemporary environment, make it extremely unlikely that some scholars will ever be able to draw near to the inner world of the New Testament. A sociological analysis of the world of the New Testament scholar may be as significant as a sociological investigation of the first century environment. The role played by fashions in philosophy can be significant. There are also communities and sub-communities within the scholarly fraternity, with groups imagining a critical consensus that cannot be questioned. Certain entrenched positions are sustained for decades, only to collapse and be replaced by new positions. It is therefore important to consult works that trace the overall history of the investigation of the New Testament and not to be overly impressed with a particular recent emphasis.[122]

5. One of the journeys taken by biblical scholarship that has not really facilitated any fresh understanding is the so-called importance of the 'delay of the *parousia*'. The idea is that Jesus predicted the imminent arrival of the Day of the Lord. As time went on without this expectation being fulfilled, the New Testament writers had to find a way to explain the delay. While earlier books (the synoptics) view the end as imminent,

later books (John) reinterpret the imminent end as the presence of the kingdom through the Spirit. Still later books (like the pastoral epistles) show an even later stage, where the expectation of the end has receded and this present time predominates. Therefore subjects such as church order and leadership reveal that the stage of 'early catholicism' has set in. Generally evangelical scholars are sceptical of this idea, as are many others.[123] This theory tends to coincide with a failure to come to terms with both 'already' and 'not yet' texts.

6. A litmus test for me is the view of the writer on the resurrection and the eschaton. If one gains the impression that the resurrection is viewed as some sort of symbol, or if the evolution of New Testament theology is supposed to have developed as if the resurrection did not occur, or if the future has no real drastic end to history, with a real final judgement and new age, then one is dealing with unbelief. It can be dressed up in all sorts of ways and be associated with excellent scholarly ability and prestige, but it is still unbelief. There is no way that such a world view can lead to an understanding of the kingdom.

The stage is set for a new generation of evangelical scholars to write new biblical and systematic theologies constructed on the kingdom, the primary theme of scripture, and to draw the implications of such a theology into every sphere of ministry and life.

# Appendix I

When one comes to working out the theology of the kingdom in the life of a local church, choices relate to the context and the people involved as well as to the biblical teaching. What follows should be viewed as one example of how the theology can be worked out in practice. This is the text given to members of our church and reflects our attempt, over the last few years, to return to a more biblical way of breaking bread.

## How we Break Bread [124]

The way we break bread is probably different from what most people expect and different from what occurs in most traditions. This does not mean that we take it less seriously. Because we have broken away from tradition, we are taking time to learn how to do it.

The way we break bread reflects the following:

- It reflects the Vineyard, a young movement able to innovate with models, plus our commitment to relevance over tradition.

- It reflects our commitment to the authority of scripture – linked to my own journey.

## Summary Statement

The norms in contemporary church life reflect traditions that have developed long after the apostolic period – traditions which have led the church far away from the biblical pattern and understanding of breaking bread. Some of these traditions are harmless, others are not.

The biblical pattern and understanding of breaking bread has its roots in Judaism, in the Passover festival and in the teaching of Jesus about the kingdom of God. If we want to be true to scripture we must return to these roots and break away from deeply entrenched but unbiblical traditions and models.

## The Biblical Terminology

There are a number of biblical names for the same thing.

| | |
|---|---|
| Acts 20.2 | Breaking bread |
| 1 Cor.11.20 | The Lord's Supper |
| 1 Cor. 10.16 | *Koinonia* (the communion or fellowship or participation) |
| 1 Cor. 10.16 | *Euchariste* (the thanksgiving or blessing) |
| Jude 12 | The love feast |

## Biblical Texts

Mt.26:26–29; Mk.14:22–25; Lk.22:14–20; 24:13–49; Jn.21:9–15; Ac.1:1–5; 2:46; 20:7, 11; 1 Cor.5:7–8; 10:14–22; 11:23–26; Heb.13:9–14; 2 Pet.2:13; Jude 12

## The Biblical Teaching

There are four contexts, or occasions in the New Testament, which are the foundation of the breaking of bread.

*We understand the breaking of bread by considering the occasion when it was instituted – the Lord's Last Supper.*

It was a combination of two Jewish traditions:

- It was a Passover meal
- It was a haburah meal

We deduce this from the fact that the Synoptic gospels and John's gospel probably follow two dating systems, the official and the Essene. In the one (Synoptics) Jesus kept the Passover meal with his disciples, while in the other (John) Jesus died during the Passover sacrifice but held a pre-festival *haburah* with his disciples.

## *The Passover meal (a 12-step meal)*

1. The Presiding Person pronounces a blessing (kiddush) over the first cup of wine (red), which was shared by all.

2. The eating of the *hors d'oeuvre* salad, bitter herbs dipped in fruit sauce (haroseth).

3. The arrival of the main course (roast lamb).

4. The question about the meaning of the meal, posed by the youngest member.

5. The explanation by the Presiding Person, which referred to the unleavened bread and the bitter herbs of the Passover event.

6. The Singing of the Hallel (Ps.113 and 114).

7. The drinking of the second cup.

8. The Presiding Person pronounced a blessing on the unleavened bread, saying 'Blessed art Thou who bringest forth bread from the earth.'

9. The Presiding Person broke the bread and handed it out, after which the main meal was eaten.

10. After the meal the Presiding Person offered a prayer of thanksgiving over the third cup, the cup of blessing, or thanksgiving.

11. The singing of the second part of the Hallel (Ps. 114–118).

12. The drinking of the fourth cup to celebrate God's kingdom.

To make it simple, it was:

- A three-course meal,
- Interspersed with worship,
- Including a biblical teaching or homily,
- In a family setting.

During the first decade or so of Christian history the church continued this tradition by keeping a Christian version of the Jewish Passover annually.

Note: The basic format, of a family dinner, presided over by a father figure, continued right up to the end of the NT and there is no evidence of anything less than a full dinner.

From this we conclude that we should break bread in small groups (extended families) at a dinner, interspersed with worship and biblical teaching about ('remembering') the meaning of Christ's saving work through death and resurrection.

### The haburah (pronounced with an 'h' as in 'Chutzpah')

The haburah was a pre-festival meal held by a company of close friends (up to ten) during which one would prepare oneself for the festival.

From this we deduce that the breaking of bread should be held in the intimate context of a friendship meal.

*We understand the breaking of bread by considering the meals associated with Christ's resurrection appearances.*

- The two who walked to Emmaus.

- The twelve who had Jesus share a post-resurrection meal with them.

- The disciples in Galilee when Jesus reaffirmed Peter's calling around a fish braai (barbeque).

- The following 40 days when Jesus often ate and drank with his disciples, teaching them about the kingdom of God (Acts 10:41; 1:1–5).

From this we deduce the following:

Every breaking of bread meal assumes that Jesus is invisibly present at the table, just as Elijah was given an empty chair at the Jewish Passover.

The fact that Jesus is invisibly present points to the future, when we will share in the marriage supper of the lamb in the New Jerusalem.

*We learn about the breaking of bread from the meals Jesus had with sinful people and the miracles of multiplying food during his ministry.*

- Jesus had meals with sinners where he extended to them the grace of the kingdom of God. His meals were not just for the sake of eating. In the OT the coming of the Messiah would introduce the Messianic banquet, where God would be the host for his people. When Jesus had meals with people, he was extending the Messianic banquet to them and blessing them with the grace of the kingdom of God.

- Jesus fed the four thousand and the five thousand. Once again the multiplication of food in the wilderness was showing that the second Moses, the one greater than Moses, was present. The meal was a vehicle for the experience of the kingdom of God.

From this we should deduce the following:

When we break bread we are receiving blessing, grace, and the coming of the kingdom. We are that blessed community who knows the visitation of the Messiah.

This meal is for the poor in spirit and the lost who need to be healed. Every time we participate in it we should re-experience that Jesus came to seek and to save the lost.

> *We learn about the breaking of bread from
> the love feasts of the early church.*

- Paul's corrective teaching to the Corinthians shows that a full meal was still the habit of the early church. Some ate too much and made others go without. Some got drunk. You cannot do this on a 'nip and a sip'.

The teaching about discerning the body had to do with the fellowship meal. The gathered family of God was one body because of the fellowship between them. To have some people selfishly forgetting others (the rich forgetting the poor) was to undermine the unity of the body. It was a *koinonia*, a communion, and fellowship.

- Peter and Jude gave warnings about excess amongst Gnostic Christians. They speak of those who 'revel in their pleasure' at the love feast. In other words their behaviour was that of excess.

We can deduce the following from this:

- We must heed the warning to beware of excess, or having too much of a party, with too much food and wine and the warning about making sure that everyone is included and has enough.

- We should assume that the occasion must have been a festive one to have this excess in the early church. The whole emphasis on the Messianic banquet and the joy of the kingdom of God was still present, as was the excitement of knowing that Jesus, the risen Lord, was invisibly present. Solemn, stiff, boring and austere occasions radically distort the biblical teaching.

## The Meaning of the Breaking of Bread

From the teaching given by Jesus and Paul, we can understand the meaning of the event as follows:

> *'Do this in remembrance of me.'*

Remembrance was what Israel did at the Passover. They looked back to the Exodus and relived the glorious act of God for their salvation, the founding history of their nation.

We look back at the life, death, burial, resurrection and ascension of Jesus, our saviour and redeemer, who delivered us from slavery to sin and made us into his kingdom people.

We look back over our lives and recall all the works he has done through the Holy Spirit, our conversion, the changes he has brought, the new life he has given, the ways we have met with God.

### 'This is the New Covenant in my blood.'

A covenant is a deep and permanent relationship. Through his death and resurrection we are brought into eternal relationship with God. We are secure in him. Nothing shall separate us from the love of God. He is our God and we are his people.

### 'This is my body ... this is my blood.'

To any Jew, the idea of literally thinking of Christ's flesh and blood as food was repulsive. That is why Jesus says in John 6:63 that he speaks words that are 'spirit and life'. The Christian church has gone on a very unfortunate journey in its preoccupation with the literal bread and wine. What has helped this is the reduction of a full meal to a 'nip and a sip', which helps one think of a magical ritual. It is difficult to sit at a three-course meal and think that every mouthful is giving you magical or holy food.

There is one truth taught in this saying. Jesus replaces the sacrificial Passover lamb. Now all OT sacrifices have been replaced by one, full, unrepeatable and perfect sacrifice which takes away the sins of the world. 'Christ, our Passover lamb, has been sacrificed' (1 Cor. 5:7).

### 'The cup of thanksgiving is a participation (koinonia) in the blood of Christ.'

Paul is teaching in the context of OT sacrifices and festivals and pagan sacrifices and festivals. The point of all such events is to participate, to enter in, to be drawn into relationship with God and with the community of God, relationship with God and relationship with the church.

So, participate! Get in there, enjoy it, celebrate your fellowship with one another. 'We proclaim to you what we have seen and heard, so that you also may have fellowship with us. And our fellowship is with the Father and with the Son, Jesus Christ. We write this to make our (your) joy complete' (1 Jn.1:3–4).

> *'As often as you do this you proclaim the Lord's death until he comes.'*

We must proclaim, or lift up, or focus on, or make much of, the Lord's death.

We must see the meal as an anticipation of the future kingdom of God, the marriage supper of the lamb.

# Appendix II

## The Vineyard Statement of Faith

WE BELIEVE that God is the Eternal King. He is an infinite, unchangeable Spirit, perfect in holiness, wisdom, goodness, justice, power and love. From all eternity He exists as the One Living and True God in three persons of one substance, the Father, the Son, and the Holy Spirit, equal in power and glory.

WE BELIEVE that God's Kingdom is everlasting. From His throne, through His Son, His eternal Work, God created, upholds and governs all that exists: the earth, every living thing and mankind. God created all things very good.

WE BELIEVE that God created mankind in His image, male and female, for relationship with Himself and to govern the earth. Under the temptation of Satan, our original parents fell from grace, bringing sin, sickness and God's judgement of death to the earth. Through the fall, Satan and his demonic hosts gained access to God's good creation. Creation now experiences the consquences and effects of Adam's original sin. Human beings are born in sin, subject to God's judgement of death and captive to Satan's kingdom of darkness.

WE BELIEVE that God did not abandon His rule over the earth which He continues to uphold by His providence. In order to bring redemption, God established covenants which revealed His grace to sinful people. In the covenant with Abraham, God bound Himself to His people Israel, promising to deliver them from bondage to sin and Satan and to bless all the nations through them.

WE BELIEVE that as King, God later redeemed His people by His mighty acts from bondage in Egypt and established His covenant through Moses, revealing His perfect will and our obligation to fulfil it. The law's purpose is to order our fallen race and to make us conscious of our moral responsibility. By the work of God's Spirit, it convicts us of our sin and God's righteous judgement against us and brings us to Christ alone for salvation.

WE BELIEVE that when Israel rejected God's rule over her as King, God established the monarchy in Israel and made an unconditional covenant with David, promising that his heir would restore God's kingdom reign over His people as Messiah forever.

WE BELIEVE that in the fullness of time, God honoured His covenants with Israel and His prophetic promises of salvation by sending His only Son, Jesus, into the world. Conceived by the Holy Spirit and born of the Virgin Mary, as fully God and fully man in one person, He is humanity as God intended us to be. Jesus was anointed as God's Messiah and empowered by the Holy Spirit, inaugurating God's kingdom reign on earth, overpowering the reign of Satan by resisting temptation, preaching the good news of salvation, healing the sick, casting out demons and raising the dead. Gathering His disciples, He reconstituted God's people as His Church to be the instrument of His kingdom. After dying for the sins of the world, Jesus was raised from the dead on the third day, fulfilling the covenant of blessing given to Abraham.

In His sinless, perfect life Jesus met the demands of the law and in His atoning death on the cross He took God's judgement for sin which we deserve as law-breakers. By His death on the cross He also disarmed the demonic powers.

The covenant with David was fulfilled in Jesus' birth from David's house, His Messianic ministry, His glorious resurrection from the dead, His ascent into heaven and His present rule at the right hand of the Father. As God's Son and David's heir, He is the eternal Messiah-King, advancing God's reign throughout every generation and throughout the whole earth today.

WE BELIEVE that the Holy Spirit was poured out in power on the Church at Pentecost, baptising believers into the Body of Christ and releasing the gifts of the Spirit to them. The Spirit brings the permanent indwelling presence of God to us for spiritual worship, personal sanctification, building up the Church, gifting us for ministry, and driving back the kingdom of Satan by the evangelisation of the world through proclaiming the word of Jesus and doing the works of Jesus.

WE BELIEVE that the Holy Spirit indwells every believer in Jesus Christ and that He is our abiding Helper, Teacher, and Guide. We believe in the filling or empowering of the Holy Spirit, often a conscious experience, for ministry today. We believe in the present ministry of the Spirit and in the exercise of all of the biblical gifts of the Spirit. We practise the laying on of hands for the empowering of the Spirit, for healing, and for recognition and empowering of those whom God has ordained to lead and serve the Church.

WE BELIEVE that the Holy Spirit inspired the human authors of Holy Scripture so that the Bible is without error in the original manuscripts. We receive the sixty-six books of the Old and New Testaments as our final, absolute authority, the only infallible rule of faith and practice.

WE BELIEVE that the whole world is under the domination of Satan and that all people are sinners by nature and choice. All people therefore are under God's just judgement. Through the preaching of the Good News of Jesus and the Kingdom of God and the work of the Holy

Spirit, God regenerates, justifies, adopts and sanctifies through Jesus by the Spirit all who repent of their sins and trust in Jesus Christ as Lord and Saviour. By this they are released from Satan's domain and enter into God's kingdom reign.

WE BELIEVE in the one, holy, universal Church. All who repent of their sins and confess Jesus as Lord and Saviour are regenerated by the Holy Spirit and form the living Body of Christ, of which He is the head and of which we are all members.

WE BELIEVE that Jesus Christ committed two ordinances to the Church: water baptism and the Lord's Supper. Both are available to all believers.

WE BELIEVE that God's kingdom has come in the ministry of our Lord Jesus Christ, that it continues to come in the ministry of the Spirit through the Church, and that it will be consummated in the glorious, visible and triumphant appearing of Christ – His return to the earth as King. After Christ returns to reign, He will bring about the final defeat of Satan and all of his minions and works, the resurrection of the dead, the final judgement and the eternal blessing of the righteous and eternal conscious punishment of the wicked. Finally, God will be all in all and His kingdom, His rule and reign, will be fulfilled in the new heavens and the new earth, recreated by His mighty power, in which righteousness dwells and in which He will forever be worshipped.

# Appendix III

## The Promise of the Kingdom in Isaiah

The book of Isaiah has the following basic structure:

|      |                                                  |
|------|--------------------------------------------------|
| 1–5  | Condemnation of Judah                            |
| 6    | The call of Isaiah                               |
| 7–12 | The coming of Emmanuel                           |
| 13–23| Prophecies against foreign nations               |
| 24–27| The end of the world                             |
| 28–31| Woes upon God's people                           |
| 32–35| The coming of the King                           |
| 35–39| A historical section, parallel to 2 Kings 18:13–20:19 |
| 40–66| The age to come                                  |

Thus apart from 1–5, 6, 13–23, 28–31 and 35–39 (twenty-five chapters), the remainder of the book is about the coming of the kingdom, 7–12, 24–27, 32–35 and 40–66 (forty chapters).

Isaiah is like a symphony, with a major theme tune that is interwoven with numerous other tunes. The theme tune is the age to come. The many other harmonies give definition to the content of the age to come. We will quote the major statements. One ought to read these in context to see the whole picture.

The age to come in Isaiah can be considered under six headings:

The coming of God
The coming of the King
The coming of the Spirit
The coming salvation
The new people of God
The new order

## *The Coming of God*

One may summarise Isaiah's promises as follows:

*"Good news! God will come to save and comfort his people and reveal his glory."*

### Good News

**40:9–10**

9    You who bring good tidings to Zion, go up on a high mountain. You who bring good tidings to Jerusalem, lift up your voice with a shout, lift it up, do not be afraid; say to the towns of Judah, "Here is your God!"

10    See, the Sovereign LORD comes with power, and his arm rules for him. See, his reward is with him, and his recompense accompanies him.

**52:7**

7    How beautiful on the mountains are the feet of those who bring good news, who proclaim peace, who bring good tidings, who proclaim salvation, who say to Zion, "Your God reigns!"

### God Will Come

**35:4**

4    Say to those with fearful hearts, "Be strong, do not fear; your God will come, he will come with vengeance; with divine retribution he will come to save you."

**59:16–19**

16    He saw that there was no-one, he was appalled that there was

no-one to intervene; so his own arm worked salvation for him, and his own righteousness sustained him.

17    He put on righteousness as his breastplate, and the helmet of salvation on his head; he put on the garments of vengeance and wrapped himself in zeal as in a cloak.

18    According to what they have done, so will he repay wrath to his enemies and retribution to his foes; he will repay the islands their due.

19    From the west, men will fear the name of the LORD, and from the rising of the sun, they will revere his glory. For he will come like a pent-up flood that the breath of the LORD drives along.

## To Save His People

### 12:1–2
1    In that day you will say: "I will praise you, O LORD. Although you were angry with me, your anger has turned away and you have comforted me.

2    Surely God is my salvation; I will trust and not be afraid. The LORD, the LORD, is my strength and my song; he has become my salvation."

### 45:22
22    "Turn to me and be saved, all you ends of the earth; for I am God, and there is no other."

## To Comfort His People

### 12:1
1    In that day you will say: "I will praise you, O LORD. Although you were angry with me, your anger has turned away and you have comforted me."

### 40:1
1    "Comfort, comfort my people," says your God.

### 61:1–3

1    The Spirit of the Sovereign LORD is on me, because the LORD has anointed me to preach good news to the poor. He has sent me to bind up the broken-hearted, to proclaim freedom for the captives and release from darkness for the prisoners,

2    to proclaim the year of the LORD's favour and the day of vengeance of our God, to comfort all who mourn,

3    and provide for those who grieve in Zion – to bestow on them a crown of beauty instead of ashes, the oil of gladness instead of mourning, and a garment of praise instead of a spirit of despair. They will be called oaks of righteousness, a planting of the LORD for the display of his splendour.

## And Reveal His Glory

### 4:5–6

5    Then the LORD will create over all of Mount Zion and over those who assemble there a cloud of smoke by day and a glow of flaming fire by night; over all the glory will be a canopy.

6    It will be a shelter and shade from the heat of the day, and a refuge and hiding-place from the storm and rain.

### 9:2

2    The people walking in darkness have seen a great light; on those living in the land of the shadow of death a light has dawned.

### 24:23

23    The moon will be abashed, the sun ashamed; for the LORD Almighty will reign on Mount Zion and in Jerusalem, and before its elders, gloriously.

### 35:2

2    … it will burst into bloom; it will rejoice greatly and shout for joy. The glory of Lebanon will be given to it, the splendour of Carmel and Sharon; they will see the glory of the LORD, the splendour of our God.

**40:5**

5   And the glory of the LORD will be revealed, and all mankind together will see it. For the mouth of the LORD has spoken.

**60:1–2**

1   Arise, shine, for your light has come, and the glory of the LORD rises upon you.

2   See, darkness covers the earth and thick darkness is over the peoples, but the LORD rises upon you and his glory appears over you.

**60:19–20**

19   The sun will no more be your light by day, nor will the brightness of the moon shine on you, for the LORD will be your everlasting light, and your God will be your glory.

20   Your sun will never set again, and your moon will wane no more; the LORD will be your everlasting light, and your days of sorrow will end.

## The Coming King

This section may be summarised as follows:

*"The King will come, to rule with justice, to establish the covenant, and to minister as God's servant."*

### The King Will Come

**4:2**

2   In that day the Branch of the LORD will be beautiful and glorious, and the fruit of the land will be the pride and glory of the survivors in Israel.

**9:6–7**

6   For to us a child is born, to us a son is given, and the government will be on his shoulders. And he will be called Wonderful Counsellor, Mighty God, Everlasting Father, Prince of Peace.

7   Of the increase of his government and peace there will be no end.

He will reign on David's throne and over his kingdom, establishing and upholding it with justice and righteousness from that time on and for ever. The zeal of the LORD Almighty will accomplish this.

**11:1–2**

1    A shoot will come up from the stump of Jesse; from his roots a Branch will bear fruit.

2    The Spirit of the LORD will rest on him – the Spirit of wisdom and of understanding, the Spirit of counsel and of power, the Spirit of knowledge and of the fear of the LORD –

**32:1**

1    See, a king will reign in righteousness and rulers will rule with justice.

**33:17**

17    Your eyes will see the king in his beauty and view a land that stretches afar.

**61:1**

1    The Spirit of the Sovereign LORD is on me, because the LORD has anointed me to preach good news to the poor. He has sent me to bind up the broken-hearted, to proclaim freedom for the captives and release from darkness for the prisoners ...

**To Rule With Justice**

**9:7**

7    Of the increase of his government and peace there will be no end. He will reign on David's throne and over his kingdom, establishing and upholding it with justice and righteousness from that time on and for ever. The zeal of the LORD Almighty will accomplish this.

**11:4–5**

4    ... but with righteousness he will judge the needy, with justice he will give decisions for the poor of the earth. He will strike the earth

with the rod of his mouth; with the breath of his lips he will slay the wicked.

5    Righteousness will be his belt and faithfulness the sash round his waist.

### 32:16–17

16    Justice will dwell in the desert and righteousness live in the fertile field.

17    The fruit of righteousness will be peace; the effect of righteousness will be quietness and confidence for ever.

### 33:5

5    The LORD is exalted, for he dwells on high; he will fill Zion with justice and righteousness.

### 33:22

22    For the LORD is our judge, the LORD is our lawgiver, the LORD is our king; it is he who will save us.

### 42:3–4

3    A bruised reed he will not break, and a smouldering wick he will not snuff out. In faithfulness he will bring forth justice;

4    he will not falter or be discouraged till he establishes justice on earth. In his law the islands will put their hope.

### 61:11

11    For as the soil makes the young plant come up and a garden causes seeds to grow, so the Sovereign LORD will make righteousness and praise spring up before all nations.

## To Establish the Covenant

### 42:6

6    "I, the LORD, have called you in righteousness; I will take hold of your hand. I will keep you and will make you to be a covenant for the people and a light for the Gentiles."

**49:8**

8    This is what the LORD says: "In the time of my favour I will answer you, and in the day of salvation I will help you; I will keep you and will make you to be a covenant for the people, to restore the land and to reassign its desolate inheritances ..."

**55:3**

3    "Give ear and come to me; hear me, that your soul may live. I will make an everlasting covenant with you, my faithful love promised to David."

## To Minister as God's Servant

**41:8–10**

8    "But you, O Israel, my servant, Jacob, whom I have chosen, you descendants of Abraham my friend,

9    I took you from the ends of the earth, from its farthest corners I called you. I said, 'You are my servant,' I have chosen you and have not rejected you.

10    So do not fear, for I am with you; do not be dismayed, for I am your God. I will strengthen you and help you; I will uphold you with my righteous right hand."

**42:1–9**

1    "Here is my servant, whom I uphold, my chosen one in whom I delight; I will put my Spirit on him and he will bring justice to the nations.

2    He will not shout or cry out, or raise his voice in the streets.

3    A bruised reed he will not break, and a smouldering wick he will not snuff out. In faithfulness he will bring forth justice;

4    he will not falter or be discouraged till he establishes justice on earth. In his law the islands will put their hope."

5    This is what God the LORD says– he who created the heavens and stretched them out, who spread out the earth and all that comes

out of it, who gives breath to its people, and life to those who walk on it:

6    "I, the LORD, have called you in righteousness; I will take hold of your hand. I will keep you and will make you to be a covenant for the people and a light for the Gentiles,

7    to open eyes that are blind, to free captives from prison and to release from the dungeon those who sit in darkness.

8    I am the LORD; that is my name! I will not give my glory to another or my praise to idols.

9    See, the former things have taken place, and new things I declare; before they spring into being I announce them to you."

## 49:1–6

1    Listen to me, you islands; hear this, you distant nations: Before I was born the LORD called me; from my birth he has made mention of my name.

2    He made my mouth like a sharpened sword, in the shadow of his hand he hid me; he made me into a polished arrow and concealed me in his quiver.

3    He said to me, "You are my servant, Israel, in whom I will display my splendour."

4    But I said, "I have laboured to no purpose; I have spent my strength in vain and for nothing. Yet what is due to me is in the LORD's hand, and my reward is with my God."

5    And now the LORD says – he who formed me in the womb to be his servant to bring Jacob back to him and gather Israel to himself, for I am honoured in the eyes of the LORD and my God has been my strength –

6    He says: "It is too small a thing for you to be my servant to restore the tribes of Jacob and bring back those of Israel I have kept. I will also make you a light for the Gentiles, that you may bring my salvation to the ends of the earth."

**50:4–11**

4    The Sovereign LORD has given me an instructed tongue, to know the word that sustains the weary. He wakens me morning by morning, wakens my ear to listen like one being taught.

5    The Sovereign LORD has opened my ears, and I have not been rebellious; I have not drawn back.

6    I offered my back to those who beat me, my cheeks to those who pulled out my beard; I did not hide my face from mocking and spitting.

7    Because the Sovereign LORD helps me, I will not be disgraced. Therefore have I set my face like flint, and I know I will not be put to shame.

8    He who vindicates me is near. Who then will bring charges against me? Let us face each other! Who is my accuser? Let him confront me!

9    It is the Sovereign LORD who helps me. Who is he who will condemn me? They will all wear out like a garment; the moths will eat them up.

10    Who among you fears the LORD and obeys the word of his servant? Let him who walks in the dark, who has no light, trust in the name of the LORD and rely on his God.

11    But now, all you who light fires and provide yourselves with flaming torches, go, walk in the light of your fires and of the torches you have set ablaze. This is what you shall receive from my hand: You will lie down in torment.

**52:13–53:12**

13    See, my servant will act wisely; he will be raised and lifted up and highly exalted.

14    Just as there were many who were appalled at him – his appearance was so disfigured beyond that of any man and his form marred beyond human likeness –

15    so will he sprinkle many nations, and kings will shut their mouths

because of him. For what they were not told, they will see, and what they have not heard, they will understand.

## 53

1     Who has believed our message and to whom has the arm of the LORD been revealed?

2     He grew up before him like a tender shoot, and like a root out of dry ground. He had no beauty or majesty to attract us to him, nothing in his appearance that we should desire him.

3     He was despised and rejected by men, a man of sorrows, and familiar with suffering. Like one from whom men hide their faces he was despised, and we esteemed him not.

4     Surely he took up our infirmities and carried our sorrows, yet we considered him stricken by God, smitten by him, and afflicted.

5     But he was pierced for our transgressions, he was crushed for our iniquities; the punishment that brought us peace was upon him, and by his wounds we are healed.

6     We all, like sheep, have gone astray, each of us has turned to his own way; and the LORD has laid on him the iniquity of us all.

7     He was oppressed and afflicted, yet he did not open his mouth; he was led like a lamb to the slaughter, and as a sheep before her shearers is silent, so he did not open his mouth.

8     By oppression and judgement he was taken away. And who can speak of his descendants? For he was cut off from the land of the living; for the transgression of my people he was stricken.

9     He was assigned a grave with the wicked, and with the rich in his death, though he had done no violence, nor was any deceit in his mouth.

10     Yet it was the LORD's will to crush him and cause him to suffer, and though the LORD makes his life a guilt offering, he will see his offspring and prolong his days, and the will of the LORD will prosper in his hand.

11    After the suffering of his soul, he will see the light [of life] and be satisfied; by his knowledge my righteous servant will justify many, and he will bear their iniquities.

12    Therefore I will give him a portion among the great, and he will divide the spoils with the strong, because he poured out his life unto death, and was numbered with the transgressors. For he bore the sin of many, and made intercession for the transgressors.

## The Coming of the Spirit

### 11:1–3
1    A shoot will come up from the stump of Jesse; from his roots a Branch will bear fruit.

2    The Spirit of the LORD will rest on him – the Spirit of wisdom and of understanding, the Spirit of counsel and of power, the Spirit of knowledge and of the fear of the LORD

3    and he will delight in the fear of the LORD. He will not judge by what he sees with his eyes, or decide by what he hears with his ears ...

### 32:15
15    till the Spirit is poured upon us from on high, and the desert becomes a fertile field, and the fertile field seems like a forest.

### 35:1–2
1    The desert and the parched land will be glad; the wilderness will rejoice and blossom. Like the crocus,

2    it will burst into bloom; it will rejoice greatly and shout for joy. The glory of Lebanon will be given to it, the splendour of Carmel and Sharon; they will see the glory of the LORD, the splendour of our God.

### 41:16–17
16    You will winnow them, the wind will pick them up, and a gale will blow them away. But you will rejoice in the LORD and glory in the Holy One of Israel.

17    The poor and needy search for water, but there is none; their tongues are parched with thirst. But I the LORD will answer them; I, the God of Israel, will not forsake them.

### 43:19–20

19    See, I am doing a new thing! Now it springs up; do you not perceive it? I am making a way in the desert and streams in the wasteland.

20    The wild animals honour me, the jackals and the owls, because I provide water in the desert and streams in the wasteland, to give drink to my people, my chosen.

### 44:1–5

1    But now listen, O Jacob, my servant, Israel, whom I have chosen.

2    This is what the LORD says – he who made you, who formed you in the womb, and who will help you: "Do not be afraid, O Jacob, my servant, Jeshurun, whom I have chosen.

3    For I will pour water on the thirsty land, and streams on the dry ground; I will pour out my Spirit on your offspring, and my blessing on your descendants.

4    They will spring up like grass in a meadow, like poplar trees by flowing streams.

5    One will say, 'I belong to the LORD'; another will call himself by the name of Jacob; still another will write on his hand, 'The LORD's', and will take the name Israel."

### 49:9–10

9    … to say to the captives, 'Come out,' and to those in darkness, 'Be free!' They will feed beside the roads and find pasture on every barren hill.

10    They will neither hunger nor thirst, nor will the desert heat or the sun beat upon them. He who has compassion on them will guide them and lead them beside springs of water.

## The Coming Salvation

As we have noted, when God comes, he will come as saviour. This salvation will include:

Forgiveness of sins,
Liberation of the captives,
Peace (*shalom*) for God's people,
The resurrection of the dead, and
Eschatological joy and praise.

## Salvation

### 12:2–3

2    Surely God is my salvation; I will trust and not be afraid. The LORD, the LORD, is my strength and my song; he has become my salvation.

3    With joy you will draw water from the wells of salvation.

### 25:9

9    In that day they will say, "Surely this is our God; we trusted in him, and he saved us. This is the LORD, we trusted in him; let us rejoice and be glad in his salvation."

### 33:6

6    He will be the sure foundation for your times, a rich store of salvation and wisdom and knowledge; the fear of the LORD is the key to this treasure.

### 49:6

6    He says: "It is too small a thing for you to be my servant to restore the tribes of Jacob and bring back those of Israel I have kept. I will also make you a light for the Gentiles, that you may bring my salvation to the ends of the earth."

### 51:4–6

4    "Listen to me, my people; hear me, my nation: The law will go out from me; my justice will become a light to the nations.

5    My righteousness draws near speedily, my salvation is on the way, and my arm will bring justice to the nations. The islands will look to me and wait in hope for my arm.

6    Lift up your eyes to the heavens, look at the earth beneath; the heavens will vanish like smoke, the earth will wear out like a garment and its inhabitants die like flies. But my salvation will last for ever, my righteousness will never fail."

## 52:7–10

7    How beautiful on the mountains are the feet of those who bring good news, who proclaim peace, who bring good tidings, who proclaim salvation, who say to Zion, "Your God reigns!"

8    Listen! Your watchmen lift up their voices; together they shout for joy. When the LORD returns to Zion, they will see it with their own eyes.

9    Burst into songs of joy together, you ruins of Jerusalem, for the LORD has comforted his people, he has redeemed Jerusalem.

10   The LORD will lay bare his holy arm in the sight of all the nations, and all the ends of the earth will see the salvation of our God.

## The Forgiveness of Sins

### 33:24
24   No-one living in Zion will say, "I am ill"; and the sins of those who dwell there will be forgiven.

### 43:25
25   "I, even I, am he who blots out your transgressions, for my own sake, and remembers your sins no more."

## Liberation for the Captives

### 29:17–19
17   In a very short time, will not Lebanon be turned into a fertile field and the fertile field seem like a forest?

18    In that day the deaf will hear the words of the scroll, and out of gloom and darkness the eyes of the blind will see.

19    Once more the humble will rejoice in the LORD; the needy will rejoice in the Holy One of Israel.

### 35:5–6
5    Then will the eyes of the blind be opened and the ears of the deaf unstopped.

6    Then will the lame leap like a deer, and the mute tongue shout for joy. Water will gush forth in the wilderness and streams in the desert.

### 42:6–7
6    "I, the LORD, have called you in righteousness; I will take hold of your hand. I will keep you and will make you to be a covenant for the people and a light for the Gentiles,

7    to open eyes that are blind, to free captives from prison and to release from the dungeon those who sit in darkness."

### 49:8–9
8    This is what the LORD says: "In the time of my favour I will answer you, and in the day of salvation I will help you; I will keep you and will make you to be a covenant for the people, to restore the land and to reassign its desolate inheritances,

9    to say to the captives, 'Come out,' and to those in darkness, 'Be free!' They will feed beside the roads and find pasture on every barren hill."

### 61:1
1    The Spirit of the Sovereign LORD is on me, because the LORD has anointed me to preach good news to the poor. He has sent me to bind up the broken-hearted, to proclaim freedom for the captives and release from darkness for the prisoners ...

## Peace for God's People

### 11:6–7

6    The wolf will live with the lamb, the leopard will lie down with the goat, the calf and the lion and the yearling together; and a little child will lead them.

7    The cow will feed with the bear, their young will lie down together, and the lion will eat straw like the ox.

### 32:15–19

15    … till the Spirit is poured upon us from on high, and the desert becomes a fertile field, and the fertile field seems like a forest.

16    Justice will dwell in the desert and righteousness live in the fertile field.

17    The fruit of righteousness will be peace; the effect of righteousness will be quietness and confidence for ever.

18    My people will live in peaceful dwelling-places, in secure homes, in undisturbed places of rest.

19    Though hail flattens the forest and the city is levelled completely …

### 60:18

18    No longer will violence be heard in your land, nor ruin or destruction within your borders, but you will call your walls Salvation and your gates Praise.

### 65:20–25

20    "Never again will there be in it an infant who lives but a few days, or an old man who does not live out his years; he who dies at a hundred will be thought a mere youth; he who fails to reach a hundred will be considered accursed.

21    They will build houses and dwell in them; they will plant vineyards and eat their fruit.

22    No longer will they build houses and others live in them, or plant

and others eat. For as the days of a tree, so will be the days of my people; my chosen ones will long enjoy the works of their hands.

23    They will not toil in vain or bear children doomed to misfortune; for they will be a people blessed by the LORD, they and their descendants with them.

24    Before they call I will answer; while they are still speaking I will hear.

25    The wolf and the lamb will feed together, and the lion will eat straw like the ox, but dust will be the serpent's food. They will neither harm nor destroy on all my holy mountain," says the LORD.

## The Resurrection of the Dead

### 25:8
8    ... he will swallow up death for ever. The Sovereign LORD will wipe away the tears from all faces; he will remove the disgrace of his people from all the earth. The LORD has spoken.

### 26:19
19    But your dead will live; their bodies will rise. You who dwell in the dust, wake up and shout for joy. Your dew is like the dew of the morning; the earth will give birth to her dead.

## Eschatological Joy and Praise

### 12:3–6
3    With joy you will draw water from the wells of salvation.

4    In that day you will say: "Give thanks to the LORD, call on his name; make known among the nations what he has done, and proclaim that his name is exalted.

5    Sing to the LORD, for he has done glorious things; let this be known to all the world.

6    Shout aloud and sing for joy, people of Zion, for great is the Holy One of Israel among you."

**24:14–16**

14  They raise their voices, they shout for joy; from the west they acclaim the LORD's majesty.

15  Therefore in the east give glory to the LORD; exalt the name of the LORD, the God of Israel, in the islands of the sea.

16  From the ends of the earth we hear singing: "Glory to the Righteous One." But I said, "I waste away, I waste away! Woe to me! The treacherous betray! With treachery the treacherous betray!"

**25:6**

6  On this mountain the LORD Almighty will prepare a feast of rich food for all peoples, a banquet of aged wine – the best of meats and the finest of wines.

**42:10–13**

10  Sing to the LORD a new song, his praise from the ends of the earth, you who go down to the sea, and all that is in it, you islands, and all who live in them.

11  Let the desert and its towns raise their voices; let the settlements where Kedar lives rejoice. Let the people of Sela sing for joy; let them shout from the mountaintops.

12  Let them give glory to the LORD and proclaim his praise in the islands.

13  The LORD will march out like a mighty man, like a warrior he will stir up his zeal; with a shout he will raise the battle cry and will triumph over his enemies.

**49:13**

13  Shout for joy, O heavens; rejoice, O earth; burst into song, O mountains! For the LORD comforts his people and will have compassion on his afflicted ones.

**51:11**

11  The ransomed of the LORD will return. They will enter Zion

with singing; everlasting joy will crown their heads. Gladness and joy will overtake them, and sorrow and sighing will flee away.

## 52:9

9    Burst into songs of joy together, you ruins of Jerusalem, for the LORD has comforted his people, he has redeemed Jerusalem.

## 55:12

12    You will go out in joy and be led forth in peace; the mountains and hills will burst into song before you, and all the trees of the field will clap their hands.

## 61:10

10    I delight greatly in the LORD; my soul rejoices in my God. For he has clothed me with garments of salvation and arrayed me in a robe of righteousness, as a bridegroom adorns his head like a priest, and as a bride adorns herself with her jewels.

### The New People of God

All nations and peoples will be gathered to Jerusalem as the city of God. A new people will be formed, out of every nation and out of all the tribes of Israel scattered abroad.

### Jerusalem, the City of God

## 2:2–4

2    In the last days the mountain of the LORD's temple will be established as chief among the mountains; it will be raised above the hills, and all nations will stream to it.

3    Many peoples will come and say, "Come, let us go up to the mountain of the LORD, to the house of the God of Jacob. He will teach us his ways, so that we may walk in his paths." The law will go out from Zion, the word of the LORD from Jerusalem.

4    He will judge between the nations and will settle disputes for many peoples. They will beat their swords into ploughshares and their

spears into pruning hooks. Nation will not take up sword against nation, nor will they train for war any more.

## 33:20–21

20   Look upon Zion, the city of our festivals; your eyes will see Jerusalem, a peaceful abode, a tent that will not be moved; its stakes will never be pulled up, nor any of its ropes broken.

21   There the LORD will be our Mighty One. It will be like a place of broad rivers and streams. No galley with oars will ride them, no mighty ship will sail them.

## 62:6–7

6   I have posted watchmen on your walls, O Jerusalem; they will never be silent day or night. You who call on the LORD, give yourselves no rest,

7   and give him no rest till he establishes Jerusalem and makes her the praise of the earth.

## 66:10–14

10   "Rejoice with Jerusalem and be glad for her, all you who love her; rejoice greatly with her, all you who mourn over her.

11   For you will nurse and be satisfied at her comforting breasts; you will drink deeply and delight in her overflowing abundance."

12   For this is what the LORD says: "I will extend peace to her like a river, and the wealth of nations like a flooding stream; you will nurse and be carried on her arm and dandled on her knees.

13   As a mother comforts her child, so will I comfort you; and you will be comforted over Jerusalem."

14   When you see this, your heart will rejoice and you will flourish like grass; the hand of the LORD will be made known to his servants, but his fury will be shown to his foes.

## The Regathering of God's People

### 11:11–12

11 In that day the Lord will reach out his hand a second time to reclaim the remnant that is left of his people from Assyria, from Lower Egypt, from Upper Egypt, from Cush, from Elam, from Babylonia, from Hamath and from the islands of the sea.

12 He will raise a banner for the nations and gather the exiles of Israel; he will assemble the scattered people of Judah from the four quarters of the earth.

### 27:12–13

12 In that day the LORD will thresh from the flowing Euphrates to the Wadi of Egypt, and you, O Israelites, will be gathered up one by one.

13 And in that day a great trumpet will sound. Those who were perishing in Assyria and those who were exiled in Egypt will come and worship the LORD on the holy mountain in Jerusalem.

### 43:6–9

6 I will say to the north, 'Give them up!' and to the south, 'Do not hold them back.' Bring my sons from afar and my daughters from the ends of the earth –

7 everyone who is called by my name, whom I created for my glory, whom I formed and made.

8 Lead out those who have eyes but are blind, who have ears but are deaf.

9 All the nations gather together and the peoples assemble. Which of them foretold this and proclaimed to us the former things? Let them bring in their witnesses to prove they were right, so that others may hear and say, "It is true."

### 49:12

12 See, they will come from afar– some from the north, some from the west, some from the region of Aswan.

## The Gathering of the Nations

### 11:10

10    In that day the Root of Jesse will stand as a banner for the peoples; the nations will rally to him, and his place of rest will be glorious.

### 55:5

5    Surely you will summon nations you know not, and nations that do not know you will hasten to you, because of the LORD your God, the Holy One of Israel, for he has endowed you with splendour.

### 60:3–4

3    Nations will come to your light, and kings to the brightness of your dawn.

4    Lift up your eyes and look about you: all assemble and come to you; your sons come from afar, and your daughters are carried on the arm.

## *The New Order*

The new order will be inaugurated by the day of judgement.

## The Day of Judgement

### 2:12–18

12    The LORD Almighty has a day in store for all the proud and lofty, for all that is exalted (and they will be humbled),

13    for all the cedars of Lebanon, tall and lofty, and all the oaks of Bashan,

14    for all the towering mountains and all the high hills,

15    for every lofty tower and every fortified wall,

16    for every trading ship and every stately vessel.

17    The arrogance of man will be brought low and the pride of men humbled; the LORD alone will be exalted in that day,

18    and the idols will totally disappear.

**24:1–13**

1    See, the LORD is going to lay waste the earth and devastate it; he will ruin its face and scatter its inhabitants–

2    it will be the same for priest as for people, for master as for servant, for mistress as for maid, for seller as for buyer, for borrower as for lender, for debtor as for creditor.

3    The earth will be completely laid waste and totally plundered. The LORD has spoken this word.

4    The earth dries up and withers, the world languishes and withers, the exalted of the earth languish.

5    The earth is defiled by its people; they have disobeyed the laws, violated the statutes and broken the everlasting covenant.

6    Therefore a curse consumes the earth; its people must bear their guilt. Therefore earth's inhabitants are burned up, and very few are left.

7    The new wine dries up and the vine withers; all the merrymakers groan.

8    The gaiety of the tambourines is stilled, the noise of the revellers has stopped, the joyful harp is silent.

9    No longer do they drink wine with a song; the beer is bitter to its drinkers.

10   The ruined city lies desolate; the entrance to every house is barred.

11   In the streets they cry out for wine; all joy turns to gloom, all gaiety is banished from the earth.

12   The city is left in ruins, its gate is battered to pieces.

13   So will it be on the earth and among the nations, as when an olive tree is beaten, or as when gleanings are left after the grape harvest.

**24:17–22**

17   Terror and pit and snare await you, O people of the earth.

18   Whoever flees at the sound of terror will fall into a pit; whoever climbs out of the pit will be caught in a snare. The floodgates of the

heavens are opened, the foundations of the earth shake.

19    The earth is broken up, the earth is split asunder, the earth is thoroughly shaken.

20    The earth reels like a drunkard, it sways like a hut in the wind; so heavy upon it is the guilt of its rebellion that it falls – never to rise again.

21    In that day the LORD will punish the powers in the heavens above and the kings on the earth below.

22    They will be herded together like prisoners bound in a dungeon; they will be shut up in prison and be punished after many days.

### 66:15–16
15    See, the LORD is coming with fire, and his chariots are like a whirlwind; he will bring down his anger with fury, and his rebuke with flames of fire.

16    For with fire and with his sword the LORD will execute judgement upon all men, and many will be those slain by the LORD.

### 66:24
24    "And they will go out and look upon the dead bodies of those who rebelled against me; their worm will not die, nor will their fire be quenched, and they will be loathsome to all mankind."

## A New Heaven and a New Earth

### 65:17
17    "Behold, I will create new heavens and a new earth. The former things will not be remembered, nor will they come to mind."

### 66:22–23
22    "As the new heavens and the new earth that I make will endure before me," declares the LORD, "so will your name and descendants endure.

23    From one New Moon to another and from one Sabbath to another, all mankind will come and bow down before me," says the LORD.

# Bibliography

Bailey, Kenneth. *Through Peasant Eyes.* Grand Rapids: Eerdmans, 1890.

Bailey, Kenneth, "Informal Controlled Oral Tradition and the Synoptic Gospels," *Asia Journal of Theology,* 5, 1991, pp. 34–54.

Bailey, Kenneth. "Middle Eastern Oral Tradition and the Synoptic Gospels," *Expository Times* 106, 1995.

Baker, H.A. *Through Tribulation.* Minneapolis: Calvary Books.

Baldwin, Joyce G. *Haggai, Zechariah and Malachi.* Tyndale Old Testament Commentaries. London: Tyndale, 1972.

Banks, Robert. *Paul's Idea of Community.* Peabody: Hendricksen, 1994.

Barth, K. *Church Dogmatics. 1.2; 111.3.* Edinburgh: T.& T.Clark, 1961.

Barth, K. *Protestant Theology in the Nineteenth Century, Its History and Background.* London: SCM, 1972.

Beasley-Murray, G.R. 'New Testament Apocalyptic – A Christological Eschatology'. *Review & Expositor,* 72, 1975, pp. 317–330.

Beasley-Murray, G.R. *Jesus and the Kingdom of God,* Grand Rapids: Eerdmans, 1986.

Berkouwer, G.C. *The Return of Christ.* Grand Rapids: Eerdmans, 1972.

Borg, Marcus. *Conflict, Holiness and Politics in the Teachings of Jesus.* Harrisburg: Trinity, 1998, reprint from 1984.

Borg, Marcus. *Jesus: A New Vision.* HarperSanFrancisco: 1987.

Borg, Marcus. *Jesus in Contemporary Scholarship.* Valley Forge: Trinity, 1994.

Borg, Marcus. *Meeting Jesus Again for the First Time: The Historical Jesus and the Heart of Contemporary Faith.* HarperSanFrancisco: 1994.

Bright, J. *The Kingdom of God.* Nashville: Abingdon, 1953.

Brown, C. (Ed.). *The New International Dictionary of New Testament Theology.* Exeter: Paternoster, 1978.

Bruce, F.F. on C.H. Dodd in *Creative Minds in Contemporary Theology.* Grand Rapids: Eerdmans, 1966.

Bultmann, Rudolf. *Jesus Christ and Mythology.* New York: Scribner's, 1958.

Catherwood, F. *The Christian in Industrialized Society.* Illinois: Inter-Varsity Press, 1980.

Charlesworth, J.H. *Jesus within Judaism: New Light from Exciting Archaeological Discoveries.* New York: Doubleday, 1988.

Charlesworth, J.H. *The Messiah: Developments in Earliest Judaism and Christianity.* Minneapolis: Fortress, 1992.

Chandler, R. *Understanding the New Age.* Dallas: Word Inc., 1988.

Chilton, Bruce. *God in Strength: Jesus' Announcement of the Kingdom.* Studien zum Neuen Testamentum und seiner Umvelt, Freistadt: F.Plochl, 1979.

Chilton, Bruce. *Pure Kingdom: Jesus' Vision of God.* Grand Rapids: Eerdmans, 1996.

Chilton, Bruce & Craig A. Evans (Eds.). *Studying the Historical Jesus: Evaluations of the State of Current Research.* Leiden: E.J.Brill, 1994.

Clouse, R.G. *The Meaning of the Millennium: Four Views.* Illinois: Inter-Varsity Press, 1977.

Conzelmann, Hans. *The Theology of Saint Luke.* London: Macmillan, 1969.

Craigie, P.C. *The Book of Deuteronomy.* New International Commentary on the Old Testament. Grand Rapids: Eerdmans, 1981.

Cross, F.L. *The Oxford Dictionary of the Christian Church.* London: Oxford University Press, 1958.

Crossan, J.D. *The Historical Jesus: The Life of a Mediterranean Jewish Peasant.* HarperSanFrancisco: 1991.

Crossan, J.D. *Jesus, A Revolutionary Biography.* HarperSanFrancisco: 1994.

Cullmann, Oscar. *Christ and Time.* London: SCM, 1952.

Cullmann, Oscar. *The Christology of the New Testament.* London: SCM, 1971.

DeMar, G. and Leithart, P. *The Reduction of Christianity: Dave Hunt's Theology of Cultural Surrender.* Atlanta: Dominion Press, 1988.

Dodd, C.H. *The Parables of the Kingdom.* London: Nisbet, 1935.

Dodd, C.H. *The Interpretation of the Fourth Gospel.* Cambridge: Cambridge University Press, 1953.

Dodd, C.H. *History and the Gospel.* London, Nisbet, 1952.

Dodd, C.H. *The Interpretation of the Fourth Gospel.* Cambridge: Cambridge University Press, 1953.

Dodd, C.H. *The Apostolic Preaching and Its Developments.* London: Hodder, 1967.

Dunn, James D.G. *Christianity in the Making, Volume I, Jesus Remembered.* Michigan, Eerdmans, 2003.

Edwards, Jonathan. *The Works of Jonathan Edwards, Volume 1.* Edinburgh: Banner of Truth, reprinted 1979.

Ellis, E.E. 'Present and Future Eschatology in Luke'. *New Testament Studies,* 12, 1965–66, pp. 26–41.

Erickson, M.J. *Contemporary Options in Eschatology: A Study of the Millennium.* Grand Rapids: Baker, 1977.

France, R.T. *Jesus and the Old Testament.* London: Tyndale Press, 1971.

France, R.T. *Divine Government: God's Kingship in the Gospel of Mark.* London: SPCK, 1990.

Francis, F.O. 'Eschatology and History in Luke-Acts'. *Journal of American Academic Religion*, 37, 1969, pp. 49–63.

Frodsham, S.H. *With Signs Following: The Story of the Latter Day Pentecostal Revival.* Springfield: Gospel Publishing House, 1926.

Fuller, R.H. *The Foundations of New Testament Christology.* London: Collins, 1965.

Funk, Robert W. *Honest to Jesus.* HarperSanFrancisco: 1996.

Funk, Robert W. *The Acts of Jesus: The Search for the Authentic Deeds of Jesus.* HarperSanFrancisco: 1998.

Funk, Robert W. *The Gospel of Jesus: According to the Jesus Seminar.* Polebridge Press, 1999.

Gerhardsson, Birger. 'If we do not cut the parables out of their frames'. *New Testament Studies*, 1991, 37, p. 321–335.

Gerhardsson, Birger. *The Reliability of the Gospel Tradition.* Peabody: Hendrickson, 2001.

Glasson, T. Francis. 'Theophany and Parousia', *New Testament Studies*, 1980, 34, pp. 259–270.

Gundry, R.H. *The Church and the Tribulation.* Grand Rapids: Zondervan, 1973.

Guthrie, D. et.al. *New Bible Commentary.* London: Inter-Varsity Press, 1967.

Hamilton, Victor P. *The Book of Genesis.* New International Commentary on the Old Testament. Grand Rapids: Eerdmans, 1990.

Harrison, R.K. *Introduction to the Old Testament.* London: Tyndale, 1969.

Harrison, R.K. *Old Testament Times.* London: Inter-Varsity Press, 1970.

Hiers, R.H. 'The Problem of the Delay of the Parousia in Luke-Acts'. *New Testament Studies*, 20, 1973–74, pp. 145–155.

Hill, D. *New Testament Prophecy.* Atlanta: John Knox Press, 1979.

Hunter, A.M. *The Works and Words of Jesus.* London: SCM, 1950.

Hunt, D. *The Seduction of Christianity: Spiritual Discernment in the Last Days.* Oregon: Harvest House Publishers, 1985.

Hunt, D. and McMahon, T.A. *Whatever Happened to Heaven?* Oregon: Harvest House Publishers, 1988.

Jeremias, Joachim. *The Parables of Jesus.* Translated S.H. Hooke, New York: Scribner's, 1966.

Jeremias, Joachim. *New Testament Theology.* Translated J. Bowden, London: SCM, 1971.

Käsemann, Ernst. "Sentences of Holy Law in the New Testament" in *New Testament Questions of Today*, London, SCM, 1969, pp. 66–81.

Kenyon, E.W. *What Happened From the Cross To the Throne.* Washington:

Kenyon's Gospel Publishing Society, 1969.

Kenyon, E.W. *In His Presence*. Washington: Kenyon's Gospel Publishing Society, 1969.

Kenyon, E.W. *The Two Kinds of Life*. Washington: Kenyon's Gospel Publishing Society, 1969.

Kenyon, E.W. *The Bible in the Light of Our Redemption*. Washington: Kenyon's Gospel Publishing Society, 1969.

Kingsbury, J.D. *Matthew: Structure, Christology, Kingdom*. Philadelphia: Fortress, 1975.

Kitchen, K. 'Plagues' in *New Bible Dictionary*. London: Inter-Varsity Press, 1962.

Kitchen, K. *Ancient Orient and the Old Testament*. London: Tyndale, 1965.

Kloppenborg, J.S. (Ed.). *The Shape of Q*. Minneapolis: Fortress, 1994.

Kloppenborg, J.S. *Excavating Q: The History and Setting of the Sayings Gospel*. Minneapolis: Fortress, 2000.

Koester, H. *Ancient Christian Gospels: Their History and Development*. London: SCM, 1990.

König, A. *The Eclipse of Christ in Eschatology*. Grand Rapids: Eerdmans, 1989.

König, A. *Here Am I!: a Christian Reflection on God*. Grand Rapids: Eerdmans, 1982.

Kümmel, W.G. *Promise and Fulfilment, Studies in Biblical Theology*. London: SCM, 1957.

Kümmel, W.G. *The New Testament. The History of the Investigation of Its Problems*. London: SCM, 1972.

Ladd, G.E. *Crucial Questions About the Kingdom of God*. Grand Rapids: Eerdmans, 1952.

Ladd, G.E. *The Blessed Hope: A Biblical Study of The Second Advent and The Rapture*. Grand Rapids: Eerdmans, 1956.

Ladd, G.E. *The Presence of the Future*. Grand Rapids: Eerdmans, 1974.

Ladd, G.E. *A Theology of the New Testament*. London: Lutterworth, 1975.

Lane, W.L. *The Gospel of Mark*. London: Marshall, Morgan and Scott, 1974.

Latourette, K.S. *A History of the Expansion of Christianity*. Grand Rapids: Zondervan, 1970.

Lloyd-Jones, M. *Studies in the Sermon on the Mount*. Leicester: Inter-Varsity Press, 1976.

MacArthur, J.F. *The Charismatics: A Doctrinal Perspective*. Grand Rapids: Zondervan, 1978.

Mack, Burton L. *The Christian Myth: Origins, Logic and Legacy*. New York:

Continuum, 2001.

Mack, Burton L. *Who Wrote the New Testament? The Making of the Christian Myth*. San Francisco: Harper and Row, 2001.

Maddox, R. 'The Sense of New Testament Eschatology'. *Reformed Theological Review*, 36, 1977, pp. 42–50.

Marshall, I.H. *I Believe in the Historical Jesus*. London: Hodder and Stoughton, 1977.

Marshall, I.H. *Luke, Historian and Theologian*. Exeter: Paternoster, 1970.

MacPherson, D. *The Incredible Cover-up: The True Story of the Pre-trib Rapture*. Plainfield: Logos, 1975.

Martin, R.P. *Mark, Evangelist and Theologian*. Exeter: Paternoster, 1972.

McConnell, Dan R. *A Different Gospel*. Massachusetts: Hendrickson Publishers, 1987.

Meier, John P. *Rethinking the Historical Jesus, The Marginal Jew, Volume I, The Roots of the Problem and the Person*. New York: Doubleday, 1991.

Meier, John P. *Rethinking the Historical Jesus, The Marginal Jew, Volume II, Mentor, Message, and Miracles*. New York: Doubleday, 1994.

Meier, John P. *Rethinking the Historical Jesus, The Marginal Jew, Volume III, Companions and Competitor*. New York: Doubleday, 2001.

Meyer, Ben F. *The Aims of Jesus*. London: SCM, 1979.

Meyer, Ben F. *Critical Realism and the New Testament*. Princeton Theological Monographs 17, Allison Park: Pickwick Publications, 1989.

Meyer, Ben F. *Reality and Illusion in New Testament Scholarship: A Primer in Critical Realist Hermeneutics*. Collegeville: Liturgical, 1994.

Moltmann, Jurgen. *Theology of Hope: On the Ground and the Implications of a Christian Eschatology*. Translated J.W. Leitch, New York: Harper and Row, 1967.

Moltmann, Jurgen. *The Crucified God: The Cross of Christ as the Foundation and Criticism of Christian Theology*. Translated R.W. Wilson & J. Bowden, London: SCM, 1974.

Moltmann, Jurgen. *The Experiment Hope*. Translated M.D. Meeks, Philadelphia: Fortress, 1975.

Moltmann, Jurgen. *The Way of Christ: Christology in Messianic Dimensions*. Translated M.Kohl, San Francisco, Harper, 1990.

Morphew, D.J. Ph.D thesis, *A Critical Investigation of the Infancy Narratives in the Gospels of Matthew and Luke*. University of Cape Town: 1980.

Morphew, D.J. *South Africa: The Powers Behind*. Cape Town: Struik Christian Books, 1989.

Morphew, D.J. *Renewal Apologetics: An assessment of materials which are critical* of the 'Toronto Blessing', the popular name for the current move of the Holy Spirit. Position Paper of Vineyard Ministries Africa. Cape Town: Vineyard Bible Institute, 1995.

Morphew, D.J. *The Spiritual Spider Web, A Study of Ancient and Contemporary Gnosticism,* Vineyard Bible Institute Course, Cape Town, 2000 and Vineyard International Publishing E-Publication, www.vineyardbi.org/vip

Morris, L. *Apocalyptic.* London: Inter-Varsity Press, 1973.

Motyer, J.A. *The Revelation of the Divine Name.* Theological Students Fellowship. London: Tyndale Press.

Mounce, R.H. *The Book of Revelation.* New International Commentary on the New Testament. Grand Rapids: Eerdmans, 1977.

Murray, Iain H. *The Puritan Hope.* Carlisle: Banner of Truth, 1979.

Neill, Stephen. *The Interpretation of the New Testament 1861–1961.* New York: Oxford University Press, 1966.

Oswalt, J.N. *The Book of Isaiah, 1–39.* New International Commentary on the Old Testament. Grand Rapids: Eerdmans, 1986.

Padilla, Rene. *Mission Between the Times, Essays on the Kingdom.* Grand Rapids: Eerdmans, 1985.

Pannenberg, W. *Revelation as History.* New York: Macmillan, 1968.

Pannenberg, W. *Jesus, God and Man.* London: SCM, 1968.

Pannenberg, W. *Basic Questions in Theology. Volume 1.* London: SCM, 1970.

Paulk, E. *Ultimate Kingdom: Lesson for Today's Christian from the Book of Revelation.* Atlanta: Dimension Publishers, 1986.

Perrin, N. *The Kingdom of God in the Teaching of Jesus.* London: SCM, 1963.

Perrin, N. *Jesus and the Language of the Kingdom.* London: SCM, 1976.

Perrin, N. 'Eschatology and Hermeneutics: Reflections on Method in the Interpretation of the New Testament'. *Journal of Biblical Literature,* 93, 1974, pp. 3–14.

Perrin, N. 'Jesus and the Language of the Kingdom' in *The Kingdom of God: Issues in Religion and Theology,* 5, edited Bruce Chilton, London, SPCK, 1984, p. 104.

Reimarus, H.S. *Fragment.* Edited Charles H. Talbert. London: SCM, 1971.

Reimarus, H.S. *The Goal of Jesus and His Disciples.* Translated G.W. Buchanan. Leiden: E.J.Brill, 1970.

Ridderbos, H. *The Coming of the Kingdom.* Philadelphia: Presbyterian and Reformed, 1962.

Robinson, J.M. *Theology as History, New Frontiers in Theology.* New York: Harper & Row, 1967.

Rushdoony, R.J. *By What Standard? An Analysis of the Philosophy of Cornelius Van Til.* Philadelphia: Presbyterian and Reformed, 1958.

Sanders, E.P. *Paul and Palestinian Judaism, A Comparison of Patterns of Religion.* Augsburg: Fortress Publishers, 1977.

Sanders, E.P. *The Historical Figure of Jesus.* London: Penguin, 1993.

Sanders, E.P. *Jesus and Judaism,* Augsburg: Fortress Publishers, 1987.

Sanders, J.T. 'The Criterion of Coherence and the Randomness of Charisma: Poring through some Aporias in the Jesus Tradition,' *New Testament Studies,* 1998, 44, pp. 1–25.

Schweitzer, Albert. *The Quest of the Historical Jesus: A Critical Study of Its Progress from Reimarus to Wrede.* London: Adam and Charles Black, 1911.

Schweitzer, Albert. *The Kingdom of God and Primitive Christianity.* Edited Ulrich Neuenschwander, translated L.A. Gerrard. New York: Seabury, 1968.

Schweitzer, Albert. *The Mystery of the Kingdom of God. The Secret of Jesus's Messiahship and Passion.* Translated by Walter Lowrie. New York: Schocken, 1964.

Saucy, Mark. *The Kingdom of God in The Teaching of Jesus in 20$^{th}$ Century Theology.* Dallas: Word Publishing, 1997.

Stern, D. *Restoring the Jewishness of the Gospel.* Jerusalem: Jewish New Testament Publications, 1988.

Stott, J. *Baptism and Fullness: The Work of the Holy Spirit Today.* Leicester: Inter-Varsity Press, 1975.

Tatum, W.B. 'The Epoch of Israel: Luke 1—2 and the Theological Plan of Luke-Acts'. *New Testament Studies,* 13, 1966–67, pp. 184–105.

Towner, P. in 'The Present Age in the Eschatology of the Pastoral Epistles', *New Testament Studies,* 1986, 32, pp. 427–448.

Twelftree, Graham. *Jesus the Exorcist: A Contribution to the Study of the Historical Jesus.* Tübingen: Mohr and Peabody: Hendrickson, 1993.

Twelftree, Graham. *A Historical and Theological Study: Jesus the Miracle Worker.* Illinois: InterVarsity Press, 1999.

Van Til, C. *The Defence of the Faith.* Philadelphia: Presbyterian and Reformed, 1955.

Wagner, C. Peter. *What Are We Missing?* Carol Stream: Creation House, 1979.

Walvoord, J.F. *The Rapture Question.* Grand Rapids: Zondervan, 1957.

Walvoord, J.F. *The Thessalonian Epistles.* Grand Rapids: Zondervan, 1967.

Walvoord, J.F. *The Blessed Hope and the Tribulation.* Grand Rapids: Zondervan, 1976.

Warfield, B.B. *Counterfeit Miracles.* Philadelphia: Presbyterian and Reformed, 1979.

Weiss, J. *The Proclamation of the Kingdom of God.* London: SCM, 1971.

Wenham, David. *The Parables of Jesus: Pictures of Revolution.* London: Hodder and Stoughton, 1989.

Wesley, J. *A Plain Account of Christian Perfection.* Kansas City: Beacon Hill Press, 1966.

White, John. *When The Spirit Comes With Power; Signs and Wonders Among God's People.* London: Hodder & Stoughton, 1988.

Willis, W. *The Kingdom of God in Twentieth Century Interpretation.* Massachusetts: Hendricksen, 1987.

Wimber, J. *Healing Seminar.* Yorba Linda: Vineyard Christian Fellowship, (no date).

Wimber, J. & Springer, K. *Power Healing.* London: Hodder and Stoughton, 1986.

Wimber, J. *Power Evangelism.* San Francisco: Harper, 1986.

Witherington, Ben. *The Jesus Quest: The Third Search for the Jew of Nazareth.* Downers Grove: InterVarsity, 1997.

Wright N.T. *Christian Origins and the Question of God, Volume I, The New Testament and the People of God.* Minneapolis: Fortress, 1992.

Wright N.T. *Christian Origins and the Question of God, Volume II, Jesus and the Victory of God.* Minneapolis: Fortress, 1996.

Wright N.T. *Christian Origins and the Question of God, Volume III, The Resurrection of the Son of God.* London: SPCK, 2003.

Young, E.J. *The Prophecy of Daniel.* Grand Rapids: Eerdmans, 1970.

# Footnotes

1    'It is always a serious misinterpretation of the New Testament as well as of the Old Testament, to think of discovering its content (after the manner of all legalism) in certain principles ... It is at once tragic and amusing to see the many points of view that have arisen in the course of time, and how without fail, from the standpoint of one of them, all the rest have been judged and discredited or else neglected as incidental and of secondary importance, as time-conditioned or even as later accretions. And then without fail there has come, not unneeded to be sure, a reaction against "over-emphasis" and "one-sidednesses," one or more of the other principles had to be played off against the one and presumably only principle, until in turn the one-sidedness of the newly erected principle became too obvious for it to conceal its essentially relative character ... Jesus Christ is not one element in the New Testament witness alongside of others, but as it were the mathematical point toward which all the elements of the New Testament witness are directed. Ultimately only the name Jesus Christ ... this eternally inexpressible name, known and still to be made known, alone represents the object which they all signify and to which they all point.' *Church Dogmatics I, 2*, p. 11. Edinburgh, T. & T. Clark, 1961.

2    One of the six possibilities scholars have explored in commenting on the plural for God is described by Victor P. Hamilton (*The Book of Genesis, New International Commentary on the Old Testament*, Grand Rapids, Eerdmans, 1990, p. 133) as the 'plural of majesty'. It is noteworthy that when dealing with man in the image and likeness of God he argues again for royal language. "Gen. 1 may be using royal language to describe simply 'man'. In God's eyes all mankind is royal" (p. 135). Later he comments, "Thus, like 'image', exercise dominion reflects royal language" (p. 138).

3    A helpful study on the 'God who Comes', linking it to Theophany, will be found in G.R. Beasley-Murray, *Jesus and the Kingdom of God*, Eerdmans, Paternoster, 1986, pp. 3–10. He links the theme of Theophany and the Day of the Lord to the revelation of the divine name, pp. 17–19.

4    My remarks on the divine name are influenced by the work of J.A. Motyer, *The Revelation of the Divine Name*, Theological Students

Fellowship, London, Tyndale.

5   The New Testament basileia (a noun) is usually translated as 'kingdom'. However, it is generally agreed that the phrase 'kingdom of God' which translated the Hebrew/Aramaic malkut(a) is poorly conveyed by this phrase, since the term refers to the act of God reigning. Scholars have made various attempts to find a suitable English phrase. Bruce Chilton has suggested 'God in Strength' and Beasley-Murray has suggested 'the saving sovereignty' of God. R.T. France prefers 'divine government' (Divine Government: *God's Kingship in the Gospel of Mark,* London, SPCK, 1990, p. 13.)

6   P.C. Craigie draws attention to the central significance of the Song of the Sea. 'Perhaps the most important new feature in the Song of the Sea is the conception of Yahweh as a warrior and the related ideology of holy war' (*The Book of Deuteronomy,* New International Commentary on the Old Testament, Grand Rapids, Eerdmans, 1981, pp. 63–64). 'Closely related to the conception of God as Warrior is the expression of the kingship of Yahweh (particularly in Exod.15:18) … In summary, these two themes – God as Warrior and God as King – are central in the Song of the Sea' (pp. 64–65). He finds a significant relationship between the Song and the book of Deuteronomy (pp. 62–66).

7   The structure of the suzerainty treaty is particularly evident in the structure of the book of Deuteronomy. For the significance of this structure and its possible implications regarding date and authorship, see Craigie, NICOT, pp. 20–24.

8   All the early leaders of Israel were 'anointed ones' in the sense that they were charismatically endowed leaders. This was true of all the Judges and leaders up to and including Saul. However David was the first to be formally described in this way.

9   *The Holy Bible,* New International Version, Hodder & Stoughton, London, 1985, p. vii.

10  Some scholars see the view of the kingdom in the Psalms as determinative for the Old Testament teaching on the kingdom. For instance Bruce Chilton, *Pure Kingdom, Jesus, Vision of God,* Grand Rapids, Eerdmans, 1996, pp. 23–44, 146–163.

11 There is a general consensus amongst Old Testament scholars that Isa.40–66 was written by a later person or group, in the post-exilic period. The section of Isaiah is usually described as Deutero-Isaiah. However, the critical reasons for this consensus have never been 'bought' by conservative evangelical scholars, who believe that presuppositions are involved in the logic. Conservative scholars continue to defend the unity of Isaiah, as does John N.Oswalt, *The Book of Isaiah, Chapters 1–39,* The New International Commentary on the Old Testament, Grand Rapids, Eerdmans, 1986.

12 The traditional view of the kingdoms in question is generally accepted by conservative evangelical scholars, but not by most Old Testament scholars. Apart from critical and linguistic issues, differing presuppositions about prediction feature in the various views. For evangelical scholars see E.J. Young, *The Prophecy of Daniel,* Grand Rapids, Eerdmans, 1970, also R.K. Harrison, *Introduction to the Old Testament, London,* Tyndale, 1969.

13 There is some doubt on the dating of Ethiopic Enoch. It may be post-Christian (*New International Dictionary of New Testament Theology, Vol. 3,* edited by Colin Brown, Exeter, Paternoster, 1978, pp. 614–617. Scholarly literature on the Son of Man is vast, see p. 665).

The view I have taken of Daniel is admittedly a backward look through the 'eyes' of the New Testament writers. I have begun at the end, with Paul's use of the new man. That has informed my understanding of Jesus' use of the 'Son of Man' which in turn has informed my view of Daniel. If one were to take a strictly historical-critical approach, then all sorts of issues would open up. Was there a Messianic understanding of the Son of Man in second temple Judaism? Was 'Son of Man' ever viewed as applying to an individual rather than a way of speaking of the future triumph of Israel over its enemies? Was the figure in Ezekiel linked to the figure in Daniel? Is the direction of the arrival of the Son of Man from earth to heaven or from heaven to earth? Both N.T. Wright and James Dunn make much of these nuances (see the references to their works in the last chapter). My approach to Daniel can be described as canonical rather than historical-critical. In other words I interpret scripture with scripture and view things from both ends of scripture at the same time. However, there is one comment that I wish to make in relation to the historical-critical approach. The stone that falls in Daniel 2 describes a decisive intervention of God in judgement. The Son of Man in Daniel 7 corresponds to the stone that falls in Daniel 2. Therefore the Son of Man becomes associated with the Day of Judgement in Daniel itself. Further, the biblical world view normally correlates what occurs in the invisible realm with what occurs in the earthly, visible realm. There is no dualism, as in Greek thought, but a co-relation between the two. I have examined this idea more fully in *South Africa: The Powers Behind,* borrowing from Klaus Nurnberger, an Old Testament theologian *(Powers, Beliefs and Equity: Economic Potency Structures in South Africa and their Intersection with Patterns of Conviction in the Light of a Christian Ethic,* Pretoria, HSRC, 1984). The point for me therefore is not really whether the Son of Man comes from within heaven or from earth to heaven. The point is that the coming of the Son of Man is synonymous with the decisive intervention of God in judgement, destroying the image/beast and replacing those powers with the kingdom of God. We may never know how developed ideas about the Son of Man were in second temple Judaism. Had they linked the Son of Man to the figure in Ezekiel? Did they therefore think of such a figure in quasi-divine terms? Maybe yes, maybe no. Did Jesus have the figure in Daniel in his mind when he used this term? Did Jesus make a synthesis of these ideas, and if so, was he the first to do so, or to what extent did he use ideas already available to him? New Testament scholarship will continue to probe such things, and the already vast literature will keep growing.

14    There is a very long scholarly debate on whether *engiken* means arrival or nearness, which was started by Dodd's insistence that it had to mean arrival. The arguments themselves almost cancel each other out, so that dogmatism is precluded. Perhaps the best solution is to observe that the Semitic words that are probably behind *engiken* themselves carry ambiguity. Imminent nearness and actual arrival do frequently overlap. My belief is that Jesus intended to convey such ambiguity, a nearness that is so near that it amounts to arrival. For reference to the critical arguments see Beasley-Murray, *Jesus and the Kingdom of God,* Grand Rapids, Eerdmans, pp. 71–74 and Chilton, *God in Strength, Jesus' Announcement of the Kingdom,* Freistadt, Plochl, 1979, p. 27f.

15 R.T. France, in *Divine Government: God's Kingship in the Gospel of Mark* (London, SPCK, 1990, chapter 4), gives a helpful discussion of ways in which the fulfilment of these sayings has been viewed. Some of the options include the transfiguration, the cross, the resurrection, the ascension, Pentecost and the fall of Jerusalem in AD 70, all of which did occur within that generation. In all of these events the future kingdom became present. When Jesus said these things the kingdom was indeed 'here' and 'almost here.'

16 This point is articulated with great clarity by W. Pannenberg in *Jesus, God and Man* (London, SCM) and *Revelation as History* (New York, Macmillan, 1968).

17 John White tells the story of the early beginnings of the Vineyard and in particular, what occurred on a certain Mothers Day, in *When The Spirit Comes With Power; Signs and Wonders Among God's People*, Part II, 'Case Studies of the Spirit's Power.'

18 I have made reference to Wesley and others and have drawn attention to the importance of the history of revival phenomena in *Renewal Apologetics: An assessment of materials which are critical of the 'Toronto Blessing', the popular name for the current move of the Holy Spirit*, Vineyard Bible Institute course, *Position Papers 5–6*, 1995, www.vineyardbi.org or *Position Papers*, Vineyard International Publishing, E-Publications, www.vineyardbi.org/vip.

19 For an authoritative work on the parables see David Wenham, *The Parables of Jesus: Pictures of Revolution*, London, Hodder and Stoughton, 1989.

20 Rudolf Bultmann, *Jesus Christ and Mythology*, New York, Scribner's, 1958.

21 Or seventy-two.

22 Is.1, Ezek.1; Dan.10; Mt.17:1–13 par; Rev.1.

23 John S. Oswalt, *The Book of Isaiah*, Chapters 1–39, The New International Commentary on the Old Testament, Grand Rapids, Eerdmans, 1986, p. 437f.

24 There are 17 references to the earth.

25 Jonathan Edwards, *The Works of Jonathan Edwards*, Volume 1, Edinburgh,

Banner of Truth, reprinted 1979, p. 395.

26  Joyce G. Baldwin places Zechariah 9 in a chiastic structure (the oracle of 9–11). The triumphal entry of the king matches the Lord being worshipped as king (14:16–21) in the chiastic structure of the second oracle (chapters 12–14). The jubilation of 9:10–10:1 is matched in the same chiasm by jubilation and restoration in 10:3b–11b and the jubilation of Jerusalem in 12:1–9. *Haggai, Zechariah and Malachi, Tyndale Old Testament Commentaries*, London, Tyndale, 1972.

27  Jesus attends the following feasts: Passover (2.13), Tabernacles (5.2), Passover (6.4), Tabernacles (7.1f), Dedication (10.22–29) and Passover (11.55f). He is viewed as the fulfilment of all the feasts, which becomes clear with the last Passover, where he dies at the same time as the Passover sacrifice is being offered.

28  There are seven signs. 1. The turning of the water into wine (2:11). 2. The healing of the official's son (4:46–54, NB verse 54). 3. The healing of the man who had been paralysed for 38 years (5:1–18). 4. The feeding of the multitude (6:1–15, 26). 5. Jesus walking on the water (6:16–21, 26). 6. Jesus healing the man who had been born blind (9:1–41, NB verse 16). 7. The raising of Lazarus (11:1–44; NB verse 47).

29  William L. Lane, *The Gospel of Mark, The New London Commentary on the New Testament*, London, Marshall, 1974, p. 106. Lane comments in note 49, 'This concept of the "messianic banquet" was also known to the scribes. An early Tannaitic saying compares the Age to Come to a banquet hall: "This age is like a vestibule before the Age to Come. Prepare yourself in the vestibule that you may enter the banquet hall".'

30  I follow George Ladd in *The Presence of the Future* (Grand Rapids, Eerdmans, 1974) quite closely in this section.

31  J.Wesley, *A Plain Account of Christian Perfection*, reprinted Kansas City, Beacon Hill Press, 1966.

32  Dan McConnel, *A Different Gospel*, Massachusetts, Hendricksen, 1987. Kenyon's theology is examined in some detail in *The Spiritual Spider Web* (Vineyard Bible Institute course).

33  E.W. Kenyon, *What Happened from the Cross to the Throne*, Washington: Kenyon's Gospel Publishing Society, 1969, p. 103.

34   E.W. Kenyon, *What Happened*, p. 105.

35   E.W. Kenyon, *What Happened*, p. 185.

36   E.W. Kenyon, *In His Presence*, Washington: Kenyon's Gospel Publishing Society, 1969, p. 61.

37   E.W. Kenyon, *What Happened*, p. 15.

38   E.W. Kenyon, *In His Presence*, p. 23

39   E.W. Kenyon. *The Two Kinds of Life*, Washington: Kenyon's Gospel Publishing Society, 1969, p. 7.

40   E.W. Kenyon, *The Bible in the Light of Our Redemption*, Washington: Kenyon's Gospel Publishing Society, 1969, p. 233.

41   E.W. Kenyon, *What Happened*, p. 129.

42   B.B. Warfield, *Counterfeit Miracles*, Presbyterian and Reformed, Reprinted 1979.

43   John F. MacArthur, *The Charismatics: A Doctrinal Perspective*, Grand Rapids, Zondervan, 1978. Similar arguments about the non-normative nature of Acts are used by John Stott, *Baptism and Fullness: The Work of the Holy Spirit Today*, Leicester, Inter-Varsity Press, 1975.

44   *Signs and Wonders and Church Growth*, John Wimber Seminar. For this and a full list of teaching materials by John Wimber refer to Alexander Venter, *Doing Church*, Vineyard International Publishing, Cape Town, 2001, pp. 249–252, or visit www.sales@doing-the-stuff.com

45   David Stern, *Restoring the Jewishness of the Gospel* (Jerusalem: Jewish New Testament Publications, 1988), p. 17.

46   Dave MacPherson, *The Incredible Cover-up: The True Story of the Pre-trib Rapture* (Plainfield: Logos, 1975), p. 85.

47   D. MacPherson, *The Incredible Cover-up*, pp. 20–21.

48   R.H. Gundry, *The Church and the Tribulation*, Grand Rapids, Zondervan, 1973.

49   E. Paulk, Ultimate Kingdom: *Lessons for Today's Christian from the Book of Revelation*, Atlanta, Dimension Publishers, 1986; Dave Hunt, *Whatever Happened to Heaven?* Oregon, Harvest House Publishers, 1988; *The Seduction of Christianity: Spiritual Discernment in the Last Days*, Oregon, Harvest House

Publishers, 1985.

50  *Encyclopedia Britannica,* Volume 12, pp. 202–203.

51  For a critique of contemporary Postmillennialism, see Mark Saucy, *The Kingdom of God in the Teaching of Jesus in 20th Century Theology,* Dallas, Word, 1997, pp. 301–304.

52  Mark Saucy, *The Kingdom of God in the Teaching of Jesus in 20th Century Theology,* Word Publishing, Dallas, 1997.

53  Saucy, *The Kingdom of God in the Teaching of Jesus in 20th Century Theology,* see particularly note 88, page 339, where he defines his position as 'progressive dispensationalism'.

54  Johannes Weiss, originally published in 1892, *Jesus's Proclamation of the Kingdom of God, Lives of Jesus Series,* edited Leander E. Keck, London, SCM, 1971.

55  Albert Schweitzer, *The Quest of the Historical Jesus: A Critical Study of Its Progress from Reimarus to Wrede,* London, Adam & Charles Black, 1911.

56  *The Kingdom of God and Primitive Christianity,* edited Ulrich Neuenschwander, translated L.A. Gerrard, New York, Seabury, 1968 and *The Mystery of the Kingdom of God. The Secret of Jesus' Messiahship and Passion,* translated Walter Lowrie, New York, Schocken, 1964.

57  H.S. Reimarus, *Fragments,* edited Charles H. Talbert, London, SCM, 1971 and *The Goal of Jesus and His Disciples,* translated G.W. Buchanan, Leiden, E.J. Brill, 1970.

58  Karl Barth, *Protestant Theology in the Nineteenth Century, Its History and Background,* London, SCM, 1972.

59  Two other criteria are normally added to these. First, the criterion of coherence means that if a number of texts come through the first two criteria and bear witness to the same message they form a coherent 'set'. Second, if such sets are found in a number of different traditions (Q, Mark, M, L, etc.) their authenticity is strengthened still further. More have been added by the third quest, as will be noted below. J.T. Sanders has questioned the viability of the criterion of coherence. On the basis that Jesus was the charismatic leader of a new religious movement, one has to assume that he would have given random, or even contradictory

teachings, as befits such a profile. One cannot therefore expect coherence. 'The Criterion of Coherence and the Randomness of Charisma: Poring through some Aporias in the Jesus Tradition,' *New Testament Studies,* 1998, 44, pp. 1–25.

60 For instance, Birger Gerhardsson believes, concerning the parables, that the synoptic writers have not misunderstood the original teaching of Jesus and argues that we must read them in their present narrative context to recover the original teaching of Jesus. 'If we do not cut the parables out of their frames' *New Testament Studies,* 1991, 37, pp. 321–335.

61 James D.G. Dunn, *Christianity in the Making, Volume I, Jesus Remembered,* Michigan, Eerdmans, 2003.

62 I have analysed the historical-critical method in chapter 3 of my Ph.D thesis, *A Critical Investigation of the Infancy Narratives in the Gospels of Matthew and Luke,* University of Cape Town, 1980. This material will be the basis of a Vineyard Bible Institute module. For a helpful introduction to the Historical Jesus refer to I. Howard Marshall, *I Believe in the Historical Jesus,* London, Hodder, 1977.

63 The best critique of Schweitzer's ideas will be found in the writings of N.T. Wright. He shows that Schweitzer misunderstood what apocalyptic meant in second temple Judaism, exaggerating the 'end of the space-time universe' concept (N.T. Wright, *Christian Origins and the Question of God, Volume I, The New Testament and the People of God,* Minneapolis: Fortress, 1992, pp. 280–298 and for a concise summary of his position, see *Christian Origins and the Question of God, Volume II, Jesus and the Victory of God,* Minneapolis: Fortress, 1996, p. 81). However, if Schweitzer overdid the more bizarre elements of apocalyptic, Wright has rather overdone the antithesis to Schweitzer, producing what Dunn describes as a definition of apocalyptic which is 'simply cosmic sound effects' (*Jesus Remembered,* p. 479).

64 The 'already-not yet' tension is similar in some ways to the 'literal' versus 'symbolic' tension. Schweitzer assumed a particular understanding of Jewish views on the eschaton and apocalyptic. Those who follow Schweitzer tend to exaggerate apocalyptic symbols and the 'Son of Man in the sky' language, which they define as mythical. However it is not that certain that Jewish apocalyptic was simplistically literalistic. T. Francis

Glasson argues that the New Testament language about the eschaton derives more from the Old Testament prophetic language of theophany. He argues that both kinds of language were largely symbolic. 'Theophany and Parousia', *New Testament Studies*, 1980, 34, pp. 259–270. Equally, if one overstresses the symbolic nature of such language one can end up with a purely symbolic eschaton.

65    C.H. Dodd, *The Parables of Jesus*, London, Nisbet, 1936; *History and the Gospel*, London: Nisbet, 1952; *The Apostolic Preaching and Its Developments*, London: Hodder, 1967.

66    W.G. Kummel, *Promise and Fulfilment; Studies in Biblical Theology*, London: SCM, 1957. In *The New Testament: The History of the Investigation of Its Problems*, London: SCM, 1972, he gives a comprehensive history of New Testament investigation.

67    Oscar Cullman, *Christ and Time*, London: SCM, 1952, also *The Christology of the New Testament*, London, SCM, 1971.

68    Joachim Jeremias, *The Parables of Jesus*, translated by S.H. Hooke, New York: Scribner's, 1966. Also *New Testament Theology*, translated by J. Bowden, London: SCM, 1971.

69    Herman Ridderbos, *The Coming of the Kingdom*, Philadelphia: Presbyterian and Reformed, 1962. His work in Dutch predated the English translation, making it coincide with Ladd's work, whose first volume is dated from 1952, *Crucial Questions About the Kingdom of God*, Grand Rapids: Eerdmans, 1952. Ladd's work was updated in *The Presence of the Future: The Eschatology of Biblical Realism*, Grand Rapids: Eerdmans, 1974.

70    George Ladd, *A Theology of the New Testament*, London: Lutterworth, 1975.

71    See notes on the relevant chapters above.

72    G.R. Beasley-Murray, *Jesus and the Kingdom of God*, Grand Rapids: Eerdmans, 1986.

73    Saucy places him in the non-eschatological camp. Although I agree that Beasley-Murray's concluding chapter does seem to be over-conscious of 'mythical' elements in apocalyptic language, he does not go all the way with the symbolic view.

74  N. Perrin, 'Jesus and the Language of the Kingdom' in *The Kingdom of God: Issues in Religion and Theology, 5,* edited Bruce Chilton, London, SPCK, 1984, p. 104.

75  Mk.1:14–15; 9:1; Mt.4:12–17; 8:11–13; 16:28; Lk.4:16–21; 9:27; 12:32; 13:28–29; 16:16, in their synoptic relationship, are rigorously analysed in *God in Strength: Jesus's Announcement of the Kingdom,* Studien zum Neuen Testamentum und seiner Umvelt, Freistadt: F. Plochl, 1979.

76  Bruce Chilton, *Pure Kingdom: Jesus' Vision of God,* Grand Rapids: Eerdmans, 1996.

77  Saucy finds that Chilton continues to be influenced by the approach of Norman Perrin and evades the fullness of the eschatological kingdom, *The Kingdom of God in the Teaching of Jesus,* pp. 99–104.

78  N. Perrin, *The Kingdom of God in the Teaching of Jesus,* London: SCM, 1963; *Jesus and the Language of the Kingdom,* London: SCM, 1976; 'Eschatology and Hermeneutics: Reflections on Method in the Interpretation of the New Testament, *Journal of Biblical Literature,* 93, 1974, pp. 3–14.

79  Chilton gives a good summary of recent discussion and argues for the new consensus in 'The Kingdom of God in Recent Discussion', *Studying the Historical Jesus: Evaluations of the State of Current Research,* edited Bruce Chilton and Craig A. Evans, Leiden: E. J. Brill, 1994.

80  T. Francis Glasson, 'Schweitzer's Influence: Blessing or Bane?' in *The Kingdom of God: Issues in Religion and Theology, 5,* edited Bruce Chilton, London: SPCK, 1995.

81  Bruce Chilton, 'The Kingdom of God in Recent Discussion', in *Studying the Historical Jesus: Evaluations of the State of Current Research,* edited Bruce Chilton and Craig A. Evans, New York: E. J. Brill, 1994, pp. 265–267.

82  A careful discussion on the subject will be found in Dunn, *Jesus Remembered,* pp. 401–406 and 478–487.

83  W. Pannenberg, *Revelation as History,* New York: Macmillan, 1968; *Jesus, God and Man,* London: SCM, 1968; *Basic Questions in Theology, Volume 1,* London: SCM, 1970.

84  Jurgen Moltmann, *Theology of Hope: On the Ground and the Implications of a Christian Eschatology,* translated J.W.Leitch, New York: Harper and Row, 1967; *The Crucified God: The Cross of Christ as the Foundation and Criticism of Christian Theology,* translated R.W. Wilson & J. Bowden, London: SCM, 1974; *The Experiment Hope,* translated M.D. Meeks, Philadelphia: Fortress, 1975; *The Way of Christ: Christology in Messianic Dimensions,* translated M. Kohl, San Francisco: Harper, 1990. For a more extensive bibliography see Mark Saucy, pp. 375–376.

85  Adrio König, *The Eclipse of Christ in Eschatology,* Grand Rapids: Eerdmans, 1989. We are particularly glad to be able to offer this as a course through Vineyard Bible Institute.

86  Adrio König, *Here Am I!: A Christian reflection on God,* Grand Rapids: Eerdmans, 1982.

87  Rene Padilla, *Mission Between the Times, Essays on the Kingdom,* Grand Rapids: Eerdmans, 1985.

88  Particularly those of Wright and Dunn.

89  Schweitzer's 'Quest' is generally believed to have destroyed the first quest. His *The Mystery of the Kingdom* (1901) and *The Quest of the Historical Jesus* (1910) indicate the turn of the century as a fair overall turning point.

90  I will take the work of Ben F. Meyer on *The Aims of Jesus* as my genesis of the third quest. Since he published this in 1979, the year 1980 is a good round figure. Dunn takes Sander's work on *Jesus and Judaism* (1985) as the real beginning of the third quest *(Jesus Remembered,* p. 89). If one views placing Jesus back in his Jewish context as the primary factor, then this is clearly right. However, I prefer to see the beginning in the area of presuppositions. As Wright has noted, 'Meyer, almost prophetically, provided a thought-out methodological basis for the Third Quest which all intending writers on Jesus would do well to study carefully' *(Jesus and the Victory of God,* p. 82, note 2).

91  See my Ph.D Thesis, particularly the section entitled: "The historical-critical method as defined by the 'Quest' for the historical Jesus."

92  Käsemann, Ernst. "Sentences of Holy Law in the New Testament" in *New Testament Questions of Today,* London: SCM, 1969, pp. 66–81.

93　See D. J. Morphew, *The Spiritual Spider Web, A Study of Ancient and Contemporary Gnosticism,* Vineyard Bible Institute, Cape Town: 2000 and Vineyard International Publishing E Publication, www.vineyardbi.org/vip

94　The works of Pannenberg are important at this point. I cover this in a section of my Ph.D thesis entitled "The new theology of the resurrection and the re-definition of the historical-critical method."

95　See my thesis, the section entitled "The attitude towards the historical-critical method in the theology of Martin Kähler and in the dialectical school."

96　James Dunn correctly describes the Jesus Seminar as "neo-liberal."

97　Ben F. Meyer, *The Aims of Jesus,* London: SCM, 1979 and *Critical Realism, Reality and Illusion in New Testament Scholarship: A Primer in Critical Realist Hermeneutics,* Collegeville: Liturgical Press, 1994.

98　John P. Meier, *Rethinking the Historical Jesus, The Marginal Jew, Volume I, The Roots of the Problem and the Person,* New York: Doubleday, 1991; *Rethinking the Historical Jesus, The Marginal Jew, Volume II, Mentor, Message, and Miracles,* New York: Doubleday, 1994; *Rethinking the Historical Jesus, The Marginal Jew, Volume III, Companions and Competitors,* New York: Doubleday, 2001. For his placing of Jesus in his Jewish environment, refer particularly to Volume III.

99　E.P. Sanders, *Paul and Palestinian Judaism,* London: SCM, 1977 and *Jesus and Judaism,* London: SCM, 1985.

100　Meier, Volume I.

101　Meier, Volume II.

102　Meier, Volume I, pp. 123–142.

103　Graham Twelftree, *Jesus the Exorcist: A Contribution to the Study of the Historical Jesus,* Tübingen: Mohr and Peabody: Hendrickson, 1993; *A Historical and Theological Study: Jesus the Miracle Worker,* Illinois: InterVarsity Press, 1999.

104　Twelftree has a helpful summary in *Jesus the Miracle Worker,* pp. 248–249.

105　N.T. Wright, *Christian Origins and the Question of God, Volume I, The*

*New Testament and the People of God,* Minneapolis: Fortress, 1992; *Christian Origins and the Question of God, Volume II, Jesus and the Victory of God,* Minneapolis: Fortress, 1996; *Christian Origins and the Question of God, Volume III, The Resurrection of the Son of God,* London: SPCK, 2003.

106 Wright, Volume I.

107 Occurring repeatedly in Volume II.

108 Wright, Volume III.

109 For which see James Dunn, *Jesus Remembered,* particularly pp. 473–477.

110 James Dunn, *Jesus Remembered,* pp. 393–396.

111 His most appropriate term, Volume III.

112 Both Wright and Dunn make use of the work of Kenneth Bailey, *Through Peasant Eyes,* Grand Rapids: Eerdmans, 1890; "Informal Controlled Oral Tradition and the Synoptic Gospels," *Asia Journal of Theology,* 5 (1), pp. 34–54; "Middle Eastern Oral Tradition and the Synoptic Gospels," *Expository Times* 106, 1995. They both feel that Bailey opens up better perspectives than Birger Gerhardsson – *The Reliability of the Gospel Tradition,* Peabody: Hendrickson, 2001.

113 Marcus Borg, *Conflict, Holiness and Politics in the Teachings of Jesus,* Harrisburg: Trinity, 1998, *Jesus: A New Vision,* HarperSanFrancisco: 1987, *Jesus in Contemporary Scholarship,* Valley Forge: Trinity, 1994, *Meeting Jesus Again for the First Time: The Historical Jesus and the Heart of Contemporary Faith,* HarperSanFrancisco:1994.

114 Dominic J. Crossan, *The Historical Jesus: The Life of a Mediterranean Jewish Peasant,* HarperSanFrancisco: 1991; *The Birth of Christianity,* HarperSanFrancisco: 1998.

115 Burton L. Mack, *Who Wrote the New Testament? The Making of the Christian Myth,* HarperSanFrancisco: 1995; *The Christian Myth: Origins, Logic and Legacy,* New York: Continuum, 2001.

116 Robert W. Funk, *Honest to Jesus,* HarperSanFrancisco: 1996; *The Acts of Jesus: The Search for the Authentic Deeds of Jesus,* HarperSanFrancisco: 1998.

117 Kloppenborg, J.S. *The Shape of Q,* Minneapolis: Fortress, 1994; *Excavating Q: The History and Setting of the Sayings Gospel,* Minneapolis: Fortress, 2000.

118 Helmut Koester, *Ancient Christian Gospels: Their History and Development,* London: SCM, 1990.

119 Ben Witherington, *The Jesus Quest: The Third Search for the Jew of Nazareth,* Downers Grove: InterVarsity, 1997.

120 So Wright, Volume II, pp. 637–639.

121 There were, of course, many parts to this general community in many contexts and places.

122 W.G. Kummel, *The New Testament, The History of the Investigation of Its Problems,* London, SCM, 1972; Stephen Neill, *The Interpretation of the New Testament 1861–1961,* New York, Oxford University Press, 1966.

123 P. Towner, in 'The Present Age in the Eschatology of the Pastoral Epistles', *New Testament Studies,* 1986, 32, pp. 427–448, examines this assumption by Dibelius and Conzelmann and concludes that even in this literature the hope of the *parousia* is still vibrant. The 'already' and 'not yet' tension is very similar to Paul's earlier epistles. The literature on the theory of the delay is quite extensive. See Hiers, R.H. 'The Problem of the Delay of the Parousia in Luke-Acts'. *New Testament Studies,* 20, 1973–74, pp. 145–155.

124 A helpful study of early church life will be found in Robert Banks, *Paul's Idea of Community,* Peabody, Hendricksen, 1994. He covers the breaking of bread service on pp. 80–85.

# BOOK ORDERS

This book and other VIP publications can be ordered
from the following Vineyard International Publishing distributors:

### South Africa
P.O. Box 53286, Kenilworth 7745
Tel & Fax: +27 21 6712633
vip@vineyardbi.org
www.vineyardbi.org/vip

### Benelux
P.O. Box 1557
3500 BN Utrecht
The Netherlands
Fax: +31 30 2340958
books@vineyard.nl

### England
Ed & Clare Evans
9 Poplar Way, Salisbury, SP1 3GR
Tel: +44 1722 326885
edevans@talk21.com

### New Zealand
VMG Aotearoa NZ
116 Wairere Rd
Waitakere, Auckland, NZ
vmg@vineyard.co.nz

### Norway
Oyvind Nerheim, Oslo Vineyard
St Halvardsgt.20
0192, Oslo, Norway
Tel: +47 24070707
nerheim@vineyard.no

### Switzerland/Austria/Germany
Mathew Mathai
Wehntalerstrasse 276
8046-Zurich,
Switzerland
Tel: +41 1 371 7151
Fax: +41 1 371 7150
mathew@vineyard.ch

### Australia
AVC Australia
P.O. Box 652
Lilydale, VIC 3140
Fax: +03 9739 7946
Tel: +03 9739 4940
office@vineyard.org.au

### Sweden
Krister Burstrom
Din Bok i Skelleftea
Stationsgatan 12
931 31 Skelleftea
krister@dinbok.net

### USA & Canada
Vineyard Music USA
12650 Directors Drive, Suite 500
Stafford, Texas, 77477
USA
Tel: +1 800 852 8463
sales@vineyardmusicusa.com